Brother Jesus

Brother Jesus

The Nazarene through Jewish Eyes

SCHALOM BEN-CHORIN

Translated and edited by
Jared S. Klein and Max Reinhart

The University of Georgia Press

Athens and London

Translation © 2001 by the University of Georgia Press

Athens, Georgia 30602

All rights reserved

Designed by Kathi Dailey Morgan

Set in 10 on 13 Minion by G & S Typesetters, Inc.

Printed and bound by Thomson-Shore

The paper in this book meets the guidelines for
permanence and durability of the Committee on
Production Guidelines for Book Longevity of the
Council on Library Resources.

Printed in the United States of America

05 04 03 02 01 C 5 4 3 2 1

Library of Congress Cataloging-in-Publication Data

Ben-Chorin, Schalom.

   [Bruder Jesus. English]

   Brother Jesus : the Nazarene through Jewish eyes / Schalom Ben-
   Chorin ; translated and edited by Jared S. Klein and Max Reinhart.

      p. cm.

   Includes bibliographical references and index.

   ISBN 0-8203-2256-3 (alk. paper)

   1. Jesus Christ—Jewish interpretations.   I. Title.

   BM620 .B213   2001

   232.9′06—dc21   00-045136

British Library Cataloging-in-Publication Data available

Contents

Indexes

Author's Foreword to the English-Language Edition

As a young man living in my native city of Munich, I wrote a poem-cycle about the *Rabbi from Nazareth*, to which I appended the following prefatory note: "Gradually, dawn is breaking into the Jewish consciousness, and Jesus is beginning to take the place that is due him in the pantheon of the people of Israel."

These words date from the year 1934.

One year later I left Germany and, following the compass of my heart, immigrated into the land of Israel.

For more than six decades now I have lived in Jerusalem, the city in which the life of Jesus came to its tragic end. Over and over again I have met him, as it were, in the streets of the Old City, but also on the hills of Galilee and especially on the banks of Kinnereth, the Sea of Gennesaret. Over and over again I have heard his brotherly voice, which calls to us and teaches us how the Law is to be fulfilled through love. This is the way I see Jesus of Nazareth. This is the way I hear him. Not as the exalted Lord but as the picture of my "eternal brother" (Stefan Zweig). This picture has engraved itself in my soul, and only from this perspective can I bear witness—Jewish witness—to the Rabbi from Nazareth, not to the Christ of the Church.

Only gradually did Jesus begin to take his place among the people of Israel. The proper, modern Jewish investigation of the life of Jesus began in 1922 with a distinguished book by Joseph Klausner titled *Jesus of Nazareth*. Written in Hebrew, this book was the first scientific inquiry by a Jew into the life of Jesus. More books on Jesus written by Jews have appeared in the last half-century since the founding of the State of Israel in 1948 than in all previous centuries together.

The impetus for the title of my book *Brother Jesus* (first published in Munich in 1967) was provided by my revered teacher, Martin Buber, in his book *Two Types of Faith* (1950). There one finds the famous sentence "From my youth onwards I have found in Jesus my great brother." For me, as well, that was the decisive consideration: Jesus, a human brother and a Jewish brother who, through his existence, his teaching, and his behavior, can be an example for us.

Of all my books, this one, my *Brother Jesus*, lies closest to my heart. I am filled with joy that it has at last been translated into English and that it can now find its way in the New World. For this I wish to express my sincere thanks to the translators, Professors Jared S. Klein and Max Reinhart of the University of Georgia.

Translators' Preface

It has been more than a century now since Christian theologians attempted to peel off the centuries-old overlay of the Christological, kerygmatic tradition in order to recover the figure of Jesus of Nazareth, the man. This search for "the historical Jesus" was not destined to attain its goal so long as it remained the sole province of Christian scholars. A moment's reflection demonstrates why this is so. Jesus was not a German, an Englishman, or a European of any provenance but a Palestinian Jew, an inhabitant of a Jewish commonwealth, who was steeped in Jewish tradition and spoke a Jewish language. The sacred scriptures of Israel were his Bible and its sacred doctrine his creed. Although his views differed in certain respects from those of the pietists or Pharisees, the prototypes of today's orthodox Jews, these differences were such as may arise anywhere and everywhere within an extended family of believers. If he was, as the Talmud brands him, a "sinner of Israel," then so are, on much more demonstrable grounds, the majority of Jews alive today.

It follows from these considerations that the scholars in the best position to penetrate to the essence of Jesus the man are either Jews who have, so to speak, drunk in the milieu of belief and doctrine in which Jesus lived from earliest childhood, or those Christians who have been willing to investigate Jewish tradition from the inside out. This means investigating not only the Hebrew Bible—lying many centuries in the past—but also the Mishna, Midrash, and Talmud as well, which often preserve traditions and beliefs already known or practiced at the time of Jesus. The everyday life of any reasonably observant Jewish family will instantiate the lore, wisdom, and customs of these texts, which have, sadly, generated little interest among Christians.

Despite these circumstances, however, the strained relations between Christianity and Judaism over most of the past two millennia, likely at any time to express itself in physical violence and oppression of Jews on the part of Christians, engendered a climate in which Jews were discouraged from investigating the sacred scripture of Christianity and its leading figures. Only with the advent of a liberal Judaism in the nineteenth century did long-standing taboos lift and Jewish scholars begin seriously to study and expound (usually to their fellow Jews) Christian scripture. Four figures preceding Ben-Chorin stand out in this scholarly tradition.

The first is Claude J. G. Montefiore (1859–1939), whose commentary on the synoptic Gospels, first published in 1909, remains to this day unique in the annals of Jewish scholarship. Montefiore's self-avowed purpose, as he indicates on the very first page, was to "concentrate attention upon those passages in the Gospels which have religious value or interest for Jewish readers." Montefiore did not deal with the figure of Jesus the man per se.

The first important Jewish scholar in the twentieth century to interest himself in Jesus the man was Joseph Klausner, whose Heidelberg dissertation on Jewish messianic conceptions in the period of the Tannaites naturally led him to explore the figure of Jesus and the origins of Christianity. His book *Jesus of Nazareth* (1922; English translation 1925) is a scholarly treatise on the life of the central figure in Christianity. Klausner wrote in Hebrew, addressing himself to Jews only; but the famous British Christian Hebraist Herbert Danby, translator of the Mishna, found Klausner's study of such importance that he translated it into English, and it remains to this day a standard reference within most Protestant seminaries. A remarkably objective work, it does not, however, avoid certain evaluative remarks, especially in the discussion of why Christianity did not make much headway within the community of nonconverted, non-Hellenized Jews.

Self-consciously in the tradition of both Montefiore and Klausner is Samuel Sandmel, *A Jewish Understanding of the New Testament* (1956). Sandmel's book differs from that of both his predecessors in being a largely nontechnical exposition "written for the average intelligent and educated American Jew" (xv). Like Montefiore's work, it is much more than a study of Jesus the man, to whom it devotes only a single chapter.

The year 1956 also saw the publication of *The New Testament and Rabbinic Judaism* by David Daube. A jurist specializing in Roman and Talmudic law, Daube was a highly original thinker, able time and again to cast surprising new light on New Testament issues through the lens of Talmud and Midrash. Although his focus was not on the figure of Jesus himself, many of the actions and statements of the Nazarene are clarified within their Jewish setting by Daube's uniquely suggestive and often compelling rabbinic parallels.

Appearing more than a decade after Sandmel and Daube, this book by Schalom Ben-Chorin is unique in that it is addressed primarily to Christians. Like Klausner's, it focuses exclusively on Jesus the man, illuminating his life and mission against the background of Jewish tradition. It is difficult to imagine a more sympathetic depiction of the flesh-and-blood figure of Jesus. Stripping off all aspects of the kerygmatic tradition, it examines the life of a Jewish man in a Jewish land. For Ben-Chorin, Jesus is a Jewish brother; and the empathy that streams forth from this perspective, as well as the pathos that is thereby evoked, is both constant and gripping. No novel, no scholarly treatise, Ben-Chorin's work is best described as a conversation with the reader, complete with personal recollections and meaningful digressions. The emotional turmoil that Jesus must have experienced when his impending fate became clear to him is depicted with a psychological penetration and a flair for the dramatic that make it the high point of the book. It will linger with readers long after the last page has been turned.

It is a matter of great sadness to the translators that Schalom Ben-Chorin did not live to see the English translation of this book but passed away in May 1999. Although widely known in continental Europe, particularly in German-speaking countries, Schalom Ben-Chorin's books have never been translated into English and are therefore almost entirely unknown in English-speaking countries. German-born and German-educated, Ben-Chorin emigrated to Jerusalem in 1935 and resided there for the rest of his life, writing in German, the language of his youth, formation, and culture. A driving force in the reform movement in Israel, he was author, coauthor, or editor of some thirty books on Jewish themes. The book we have translated here, his self-described "keystone work," is the first volume of a trilogy titled *Die Heimkehr* (The Homecoming), whose three volumes deal respectively with the lives of three seminal Jewish figures of early Christianity: Jesus, Mary, and Paul. Ben-Chorin served as visiting professor at the Universities of Tübingen and Munich, was the recipient of honorary doctorates from the Universities of Munich and Bonn, and was honored with numerous medals and prizes for his untiring labors on behalf of interfaith understanding and German-Jewish relations.

Editorial Apparatus

Brother Jesus is a very readable and understandable book. Nevertheless, the arguments that Schalom Ben-Chorin develops are often based on a complicated comparison or interweaving of texts and words from various traditions and languages. In order to make these traditions and sources transparent and to enhance the book's general usefulness to readers, we have fitted it out with several indexes: they list biblical citations, citations from classical Jewish texts, persons, subjects, classical exegetical sources and translations, and words and phrases from Hebrew, Aramaic, Greek, and Latin. The editorial notes we have added to those of the author consist largely of Jewish background information to help the reader better understand the various points that Ben-Chorin discusses. In addition, we have updated the bibliography, and substituted English translations of German texts cited by the author wherever they exist. Where they do not, the translation of quotations from German sources is ours.

A Note on Transliteration and Pronunciation

Ben-Chorin's somewhat informal transliteration of Hebrew and Aramaic follows the principles of German orthography, which differ substantially from those that are standard in English. Our methodology therefore requires a word of explanation. Although it has been our wish to follow consistent guidelines, we have also made an effort to avoid pedantry as well as exotic-looking orthographic sequences and the accumulation of formal diacritical markings. Consequently, we have chosen a twofold system. On the one hand, in the case of names and terms that are known to readers of the Bible in English, we have generally followed the traditional spellings of the King James Version as they have been taken over by the New Revised Standard Version, our source for biblical quotations (e.g., *Saul* rather than *Sha'ul, Joshua* rather than *Yehoshua'*). On the other hand, in the case of Hebrew and Aramaic terms and names from the Talmud and Midrash, we have provided transliterations.

It should be pointed out that classical Hebrew possessed three consonants called laryngeals not found in English: *'alef* ('), *'ayin* ('), and *cheth* (*ch*). The first of these is pronounced with the same glottal catch one hears before the initial *i* of *ice* when one distinguishes the phrases *a nice man* and *an ice man*. The *'ayin* is not comparable to any English sound but often, especially at the beginning of a word, struck Hellenistic Greek speakers as similar to *g:* hence *Gaza, Gomorrah,* transliterating Hebrew place names beginning with *'ayin.* In modern Hebrew as well as in traditional pronunciations of biblical Hebrew in the Western world, neither the *'alef* nor the *'ayin* is pronounced. The third laryngeal, *ch,* may be assigned the pronunciation heard at the end of the interjection of disgust *ach.* A similar pronunciation is to be assigned to *kh,* a variant of *k* occurring after vowels and paralleling *f* and *th,* the postvocalic variants of *p* and *t,* respectively. Following standard (nonphilological) practice, we have indicated the postvocalic variant of *b* by *v* but have not employed any special marking to note the corresponding variants of *d* (the initial *th*-sound of English *thy* as opposed to *thigh*) and *g* (similar to the sound one makes when gargling). Moreover, we have regularly transliterated the Hebrew *waw* as *v* rather than *w*, which must have been its pronunciation in classical times.

Another point to note is that in most instances where Hebrew writes -*h* at the end of a word, it is not a consonant but a signal that the preceding vowel is long. We have left off this final -*h*, except where it appears in words that have passed into general currency (e.g., *Torah*, but *mitsva*). We have written double consonants selectively, retaining them in words derived from the Hebrew conjugational pattern known as the "intensive" (e.g., *kiddush, Kabbala,* [*Choni*] *Hame'aggel*) but eschewing them following the definite article *ha-* (e.g., *barukh haba',* *Hame'aggel, kos hatar'ela*). Moreover, we have not distinguished the two classical Hebrew *t*-sounds (*taw* and *teth*), *k*-sounds (*kaf* and *qof*), and *s*-sounds (*samekh* and *sin*); and we have transliterated the "emphatic" *s*-sound (*tsade*) as *ts*.

Additionally, Hebrew possesses a construction in which two nouns are juxtaposed in order to produce the equivalent of an English *of* phrase. In many such instances the first noun takes on a form somewhat different from that which it possesses in isolation. Where this is so, we have placed a hyphen after the noun (e.g., *beth-hakeneseth,* 'house of assembly/worship,' beside *bayith,* 'house'; *'aniyei-haruach,* 'the poor of spirit,' beside *'aniyim,* 'poor [people]'; but *kol chathan,* 'voice of a bridegroom,' with unchanged *kol,* 'voice').

Finally, in the course of translating we encountered a few instances where we felt the exposition was not clear in the original and thus exercised our prerogative to make such changes as we believed would render the argument clearer to the reader. Similarly, we have silently corrected occasional erroneous references in the Jewish literature.

Brother Jesus

1 *The Figure of Jesus*

The author of the Gospel of John concludes with a personal note that might well be appended to every new reexamination of the life of Jesus: "But there are also many other things that Jesus did; if every one of them were written down, I suppose that the world itself could not contain the books that would be written" (21:25).

Since the time this statement was made, innumerable books about Jesus of Nazareth have in fact been written in the attempt to reconcile the contradictions between the synoptic writers (Matthew, Mark, Luke) and John, beginning with the earliest gospel harmonies and continuing all the way down to the nineteenth-century reconstructions of a quasi-historical Jesus.

Christians of all denominations, but also Marxists and other opponents of Christianity, have offered their respective versions of Jesus. Only in the twentieth century, however, have Jewish scholars been able to bring their own focus to the figure of Jesus. The reason for this is obvious. So long as ecclesiastical authorities threatened to censure any representation of Jesus that deviated from dogma, it was impossible for Jewish scholars to stake out a position for their own point of view.

In the nineteenth century, when liberal Protestantism freed theology from, on the one hand, the bonds of the Inquisition and, on the other, the bonds of Protestant orthodoxy, the first tentative steps toward this Jewish contribution were made. The motivation of these Jewish scholars was primarily apologetic in nature and concerned with demonstrating that the Jews were not guilty of killing Jesus. Such efforts continue into our own times. We think, for example, of Paul Winter's book *On the Trial of Jesus* (1961).

Whereas in the nineteenth century much energy and learning were applied to the discovery of the historical Jesus, today few scholars are inclined to deal with this question any further. One of the leading experts on the life of Jesus, the New Testament scholar Ernst Käsemann, has remarked,

> In writing a life of Jesus, we could not dispense with some account of his exterior and interior development. But we know nothing at all about the latter and next to nothing about the former, save only the way which led from Galilee to Jerusalem, from the preaching of the God who is near to us to the hatred of official Judaism and execution by the Romans. Only *an uncontrolled imagination* could have the self-confidence to weave out of these pitiful threads the fabric of a history in which cause and effect could be determined in detail. (*Essays*, 45)

Although Käsemann and other disciples of Rudolf Bultmann are careful not to appear overly pessimistic in this regard, in fact they are interested not so much in the historical Jesus as in the kerygma: the risen Lord proclaimed by the original Christian community. For Bultmann and his followers the *sitz im leben*, the cultural and historical context, is precisely the preaching, not the actual event; events are no longer considered to be reconstructible. These scholars base their premises on the undeniable fact that the Gospels do not represent a historical report but attest only to the missionary purpose of the risen Lord, the savior of Israel and the world. In academic circles it is commonly held today that missionary documents of this type cannot yield a valid historical picture. The elements of the picture are of course lacking, since it was not the intention of the New Testament authors to provide a historical report. The few sources we do have beyond the New Testament are, if anything, even less useful for historical evaluation.

The apocryphal gospels, for example, certainly have no historical value, even where they preserve a statement of Jesus here and there that has an authentic ring to it. The few passages in the Talmud and the Midrash that may refer to Jesus (these have been compiled by Joseph Klausner in his *Jesus of Nazareth*) are likewise of little historical value, since they grew out of the polemic with the early Christian community. For example, the following is one of the few citations from the Talmud in which Jesus is referred to by name:

> Only then he ['Onkelos] went off and conjured up Jesus and asked him, "What is the most important thing in this world?" Jesus said to him, "Israel." 'Onkelos asked, "And if I join their ranks?" Jesus said, "Seek their well-being. Do not seek their harm. Whoever lays a hand on them does the same thing as if he were to lay a hand on the apple of [God's] eye." 'Onkelos asked Jesus, "And what is his punishment?" Jesus said to him, "Boiling excrement." As a baraitha[1] says, "Whoever mocks the words of the wise is punished with boiling excrement. — Come and see how different are Israel's mockers from the prophets of the nations of the world." (Babylonian Talmud [BT], Gittin 57a)

As this example shows, many utterances made about Jesus have not the slightest historical worth. Some of these statements in the Talmud are apologetic. For example, it is said that forty days after the condemnation of Jesus a herald went before him and urged everyone to present something in his defense, but no such witness could be found (BT, Sanhedrin 43a). In this we can perhaps hear an echo of Peter's denial; clearly, however, no useful historical evidence is transmitted even here, because no such process of exoneration is mentioned anywhere else in Jewish law.

Must we therefore resign ourselves to the thought that a life of Jesus can be created only from fantasy, as so many novelists, among them Jewish ones, have sought to do?

I emphatically reject this. "I hate, as something vile, any unrestrained fablization; and any poetic license that lacks strict reasoning would seem to me inartistic and destructive nonsense. For what remarkable people these are! What seriousness of purpose they have! What eternal significance for human history we find here!" It was the great Jewish poet Franz Werfel who attached this confession to his drama *Paulus unter den Juden* (Paul among the Jews). Anything of a purely fantastic quality was entirely unacceptable to him.

Several books of the fantastic kind have been written since about the mid-1950s. One is by the French Jew Robert Aron, *Jesus of Nazareth: The Hidden Years,* who creates ex nihilo the childhood and youth of Jesus. There is also the popular book by Joel Carmichael, *The Death of Jesus,* which makes Jesus of Nazareth into one of the leaders of the Jewish resistance forces—a thesis that had already been proposed decades earlier by the Viennese Jewish historian Robert Eisler. If Carmichael is still considered an original thinker, it is owing only to the public's forgetfulness. Pure fantasy as well is Robert Graves's book *King Jesus,* which makes Jesus into the son of Herod. Such "theses" always cause a stir but do not serve to uncover a genuinely historical picture of Jesus.

According to a saying of Jesus, all sins but that against the Holy Spirit may be forgiven (Matt. 12:31; Mark 3:29). Like many of his sayings, this one is susceptible to multiple interpretations. The simple and obvious sense of the word seems to me to be the right one here: namely, that any *arbitrary* reinterpretation of sacred tradition is a sin against the Spirit and cannot be forgiven.

For me, the New Testament is certainly not holy scripture in the canonical sense. Nevertheless, I agree with Rabbi Leo Baeck ("Gospel") that it is a document that belongs to the history of Jewish faith and preserves much of relevance to the salvation of Israel. Accordingly, I find it unjustifiable to alter the figure of Jesus in any arbitrary fashion, just as it seems wrong to me to make an Egyptian of Moses, as Sigmund Freud did in his late work *Moses and Monotheism* (1939).

What may perhaps be forgiven a genius like Freud, however, is unpardonable for many other authors who deal all too capriciously with biblical figures. This holds true as much for non-Jewish as for Jewish authors. One thinks, for instance, of Ethelbert Stauffer. Stauffer maintains that a sharp contradiction existed between the (positive) teachings of Jesus and the (negative) teachings of the Torah and projects this Marcionite tendency against Judaism onto the figure of Jesus (*Jesus and His Story,* 75–78).

What middle ground can we discern, then, between an unverifiable historical position, on the one hand, and theological-literary fantasy, on the other? *Intuition.*

Intuition and fantasy are not identical. Intuition, as I understand it, grows out of a lifelong familiarity with the text and allows it to be interpreted subjectively. Subjectively, to be sure, but not in an unbridled fashion.

Intuitive interpretation proceeds from a deep kindred empathy with Jesus within the Jewish world in which he lived, taught, and suffered.

The loyal collaborator of Theodor Herzl in the early period of Zionism, Max Nordau, wrote in 1899 to Father Hyacinthus Loyson, "Jesus is the soul of our soul as he is the flesh of our flesh. Who should want, therefore, to exclude him from the Jewish people? St. Peter remains the only Jew to say of this descendant of David, 'I do not know the man'" (Matt. 26:72).[2]

It was Martin Buber who made the famous comment about his "brother Jesus" in his book *Two Types of Faith:*

> From my youth onwards I have found in Jesus my great brother. That
> Christianity has regarded and does regard him as God and Savior has
> always appeared to me a fact of the highest importance which, for his
> sake and my own, I must endeavor to understand.... My own fraternally
> open relationship to him has grown ever stronger and clearer, and today
> I see him more strongly and clearly than ever before. I am more than
> ever certain that a great place belongs to him in Israel's history of faith
> and that this place cannot be described by any of the usual categories.
> (12–13)

Buber's confession defines my own position. Jesus is for me an eternal brother—not only my human brother but my *Jewish brother.* I sense his brotherly hand clasping mine and asking me to follow him. It is *not* the hand of the Messiah, this hand marked by a wound; it is certainly *no divine hand.* It is rather a *human* hand, in whose lines the deepest sorrow is inscribed.

That distinguishes me, the Jew, from the Christian, yet it is the same hand that stirs both of us. It is the hand of a great and faithful witness in Israel. His belief, his unconditional belief, his simple trust in God the Father, his willingness to humble himself completely before the will of God—that is the attitude of which Jesus is the supreme example, the attitude that can join us, Jew and Christian, together. The belief of Jesus unifies us, but the belief in Jesus divides us.

The belief *of* Jesus as expressed in the Sermon on the Mount, in his parables of the fatherhood of God and his kingdom, and in the prayer that Jesus teaches his disciples, the Our Father, unifies us.

The belief *in* Jesus as the Messiah, as the second person of a trinity nowhere attested in the New Testament, as the sole Just One who takes upon himself the vicarious suffering for sins, necessarily distinguishes us, divides us. This is entirely foreign to the *Jewish insight* into Jesus that we wish to describe here. Today there are important streams in modern evangelical theology whose views more and more approximate the view of Jesus presented here. One thinks, for example, of the New Testament scholar Herbert Braun who, in his book *Jesus of Nazareth: The Man and His Time*, defines Christian discipleship as the attempt to believe with Jesus and as Jesus, not primarily in Jesus.[3]

After centuries of a Christology that has sacrificed the human side of Jesus more and more to his divine nature, attempts are being made today to see the person Jesus, the *human being Jesus*. Nevertheless, the prevailing tendency is still to view Jesus as the mediator, divested of his bodily nature. For example, in her book *Christ the Representative: An Essay in Theology after the Death of God*, Dorothee Sölle maintains that today belief is possible only representatively through Jesus. But this is not a realistic view of the *Jew Jesus*—not merely *a* Jew but *the* quintessential Jew, to whom representational faith was entirely alien.

The Jewish person's relationship to Jesus must be essentially different from that of the Christian—though Jesus comes to Jews with an immediacy, to be sure, only after we have rediscovered the true features of the Jewish man from Nazareth under the painted overlay of Christian iconology. Layer after layer must be removed in order to penetrate to the original countenance of Jesus. But this countenance and this form do not stand in an empty space; they must be examined within the context of the Palestinian Judaism contemporary to him. Any other viewpoint fails to see the true nature of Jesus.

My own path in life has led me closer and closer to Jesus, though only as a result of personally undertaking to recover Jesus' picture from the Christian overpainting. My path to the land of Jesus, the land of Israel, and to the city of his passion, the city of Jerusalem—where I have lived since the mid-1930s—led me out of Catholic Bavaria. There I had encountered the Crucified One in churches and chapels, on little field crosses and in the Holy Savior nooks of farmhouses—an image that impressed itself painfully on me as a Jewish child. I have always found so much in this land of Israel, in this city of Jerusalem, and so much in Judaism, even in our own day, that lent to the reports of the Gospel a burning actuality that is always with me. Jesus is certainly a central figure of the Jewish past and the history of Jewish faith. But he is simultaneously a piece of our present and our future, no different from the prophets of the Hebrew Bible, who have for us more than merely historical relevance.

This view furthermore binds me to the many Christians for whom Jesus is the "One who has come," the Christians for whom Jesus is both the centerpiece of their lives and, ultimately, the Coming One. The New Testament closes with the words of the *Maran 'atha* (The Lord has come): "Amen. Come, Lord Jesus!" (Rev. 22:20). This Coming One interpreted messianically, however, is for me, a Jew, *not* what Jesus is. I also believe, moreover, that Jesus did not think of himself as the Messiah, even if here and there the presentiment of a messianic calling, as an unresolved question of his own existence, may have broken through.

The intimacy with which we wish to examine the figure of Jesus allows the messiahship of Jesus *to remain a valid question.* It is not my intention here, however, to address the apotheosis of Jesus. Rather, I share the sentiment expressed by Goethe in his late poetic cycle *West-östlicher Divan:*

Jesus fühlte rein und dachte
Nur den Einen Gott im Stillen;
Wer ihn selbst zum Gotte machte
Kränckte seinen heiligen Willen.[4]

[Jesus felt purely and thought
in his silence only on the *one* God;
whoever would turn Jesus himself into God
would distort his holy will.]

The question of the divinity of Jesus cannot exist for the historian or for the Jew. Even the question of the messiahship of Jesus must be bracketed here, since it exists apart from historical knowledge and Jewish belief.

The messianic *self-understanding* of Jesus is quite another matter, however. Käsemann, in addressing the issue of whether Jesus considered himself to be the Messiah, says, "I personally am convinced that there can be no possible grounds for answering this question affirmatively. I consider all passages in which any kind of Messianic prediction occurs to be kerygma shaped by the community" (*Essays*, 43). I have nothing to add to this, because I too can find no evidence that Jesus proclaimed himself the Messiah. It is true that a *messianic secret* exists in Jesus, which suggests that he occasionally became conscious of some messianic mission; but he forbids his disciples to publicize proclamations of this kind (Luke 9:21), as he is probably waiting for the hour when his true being is revealed to himself, his disciples, and the world.

Jesus can, therefore, not be taken as the Messiah, even if messianic features in the image of Jesus are clearly transmitted to us. They are products of kerygmatic revisions of a later hand.

Since the nineteenth century a liberal theology, in Judaism as well as Christianity, has readily designated Jesus as a *prophet*. But this definition, too, strikes me as untenable. Jesus was no prophet, no *navi'*, in the Old Testament sense of the word. What characterizes the *navi'* is his office as proclaimer. The *navi'* proclaims the utterance of Yahweh; he becomes the mouth of the deity. The character of the *navi'* is most clearly reflected in the story of the heathen seer Balaam, who can say only what God has placed in his mouth and who therefore must bless Israel, despite his intention of cursing the people (Num. 22–24).

The prophetic oration begins usually with formulas such as "Thus saith the Lord" or "Hear the Word of the Lord," or as a charge to the prophets such as "Speak to the children of Israel," or as a self-expression such as "And the word of the Lord came to me and said. . . ."

Introductory formulas of this sort are foreign to the speeches of

Jesus. He speaks upon personal authority, without conveying the dicta of God.

The nature of the prophet encompasses the quality of the seer, documented in visions of a particular type, such as that of Isaiah (6:1), who sees the Lord sitting on high in the temple, or of Jeremiah (1:11), to whom God speaks from the blooming almond branch (here one might recognize a parallel in Jesus' parable of the fig tree), or in that of the enthroned wagon of the prophet of the Exile, Ezekiel (1). Visions of this kind are missing in Jesus.

Revivals of the dead are found in the oldest prophets, Elisha (2 Kings 4:8–37) and Elijah (1 Kings 17:17–24), as well as in Jesus; the Evangelists, however, emphasize clearly a qualitative difference. Whereas the old prophets prayed when they raised someone from the dead, Jesus simply commands Lazarus to come forth from the grave (John 11:1–44), or the daughter of Jairus to stand up and walk (Luke 8:40–56).

Prophetic traits in the Old Testament sense are lacking in Jesus. Jesus appears rather to act in the manner of the contemporary teachers of the law, the Tannaim.[5] The tannaitic element is documented in the fact that Jesus, like the contemporary experts in scriptural law, teaches in two ways typical of the period: through *interpretation* of given canonical texts, and through parables (*meshalim*).

It is true that he taught "powerfully" and interpreted publicly with greater authority than others dared (Mark 1:22). Interpretations with the opening formula "But I say to you" give his exegesis its particular impact and nuance. And yet I find it misleading to insist that a rupture exists here with the tradition of Judaism, as Christian theologians up to the present day have done in the obvious attempt to isolate the figure of Jesus in order to arrive at the concept of the "exalted Lord."

Pharisaic Judaism at the time of Jesus was typified by the two great schools of Hillel and Shammai. The corpus of the Halakha, that body of religious law born from the interpretation of the Old Testament, especially of the commandments in the Pentateuch, acquired its definitive form in these two schools. The school of Hillel favored a milder, less stringent interpretation, which therefore found greater favor by virtue of its greater practicality; the school of Shammai took the path of stricter interpretation. Nevertheless, the decisions of both schools were considered to have the validity of "words of the living God."

I do not hesitate to declare that I see in Jesus of Nazareth a *third authority,* whose views are to be placed alongside those of Hillel and Shammai. It is not easy, however, to define Jesus' interpretation of the law. Jesus interprets the law at times mildly, like Hillel, and at other times harshly, like Shammai. And yet I believe that we can recognize in Jesus' interpretation a clear tendency toward the *internalization of the law,* whereby *love* constitutes the decisive and motivating element.

In the school of Hillel in particular, to which we owe the Golden Rule, likewise found in the New Testament (Matt. 7:12), *brotherly love* is central. The Haggada,[6] the body of talmudic legend, tells of a heathen man who wished to be introduced to Judaism within the period of time in which a person could stand on one foot. The furious Shammai chased the questioner out of the house, whereas the patient Hillel explained to him the law of brotherly love, noting that all else was only commentary and that he could now proceed to learn (BT, Shabbath 31a).

This reply could very well come from Jesus, yet he expresses the commandment of love more radically than does Hillel. Indeed, the radical quality of this love often turns into a radical hatred, particularly self-hatred. The statement in John 12:25, "Those who hate their life in this world will keep it for eternal life," appears to me typical only of Jesus' manner of teaching.

We know nothing about any teacher of Jesus, unlike Paul, for example, whose teacher was said to be Rabbi Gamaliel (Acts 22:3). It was probably the intention of the authors of the New Testament to represent Jesus as the Inspired One, who stood in need of no earthly teacher. On the other hand, it is probable that Jesus was not a *talmid chakham,* 'scholarly student,' but knew only the Hebrew Bible and interpreted it in his own way.

There is, however, a talmudic tradition according to which Yehoshua' Ben-Perachia is presented as the teacher of Jesus (BT, Sota 47a). The historical reliability of the reference in the Talmud—as well as in a *baraitha*—to this alleged teacher was never given serious credence by historians. But a related statement exists that on reflection has the force of credibility: namely, in a *baraitha* that reads, "Let the left hand push away, the right hand draw near; not as Elisha, who pushed aside Gechazi with both hands, and not as Yehoshua' Ben-Perachia, who pushed aside Jesus the Nazarene with both hands" (cf. Klausner, *Jesus,* 24–26).

This may be echoed in Matthew 6:3: "Do not let your left hand know what your right hand is doing." Might this relate to an answer that Jesus made to his teacher Yehoshua' Ben-Perachia? Further passages in the Talmud (e.g., BT, Sanhedrin 107b) indicate that Jesus, together with his teacher, fled to Egypt, which may be connected to the flight into Egypt recorded in Matthew 2:13–15. Yet the talmudic source places the flight of Jesus and his teacher in the time of King Alexander Jannaeus, who reigned from 103 to 76 B.C.E. Here, obviously, Alexander Jannaeus and Herod are reversed. The bases of the supposed controversy between Jesus and his teacher are very unclear in the versions of this legend that have been handed down to us. One of the later versions suggests that it was because Jesus subscribed to magic (a negative interpretation of the miracles of Jesus) that his teacher had a falling-out with him.

The evidence is so unreliable, however, that we must admit to knowing nothing about the teachers and education of Jesus.

Given this predicament, the question arises whether Jesus may have belonged to one of the currents, groups, or parties of his time. Although these groupings undeniably possess political character as well, they must be defined primarily in terms of their origin and, especially, as schools in the broader sense.

They were divided into two major feuding parties: the *Pharisees* and the *Sadducees.* The Pharisees were the party of those learned in scriptural law. In the New Testament the designations "Pharisees" and "scribes" are used interchangeably to designate the same group.[7] Historically, the Pharisees, a group characterized by quasi-democratic principles, were responsible for the institution of the synagogue, which represented a democratic expression of the ritual at once opposed to and complementing the temple cult; the latter had a sacramental character and was administered by two castes, the priests (*kohanim*) and the Levites.

The Pharisees themselves created the type of the *talmid chakham* and traced their intellectual lineage back to Ezra, the leading force in the reconstruction of Judaism following the return from the Babylonian Exile. In the New Testament the Pharisees appear in a distorted light because of their conflict with Jesus and his disciples. The later polemics between the original Christian community and the synagogue are likewise reflected in this controversy.

The situation in which the authors of the New Testament wrote did not allow an objective representation of the Pharisees, which explains their "bad press." In fact, the many positive traits of the Pharisees were suppressed in the New Testament in a polemical fashion. The Pharisees strove to sanctify all aspects of life, which in law and custom was to be subordinated to the revealed will of God. Nothing lay outside this sanctifying sphere: eating and drinking, work and rest, sexuality and hygiene, clothing and hairstyle. Nothing was considered too trivial to be integrated with the service of God in the most profound reverence. Thus the Pharisees, whose high ethical conceptions are preserved in the collection of wisdom known as Pirkei-'Avoth (Sayings of the Fathers), became the intellectual fathers of later Jewish orthodoxy. The Pharisees of the New Testament are mirrored in the reality and problems of modern Jewish orthodoxy. Deep seriousness, unconditional devotion to the law of God, minute attention to one's duty with regard to this law—these traits mark the descendants of the Pharisees even today. But we also witness in them the dangers of the degeneration of which the New Testament speaks almost exclusively. This degeneration is the result of being wrapped in an armor of 613 commandments and prohibitions and thereby losing the freedom necessary for the stirrings of living faith. The world of the Pharisees, like the world of contemporary Jewish orthodoxy, is a closed system, seamlessly knit together by a relentlessly consistent logic.

Faith, however, represents a kind of daring that must be retained in the freedom of love beyond all assurances. It is here, probably, that the antagonism arose between Jesus and the Pharisees. Even within the pharisaic school we find a tendency toward unconditional faith, expressed in the beautiful injunction "Be not as servants who serve for reward, but as those who serve out of love" (Pirkei-'Avoth 1.3). That point is emphatically made in a Haggada concerning the heretic 'Elisha' Ben-'Avuya, whom the problem of theodicy turned into one who denied heavenly justice. A heavenly voice says to him, "All creatures are forgiven except for 'Elisha' Ben-'Avuya." Thereupon Rabbi 'Akiva answers, "Blessed art thou, Ben-'Avuya. All creatures serve for reward; you, however, can now serve out of love."

If in light of the New Testament one faults the Pharisees' insistence upon punctilious adherence to justification by works, we should recall the words of Rabbi 'Akiva, preserved for us in the Babylonian Talmud (Kiddushin 40b): "So Rabbi Tarfon and the elders were gathered in the upper room of the house of Nitheza in Lod, and the question was raised, 'What is more important: doctrine or deed?' Rabbi 'Akiva answered, 'Doctrine.' Then all agreed unanimously that doctrine is superior because doctrine leads to deed."

Doctrine here means Torah. Viewed in this way, the religion of the deed, which is a hallmark of the Pharisees, may be properly understood.

The Pharisees were not beyond self-criticism. The Jerusalem Talmud (JT) says the following in Berakhoth 9.5:

> There are seven kinds of Pharisees (*perushim*) . . . the shoulder Pharisee carries his good deeds on his shoulder [i.e., openly, before the whole world]; the gleaning Pharisee says, "Wait for me. I must fulfill the commandments [and have no time for you]"; the balancing Pharisee pays off each debt [i.e., sin] by performing a commandment; the frugal Pharisee says, "From the little I have, what can I set aside for performing commandments?"; the debtor Pharisee says, "Tell me what sin I have committed, and I will perform a commandment to offset it"; the fearing Pharisee is like Job; the loving Pharisee is like Abraham.

The five negative types of Pharisees here are clearly depicted in the New Testament, whereas the two positive types, those in the tradition of Job and Abraham, are visible hardly anywhere in the Gospels.

The most dangerous type of Pharisee, however—and it is on him that the light of the Gospels falls—is the "colored" Pharisee: that is, the hypocrite. We are warned of this type of Pharisee in the Babylonian Talmud (Sota 22b): "Fear neither the Pharisees nor those who are not Pharisees but only the colored ones who seem like Pharisees, who do the works of Zimri and demand the reward of Phinehas." This passage alludes to Numbers 25:6–15, which narrates the incident surrounding the Israelite Zimri, who is involved in an unseemly relationship with the Midianite Cozbi and for that is killed by the zealot Phinehas. This criticism of the colored ones implies that they are *hypocritical moralists*. They are outwardly zealous, but internally they lead unbridled lives.

Among the Pharisees themselves there is much vocal criticism, hardly outdone even by that of the Gospels. For example, Rabbi Yehoshua' says (Mishna, Sota 3.4), "The foolishly pious, the cunningly wicked, the pharisaical woman, and the fleshly mortifications of the Pharisees are ruining the world." A Pharisee himself says this!

In this light, it is probably not wrong to reckon Jesus among the Pharisees, albeit as part of an internal opposition movement within this largest Judaic group of his day. Jesus himself talks like a pharisaic rabbi, although from a greater position of authority; his extraordinarily forceful manner of speaking is, however, most likely a product of the kerygmatic tradition. Nevertheless, the authority with which the Pharisees themselves spoke should not be underestimated. They must be distinguished from their opponents, the Sadducees, who held firmly only to the written Torah, the Pentateuch, as well as to some later parts of the Old Testament. The Pharisees' consciousness of their own authority is exemplified by a legend that tells how the experts in scriptural law decided *against* a heavenly voice, justifying their decision upon Deuteronomy 30:12: "It [the Torah] is not in heaven." Thereupon a heavenly voice declares, "My children have defeated me."

One can reject this attitude of the Pharisees as theological bluster; one can also recognize in it, however, the "freedom of the glory of the children of God" proclaimed in the New Testament (Rom. 8:21). In any event, it is clear that the experts in scriptural law among the Pharisees themselves taught with an authority based on the belief that they, conscious of their succession from Moses, were the fully empowered bearers of revelation.

Jesus stands at an even greater distance from the Sadducees, also called "the high priests" in the New Testament—a false classification, since there was at any given time only one officiating high priest (*kohen gadol*, lit. 'the great priest'). "The high priest" is probably meant to signify the party of the one high priest, his dynasty, and his intimate clique. He represented the leading stratum of the Sadducees, whose name *tsedukim* derives from that of the ruling dynasty of the house of Tsadok. In the New Testament as in the Talmud we can discern a major distinction between the Pharisees and the Sadducees: the Sadducees deny the resurrection of the dead (Acts 23:6–10). That explains their narrow focus on only the written Torah, the five books of Moses, which indeed never speak of the resurrection of the dead. This conception is documented much later, probably during or after the Exile, and only very sparsely in the Old Testament (Isa. 25:8, 26: 19; Ps. 49:15; Dan. 12:2). Even that most famous resurrection passage in Ezekiel 37 refers to the national resurrection of Israel, not to the individual resurrection of the dead.

The Sadducees laid greatest stress on the proper temple service and thus denied the laical element accentuated by the Pharisees. Socially, the Sadducees formed the aristocratic upper crust; Jesus, therefore, who stemmed from very humble origins, stood also in social opposition to them. The reason we know so much less about the Sadducees than about the Pharisees is that the Jewish traditional literature passed through pharisaic redaction. The Sadducees thus appear only in the reflection of their opponents, which is certainly distorted. Not until the beginning of the twentieth century, when Solomon Schechter discovered the so-called Damascus document in the Cairo Geniza (synagogue archives), did a text attributable to the Sadducees become available. Further, a portion of the papyrus rolls from Qumran may be ascribed to the tradition of the Sadducees. Jesus has absolutely nothing in common with the Sadducees. He silences them much more easily (Matt. 22:34) than he does the Pharisees, who stand closer to him.

Concerning the Essenes, we formerly knew even less than we do about the Sadducees. But the papyrus rolls of Qumran, *if* they are ascribable to the Essene sect, help to clarify the picture of this monastic community at the time of Jesus. In the nineteenth century the tendency was to count Jesus among the Essenes, but that now appears to be incorrect, given that he did not share their abstinence and in no way rejected the enjoyment of wine.[8]

There were obviously groups related to the Essenes, such as the 'Evionim (the poor) and the 'Anavim (the wretched), with whom Jesus felt an affinity, as we see particularly in his conversation with the rich young man and in the sharp paradox, "It is easier for a camel to go through the eye of a needle than for someone who is rich to enter the kingdom of God" (Mark 10:25). The blessing of the poor in the Sermon on the Mount belongs here as well, as we shall see. To what degree the Chasidim (Hasideans), the particularly God-fearing group, and now also the Qumranians are to be considered as actual parties cannot yet be determined. They may simply have amounted to currents or splinter groups within larger groupings.

On the other hand, the Zealots, or Sicarians (the word derives from the short daggers [Latin *sica*] that they carried), constitute a well-defined group of political and messianic activists who "pressed for the end of time." They prepared themselves for armed resistance against Rome, and there may very well have been, in the circle of Jesus' disciples, representatives of this Jewish underground movement, especially the dark disciple Judas, who wanted to turn Jesus into the messianic claimant. As far as I can see, there is only one documented saying of Jesus that might associate him with these activists: "But now, the one who has a purse must take it, and likewise a bag. And the one who has no sword must sell his cloak and buy one" (Luke 22:36). Only two verses later (v. 38), however, this statement is considerably weakened: "They said, 'Lord, look, here are two swords.' He replied, 'It is enough.'"

We recall, on the other hand, Jesus' warning to Peter that whoever takes up the sword is killed by the sword (Matt. 26:52)—a saying that stands in line with Hillel, who emphasized that the assassin is assassinated and every violent act repaid by a violent act. If Jesus was satisfied with the presence of only two swords, it is hard to understand why authors such as Robert Eisler and Joel Carmichael have sought to redefine Jesus as belonging to the class of Zealot activists. It is true that no polemic against the Zealots is found in the New Testament, but neither is a polemic found against their rivals, the mild Essenes.

We may conclude that Jesus cannot be reckoned entirely to have belonged to any single group known to us, although it is to the Pharisees—as peculiar as that may sound—that he has the closest links.

Jesus must simply walk the path prescribed for him alone, and he calls out of his solitude to those who would follow him. I cannot agree with Käsemann that there is no discernible development in Jesus (*Essays*, 35). Albert Schweitzer long ago recognized an internal development in Jesus' personality occurring within the brief period of work between his thirtieth and thirty-third year of life.

I myself recognize three stages of development, or tragic disappointment, in the life of Jesus: eschatology, introversion, and passion.

Eschatology. The first phase in the life of Jesus stands under the sign of the imminently expected appearance of the kingdom of God. Jesus sends the disciples forth and assures them, "You will not have gone through all the towns of Israel [to preach the gospel to them] before the Son of Man comes" (Matt. 10:23). The disciples return, but nothing has changed. Jesus must subject his message to a revision.

Introversion. What was first expected as an event of history, the advent of a new age, is now understood as having already attained completion in the soul: "The kingdom of God is among you" (Luke 17:21; some exegetes construe this passage to say that Jesus is referring to himself as the incarnation of the kingdom among his disciples). But neither does this internalized kingdom of God suffice, since the external force cannot be overcome by the kingdom-of-God community already established in his circle of disciples. Thus Jesus is stirred on to the ultimate tribulation: a freely chosen self-sacrifice provoked by the Jewish and Roman authorities.

Passion. This sacrificial path ends with the crucifixion and the despairing cry of Jesus, "Eli, Eli, lema sabachthani?" (Matt. 27:46, based on Ps. 22:1; the reading "Eloi, Eloi, lema sabachthani" is found in Mark 15:34). There is every reason to accept the despairing cry, "My God, my God, why have you forsaken me?" as the *true* final words of Jesus. The Martyred One gives up the ghost with the horrifying realization of having been abandoned by God, precisely in this third and final station of his thorn-strewn path toward the kingdom of God.

And thus, in the Jewish historical view, Jesus ends up a tragic failure. That does not, however, belittle his greatness, not even in terms of Jewish historical understanding. Rabbi 'Akiva himself, who considered Bar-Kokheva the Messiah, proved to be tragically wrong and ended up a martyr for his faith. Nevertheless, his tragic mistake did not rob him of any of his greatness within the Jewish folk consciousness. Quite to the contrary, the Jewish tradition explains this kind of error with the saying, "Out of love for Israel, God sometimes blinds the eyes of the wise."[9]

Jesus of Nazareth was also such a tragic erring one whose eyes were blinded out of love for Israel.

The Jesus revealed to us in both exegesis and intuition (these do not exclude but condition each other) is a historical figure, even if not all details of his life can be historically validated. But for what personality who lived two thousand years ago could it be otherwise? The school that once insisted upon the unhistoricity of Jesus and sought to describe him in terms of an astral myth or the like may be assigned now to the definitive past. Rousseau already noted in the famous digression "Profession of Faith of the Savoyard Vicar" from his novel *Emile* that if the Gospels had been fabricated, their contrivers would have been greater than Jesus himself. In his book *The Son of Man* (xiv), Emil Ludwig makes reference to this profound insight of Rousseau, noting that the authors of the Gospels speak of a real person according to the testimony of those who knew Jesus "in the flesh." There are so many contradictory features, traits, and details in the reports of the Gospels that we must conclude, on this fact alone, that we are dealing not with a didactic abstraction or invented messianic myth but with the living reminiscence of a son of man—a son of *a* man—notwithstanding the aura of apotheosis surrounding him.

German historians and theologians of the nineteenth century often fell under the suggestive power of a famous passage in Friedrich Schiller's poem "An die Freunde" (To friends):

> Alles wiederholt sich nur im Leben,
> Ewig jung ist nur die Phantasie,
> Was sich nie und nirgends hat begeben,
> Das allein veraltet nie!

> [Everything returns only in life,
> only fantasy is forever young;
> what never and nowhere existed,
> that alone never grows old!]

But the fact that the happy and tragic mission of the life of Jesus has not grown old after two thousand years must not lead to the assumption that it is "only fantasy." Of these four lines of Schiller, the first is especially important: "Alles wiederholt sich nur im Leben." Prefigured in the life of Jesus was much that has been repeated in the lives of his followers. Fantasy and belief have extracted much from his life, transporting it from the sphere of secular history into the higher sphere of salvation history. But the *sitz im leben,* the real context of these episodes in the historical report of Jesus, is unmistakable to Jewish eyes.

Jesus of Nazareth lived. He continues to live, not only in the church that rests on him—or, more precisely, in the many churches and denominations that claim him—but also in his Jewish people, whose martyrdom he embodies. Is not the suffering Jesus, the Jesus scorned as he hangs dying on the cross, a likeness for his entire people who, tortured and bloodied, have been hanged time and again on the cross of anti-Semitism? And is the Easter message of the resurrection not a parable for postwar Israel, which has risen out of the abasement and disgrace of the darkest twelve years in its history to a new incarnation?

2 *Birth and Rebirth*

The birth of Jesus lies in darkness. A light falls only on the hour of his rebirth: that is, the Jordan baptism by John. That is no coincidence but corresponds to the conception of Jesus echoed in the conversation with the Pharisee Nicodemus: "No one can see the kingdom of God without being born from above" (John 3:3).

The concept of rebirth is in Judaism at the time of Jesus clearly a folk belief. John the Baptist is identified in the New Testament as the returned Elijah; Jesus is also presumed to be Elijah. But we must examine the figure of Elijah more closely, for according to biblical legend he did not die but was carried away in a fiery chariot (2 Kings 2:11). Thus the prophet Malachi (4:5)[10] expected Elijah's return—a motif that comes up repeatedly in the later Haggada. Elijah and Enoch (Gen. 5:24) are the only personages of the Old Testament who are held not to have died and whose return was therefore anticipated.

We encounter the idea of rebirth also with respect to the deceased. This explains why people considered Jesus to be one of the old prophets who had returned (Luke 9:8,19). In the Talmud there are striking allusions to a belief in the transmigration of souls, or rebirth, such as the remark, "Mordecai, that is, Samuel." The comment implies that the Jew Mordecai, the uncle of Queen Esther, was a reincarnation of the prophet Samuel. The doctrine of the transmigration of souls, which is organic to the concept of rebirth, is developed in Jewish mysticism in the Kabbala and continues into chasidic folk belief. According to this conception a person is born and reborn over and over, undergoing in this way a *gilgul neshama,* a transmigration of souls, or becoming attached to another soul *('ibbur neshama,* or *dibbuk);* rebirth occurs as often as necessary until redemption *(tikkun)* is achieved.

The antiquity of these conceptions in Judaism is not important here. Traditionally, they go back to the origins of mankind and were revealed most fully through Rabbi Shim'on Ben-Yochai (a contemporary of Rabbi 'Akiva) in the *Zohar,* which is ascribed to him.[11] We know with certainty today that the *Zohar* was a medieval work, though that is not to deny the possible literary refashioning of old traditions and the pseudepigraphal attribution to some revered figure of antiquity. In any event, the New Testament shows that belief in rebirth was current at the time of Jesus. The extent to which Far Eastern influences were present cannot be considered here; besides, there is no immediate evidence of such influences, and we should rather speak of archetypal conceptions of the soul which may arise among various peoples and cultures more or less independently.

Jewish folk belief, at the time of Jesus and later, connects rebirth with the transmigration of souls; Jesus himself, at least in the doctrine attributed to him, deepens and reinterprets the concept. (It is typical of Jesus' manner of teaching that he borrows generally familiar concepts and reinterprets them, rather than actually creating new ones.) The word *palingenesia,* 'rebirth,' is found in the New Testament only twice (Matt. 19:28 and Titus 3:5) and is employed in both instances in allusion to a messianic era: the citizens of the coming kingdom of God have been reborn. But the conversation with Nicodemus in John 3:1–21—though it may be a later kerygma—penetrates deeply into the conceptual sphere of rebirth as understood by Jesus. In this dialogue Nicodemus asks the naive question, "How can anyone be born after having grown old? Can one enter a second time into the mother's womb and be born?" (v. 4). Jesus' answer is *not* that a person dies and then is reborn, which would correspond to the concept of the transmigration of souls, but that a person can be reborn from water and spirit; spirit, of course, or wind, "blows where it chooses" (v. 8). Only in being reborn in this manner can a person become a citizen of the kingdom of God.

From water and spirit! Spirit must be understood in the double meaning of the Hebrew word *ruach* and of the Greek word *pneuma*. *Ruach-pneuma* in the biblical sense means both 'wind' and 'spirit' together. In his translation of the Bible, Martin Buber rendered this critical word as *Braus* 'a roaring.'

Jesus' conversation with Nicodemus, which teaches rebirth from water and spirit, is clearly the basis of the (later) sacrament of baptism. Baptism itself, however, is by no means an institution of Jesus. He himself did not baptize but did let himself be baptized by John (Mark 1:9). This baptism by John presents no novelty in Judaism, for it was a ritual widely practiced by Jews at the time, as it is today. The word *baptism* became misunderstood, however, through its later ecclesiastical development; more accurately, it refers to *tevila*, 'bath of immersion.' Jesus in fact takes a bath of immersion in the Jordan, no differently than hundreds or even thousands of his contemporaries who went down to the Jordan in order to complete the ritual of purification. The law of the Torah (e.g., Lev. 22:6) prescribes the bath of immersion for numerous types of ritual impurities, especially that of touching a corpse or a skeleton. The Essenes and the sects of Qumran increasingly conceptualized the bath of immersion as a spiritual means of purification: a catharsis. Rabbi 'Akiva went even further in his famous wordplay at the end of the Mishna tractate Yoma: "Happy are you, O Israel. Before whom do you purify yourselves? And who purifies you? It is your Father in heaven. As it is written, 'I will sprinkle clean water upon you, and you shall be clean'" (Ezek. 36:25). He goes on to say, "'O hope [*mikve*] of Israel! O Lord!'" (Jer. 17:13). "If the bath of immersion [*mikve*] purifies the impure, so then does the Holy One, blessed be he, purify Israel" (Yoma 8.9). The word *mikve* used in the text has both meanings: hope and bath of immersion.[12]

The so-called baptism of John, which Jesus undergoes and which we can characterize as the act of his rebirth and the beginning of his public work, must be seen within this Jewish tradition.

But in his discussion with Nicodemus, Jesus emphasizes that the spirit belongs to the water (the immersion bath). This is an obvious allusion to Genesis 1:2: "A wind from God swept over the face of the waters." The classical rabbinic exegete Rabbi Shelomo Ben-Yitschak, called Rashi (from southern France, 1040–1105), cites a midrash in his commentary on this passage: "The spirit of God hovered like a dove that hovers over its nest" (BT, Chagiga 15a). In this we have a conception of the spirit of God, which in the figure of a dove hovers over the water at the rebirth of Jesus in the hour of his Jordan baptism by John. The word used in Genesis, *merachefeth,* means 'hover' or 'brood'; the same image is found in the final song of Moses (Deut. 32:11), which speaks of a brooding eagle.

Jesus of Nazareth was probably about thirty years old when he came to the Jordan in order to complete, like others of his contemporaries, the purification ritual under the guidance of John. Clearly, in this ceremonial act he becomes self-consciously awakened to his mission. Only at this moment does he become visible to us. The *tevila,* the immersion, represents the actual rebirth, for the person being immersed is buried by the waters; he goes under in order to rise again symbolically as a new man, purified of his sins.[13] This conception has remained vital in the community of Jesus.

The physical birth of Jesus, as we said, is shrouded in darkness. Matthew 1:1–17 and Luke 3:23–38 both offer a family tree of Jesus, but these contradict each other, as is well known. Matthew describes a genealogical tree from Abraham to Jesus in 3 groupings of 14 generations each ($14 = 2 \times 7$, the sacred number): Abraham to David $= 14$; David to the Babylonian Exile $= 14$; the Babylonian Exile to Jesus $= 14$ (for a total of 42 generations). In Matthew's account, Joseph, the husband of Mary, Jesus' mother, is a son of Jacob. According to Luke, that same Joseph is a son of Eli.

The darkness that lies over the bodily origin of Jesus has led his enemies to the inevitable claim that his was a birth out of wedlock. We have in the Talmud the so-called Pandera, or Panthera, tradition, according to which a Roman official by that name seduces one Miriam, who was betrothed to Joseph, and impregnates her; the fruit of this sin, it is said, was Jesus (cf. Klausner, *Jesus,* 23).

The distant relationship (to state it mildly) of Jesus to his mother, whom he never addresses by any name other than "woman"[14] (John

2:4, 19:26), may reflect the painful consciousness of an illegitimate birth. Jesus does not honor his mother, and he denies his bodily father, since it appears that he is aware of his unlawful and foreign— that is, non-Jewish—origin.

In the Gospel this darkness is illuminated by the light of a miracle. Jesus is proclaimed to be the Son of God born of the Holy Spirit. Matthew 1:21 adds a wordplay to the announcement made to Joseph of this miraculous birth: "She will bear a son, and you are to name him Jesus, for he will save his people from their sins." This wordplay is understandable only in Hebrew: his name is to be called Yeshua', for he will save (*yoshia'*) his people, the Jews, from their sins.[15] That Isaiah 7:14 is adduced in this context is in itself unfounded. All that is said in Isaiah is that a young woman (*'alma*), not a virgin, will become pregnant and bear a son and call him Immanuel, not Yeshua'. Equating a young woman with a virgin goes back to the Greek Bible translation, the Septuagint, in which the word *'alma* is translated as *parthenos* 'virgin.' Had the Hebrew text intended to speak of a virgin, it would have used the term *bethula,* which is not the case.

The wordplay Yeshua'/yoshia' in the Jewish-Christian Gospel of Matthew is lacking in Luke (1:31). Luke, a non-Jewish physician, is writing to a certain Theophilus, who, presumably, was a patrician in Antioch and would not have understood the Hebrew wordplay (it was in fact foreign to Luke himself).

The story of the birth of Jesus is permeated by typical legend motifs: The wise Magi from the East belong to the realm of fairytales. The myth of the birth of the hero, as it echoes in the Nativity story, has many parallels in legends associated with famous personages from antiquity. King Herod's fear of the chosen king who will challenge him for the throne is prefigured, for example, in the fear of King Laius of Thebes, who maims and expels his son Oedipus at birth. The father of Theseus, King Aegaeus of Athens, keeps the birth of his son secret. But we are particularly reminded of the myth of the birth of Moses, which also provides a model for the alleged infanticide in Bethlehem. This event in fact never took place. Before the birth of Moses, the gruesome Pharaoh orders that all newborn Jewish males are to be killed and thrown into the Nile (Exod. 1:22), but the chosen one is miraculously saved. The infanticide in Bethlehem is further related by

Matthew (2:16–18) to the figure of Rachel weeping for her children (Jer. 31:15); Rachel's grave was traditionally located in Bethlehem.

The gospel assertion of Bethlehem as the birthplace of Jesus, who was known to have come from Nazareth, is owing to the prophecy of Micah (5:2): "But you, O Bethlehem of Ephrathah, who are one of the little clans of Judah, from you shall come forth for me one who is to rule in Israel, whose origin is from of old, from ancient days." [16]

That many legendary elements exist in the Bethlehem tradition is demonstrated by the confusion of two places bearing this name. The Bethlehem intended in the Gospels as Jesus' birthplace is the one near Jerusalem, the city of David. Micah's prophecy, however, refers to Bethlehem-Ephrath, the well-known place of death of the matriarch Rachel (Gen. 35:19). The grave of Rachel, as previously noted, was also subsequently worshiped in the Bethlehem near Jerusalem.

For the later pagan Christians, another element may have figured into the birth myth as well: an Adonis grotto worshiped in the Bethlehem near Jerusalem. It is mentioned as early as the church father Jerome, who himself lived in this Bethlehem and there translated the Bible into Latin.

Equally mythical is the tale of the flight of the baby Jesus into Egypt. It too is traceable to a prophetic passage: "Out of Egypt I called my son" (Hos. 11:1). This son is, in Hosea, the entire people of Israel, and the prophet is alluding to the Exodus from Egypt. In the Jesus tradition, the prophecy is interpreted as having its fulfillment only with the life of Jesus. The childhood history remains so shrouded in darkness that only the apocryphal gospels (the proto-gospel of Jacob, the pseudo-Matthew, etc.) report any further details about it; there are also Armenian and Arabic childhood gospels (twentieth-century finds in Nag Hammadi have brought to light similar ones). All of these bear purely fairytale traits. Jesus is depicted as a wunderkind. For example, in the company of his comrades he throws stones at clay doves and afterward bestirs the broken figures to life.

There is of course not a scintilla of biographical worth to any of these narratives. Even the church refused to accept them into the New Testament canon.

The disputation in the temple between the twelve-year-old Jesus and the experts in scriptural law belongs also only to legend (Luke 2:

41–52). Its point is merely to emphasize that Jesus was no scholarly student who had received his knowledge from a teacher. He appears rather as the Inspired One of God, who even as a boy is superior to the experts. It is significant that Jesus is introduced as a twelve-year-old, since according to a sacred Jewish conception that continues to be valid today, a thirteen-year-old boy is a *bar-mitsva,* a son of the law (Pirkei-'Avoth 5.25). Luke's narrative means to convey that before his religious maturity, Jesus already had a knowledge of the Torah that surpassed even that of the experts in scriptural law.

All evidence indicates that Jesus came from Nazareth. Here too, however, we recognize a certain forcible attempt to relate his lineage to a biblical text—namely, to the vision of the coming kingdom of peace (Isa. 11:1): "A shoot shall come out from the stump of Jesse, and a branch shall grow out of his roots." This shoot, or twig, is called in Hebrew *netser* and is associated with Nazareth (Matt. 2:23).

An etymological connection of this sort is known in the Hebrew tradition as an *'asmakhta.* An *'asmakhta* does not possess any immediate exegetical value but, rather, bears homiletic character; it is an essential element of the Midrash, the legendary exposition of scripture.

We see in the motifs both of Bethlehem and the flight into Egypt simply the wish to present the Jesus who was preached to the Jews as the Messiah promised by the prophets and to represent his life as the fulfillment of the prophecies; in the Nazareth tradition, however, we see exactly the opposite. There is an almost embarrassing insinuation in the question "Can anything good come out of Nazareth?" (John 1:46). The Messiah had to be born in Bethlehem or in the Holy City of Jerusalem. Jesus comes, however, from completely unsung Nazareth, a place not mentioned in the Old Testament at all. Some kind of link to a biblical text—preferably to a messianic prophecy—needed to be discovered in the manner of the *derash,* or homiletic interpretation.

But lineage and birth, childhood and education, sink into insignificance at the hour of the rebirth. That explains why we know nothing about the childhood and early education of Jesus. It is generally accepted that he acquired the carpentry trade from his father, or foster father, Joseph, but that is only a supposition. The claim made by Erich

Zehren in *Der gehenkte Gott* (The crucified God) that Jesus was entirely unlearned must be rejected, for in the synagogue at Nazareth Jesus in fact reads aloud the prophet section, the *haftara,* which is something that no *'am-ha'arets* (a wholly unlearned person) could do. We have every reason to assume that Jesus knew the Hebrew Bible very well. He lived in and with it, especially the Torah and the Prophets. The instructional manner of the Tannaim, his scholarly contemporaries, was familiar to him, though that does not imply that he himself was necessarily a student of some famous master. The fact that he is addressed as "rabbi" suggests that he appeared to those around him as a man fully conversant with the law. At the trial, even his opponents do not accuse him of lack of knowledge. Only Jesus himself says of his enemies that they do not know what they are doing. In one of the apocryphal gospels Jesus sees a man working his field on the Sabbath and speaks to him in a paradox: "If you know what you are doing, you are blessed; if you do not know what you are doing, you are accursed and a violator of the law" (Codex Bezae reading following Luke 6:4).[17] That is very much in keeping with Hillel's saying that no unlearned person can be pious (Pirkei-'Avoth 2.5). Every deed must be thought through in terms of the law. We should therefore think of Jesus as a self-educated man, who acquired elementary knowledge of the Bible in his little town of Nazareth and then later continued his studies, attaining at last a revolutionary level of knowledge.

But as we noted, all of that sinks into the waters of the Jordan at the moment of the immersion bath that leads to rebirth. It is the Risen One, the one risen from the watery grave, who carries on into history. The man who facilitates this rebirth with spiritual aid and who can thus claim to be the proper father of Jesus, his father in spirit, is John the Baptist. Who was John?

According to Luke 1:5–25, John was the son of a devout priest, Zechariah (Zecharias), of the priestly dynasty of Abijah (1 Chron. 24:10), and his wife Elizabeth ('Elisheva'), who had long been barren.

The angel Gabriel—the same one who will foretell the birth of Jesus—announces the birth of John to the priest Zechariah in the temple during the service. In the birth myth of John, numerous elements from the Old Testament are interwoven. Zechariah and Elizabeth are equal in age and barrenness to Abraham and Sarah. The announcement of the miraculous birth of John recalls that of the judge Samson; like Samson, John (Yochanan) is to be a *nazir* (Nazirite; Judg. 13:4–5), one who abstains from wine and intoxicating beverages (Luke 1:15). The Nazirite institution—a group of men who for either a specifically limited period of time or for an entire lifetime maintained the vow of abstinence from alcohol and wore their hair long, becoming thereby identified as men dedicated to God—is set forth in the law of the Nazirites (Num. 6:1–21).[18] At the time of John it was so strongly observed that the Mishna devoted an entire tractate, titled Nazir, to this institution.

The Nazirite institution shared certain barbaric features with other ascetic movements and was consequently associated with the Rechabites (1 Chron. 2:55; Jer. 35), who likewise rejected alcohol and who lived in tents in the wilderness rather than in permanent dwellings. A remark in Luke 1:80 suggests that as a boy John was close to the Rechabites—astonishing for the son of a priest: "The child grew and became strong in spirit, and he was in the wilderness until the day he appeared publicly to Israel." Recently, there has been a tendency to see a connection between John and Qumran. In this view, the child cannot have remained alone in the desert but was probably reared in the monastic society of Qumran in the spirit of that sect, about which we have gained some knowledge as a result of the discovery of the Dead Sea scrolls. One can imagine John being reared in that spirit and later taking the message from the wilderness to the people. In the announcement of the birth of John the Elijah motif is struck in a manner reminiscent of Malachi, who prophesied the return of Elijah, the reconciler of the generations. John is viewed, quite beyond his violent death (Mark 6:27–29), as a reincarnation of Elijah, who was himself intimately connected with the wilderness.

On the basis of the purely legendary story of the Visitation (Luke 1:39–56), Jesus and John must have been approximately the same age, John being only a few months older, since both mothers, Mary and Elizabeth, were pregnant at the same time. The tradition of the Visitation, however, is so unclear that the place of the encounter of the two women is identified only as "a Judean town in the hill country"

(v. 39), later thought to be Ein Karem in the neighborhood of Jerusalem. Though this report has no historical value, its kerygmatic significance is nonetheless clear. John must be at least a few months older than Jesus in order that his role as the "precursor" may appear sensible. The two blessed mothers must meet each other so that the salvation plan of God may be made visible. The legend, however, is completely transparent. One can easily recognize that an older tradition of the disciples of John transformed the birth of their master into a miraculous one. The disciples of Jesus could not simply discard this tradition, and so they outdid it with an even more miraculous birth myth. It is striking that we have no birth notice of any of the disciples or apostles but such a detailed birth legend about John. That is explainable only by an independent tradition emanating from the circle of John, possibly related in some way to Qumran.

In the birth myth of John one must also note the temporary loss of the faculty of speech suffered by his father, Zechariah. It is presented as a punishment for the doubt with which Zechariah received the announcement of the birth of a child that he no longer expected. But on a deeper level a different motive is discernible. The great preachers were often afflicted with temporary loss of speech or with a speech impediment; in the language of myth this symbolizes the heaviness of the Word of God in the mouths of men. Moses was a man of heavy lip and tongue (Exod. 6:12), and the lip of Isaiah first had to be burned pure by a coal taken from the altar by an angel (Isa. 6:5–7).

John is introduced as a herald, specifically as a "crier" in the wilderness. A hindrance of speech must precede this cry—here, however, transferred to the father.

At his circumcision John was originally supposed to be named after his father, Zechariah (Luke 1:59). The custom of naming a son after his father is very rare among Jews; at any rate, it is certainly not a given, as the pagan Christian Luke assumes. (We do know of such cases: for example, in the book of Tobias, both the father and the son are called Toviya, Tobias.[19] In the Talmud as well there are a few cases in which father and son bear the same name. Today in Jewish society the name of the father is usually given to the son only when the birth occurs after the death of the father.) Here, however, mother and

father want the child be called Yochanan (John), which causes confusion among their acquaintances, since no one in the family is
known to have had this name.

This passage in Luke is specious, for the name Yochanan enjoyed
wide popularity, as we can gather from the New Testament alone.
The beloved disciple of Jesus bears this name; there are also three
John epistles, a John Gospel, and the Apocalypse of John of Patmos;
and we should by no means assume that these Johns represent the
same person. The personage of Rabbi Yochanan is known to us from
the Talmud. What is remarkable is that no explanation for the name
John is given in the story of John the Baptist. Apparently, the meaning of the name *Yochanan,* 'God favors,' escaped the pagan Christian Luke.

There are few figures in the New Testament about whom we have
such exact information as for John the Baptist. The comment in
Luke 3:1–2 even provides a double dating: "In the fifteenth year of
the reign of Emperor Tiberius, when Pontius Pilate was governor
of Judea, and Herod was ruler of Galilee, and his brother Philip ruler
of the region of Ituraea and Trachonitis, and Lysanias ruler of Abi-
lene, during the high priesthood of Annas and Caiaphas, the word of
God came to John son of Zechariah in the wilderness."

In this double-dating both the secular and religious authorities are
named. One could even speak of a threefold dating: according to the
calculation of the Imperium Romanum; according to the regency of
the governors; and according to the office term of the high priests.
Within the same chapter (v. 23) we also have an exact datum about
Jesus: "Jesus was about thirty years old when he began his work. He
was the son (as was thought) of Joseph son of Heli."

Despite this ostensible precision, however, the figure of John remains shrouded in darkness; later retouches have distorted the image
of the Baptist.

Over the course of kerygmatic and dogmatic development, John
came to be viewed as the last prophet of the Old Covenant and the first
prophet of the New Covenant, the "first exegete of Jesus," as Claus
Westermann calls him. A later ecclesiastical interpretation brought
John the Baptist into a connection with Mary, the mother of Jesus,
whom he in fact probably never knew. Above all, however, John was

viewed as the precursor of Jesus and necessarily lost significance in the same measure as Jesus gained in significance.

In order to view the figure of John properly, one must first become freed of all of these Christian conceptions.

John, or Yochanan, as he probably called himself, is viewed rightly by Josephus as one of the most successful preachers of repentance of his time, not some out-of-the-way figure. He had his own band of disciples, probably larger than that of Jesus. Thus in Acts 18:24–28 there is the report of an Alexandrian Jew, with the purely Greek name Apollos, who came to Ephesus and there continued the tradition of John's baptismal practice. This Apollos is clearly a diaspora Jew who became associated with John's group or sect before going over to the Jesuan community. We do not know, however, how many disciples of John, both domestic and foreign, did *not* take this step. To see John only in relation to Jesus is shortsighted. We must first look at John from a broader perspective: namely, from that of the repentance movement of his time, in which many revivalist preachers like him were involved.

The foreign Roman governorship in the land and the violent regime of Herod Antipas were perceived, like many other critical moments in Jewish history, as messianic birth pangs. At the conclusion of the mishnaic tractate Sota (Water of Jealousy), the phase immediately preceding the messianic period is painted in drastic colors: "The countenance of this generation will be like the face of the dog, and the son will not show respect in the presence of his father" (9.15). The latter remark is an allusion to Amos 2:7, which speaks of the father and the son going in to the same harlot. The dog simile is probably an allusion to the female slaves of the male temple prostitutes. Later exegetes interpret the dog simile in yet a different way: just as the dog runs before his master but does not determine the direction, turning instead each time with his master, so also this generation and its leadership. The dog of this simile could certainly be interpreted as a messianic precursor.

The Mishna text adduced here depicts relationships as they repeatedly occur in the eschatological preaching of the New Testament: families breaking apart; a man surrounded by his enemies in his own house (Micah 7:6; Matt. 10:35); strong bonds in dissolution. In this chaotic time, of which John the Baptist says, "Even now the ax is lying at the root of the trees" (Matt. 3:10), there is still but one refuge: God himself. The tractate Sota now confesses, "On whom can we depend (in the tumult of such a dire age)? On our father in heaven" (9.15).

The preaching of John is a manifestation of the imminent expectation of that "great and terrible day" spoken of by the prophet Malachi (4:5): "Lo, I will send you the prophet Elijah before the great and terrible day of the Lord comes." John too was seen by his contemporaries, in light of these words of Malachi, as the reincarnation of Elijah. He chooses the Judean wilderness around the Jordan as the stage of his activity. The identification of John in this context as "the voice of one crying out in the wilderness" (Matt. 3:3; Luke 3:4; John 1:23) again rests on a mistake in translation that derives from the Septuagint. John is supposed to appear as the fulfillment of Isaiah 40:3, the first chapter of the Consolation from the Babylonian Exile.[20] According to the Septuagint, this verse reads as follows:

> The voice of him that crieth in the wilderness, Prepare ye the way of the Lord, make straight in the desert a highway for our God.[21]

We must read this text, however, in accordance with the punctuation suggested by the cantillation of the Masoretic text:[22]

> A voice cries out:
> "In the wilderness prepare the
>   way of the Lord,
> make straight in the desert a
>   highway for our God."

The concern here is not with "the voice of one crying out in the wilderness." Rather, a voice calls, and this call resounds beyond the wilderness as well—presumably even to the metropolis of Babylon—with the message to return, in accordance with the old nomadic ideal of the Rechabites, to the wilderness, the "innocent land of Israel," where the Jews once obediently followed their God. That is a motif often found among the prophets.

John is not the personification of "the voice of one crying out in the wilderness," even if his call does penetrate beyond the wilderness to Jerusalem and the entire land, even into the diaspora.

The question arose in the mid–twentieth century as to whether John belonged to the Qumran sect. There is still no definite answer. Nonetheless, Hans Wildberger is correct in asserting, "Without exact knowledge of the conceptual world and theology of the Qumran writers, the New Testament can no longer be scientifically investigated. . . . Like John the Baptist, the people of Qumran are also, if rather differently . . . precursors of the Lord" (*Handschriftenfunde*, 37). I would restrict this remark somewhat by calling them precursors of a messianic movement.

Regarding John's lifestyle, we know that he dressed in a suit of camel hair, wore a leather belt, and nourished himself on wild honey and locusts. Eating locusts did not violate the food laws, since certain locusts are expressly allowed by the Torah (Lev. 11:22); the Mishna later discusses particular characteristics of those locusts that are acceptable for consumption. In this case, though, eating locusts probably also provides a figurative interpretation of the prophets' handling of symbols (as in Hosea and Ezekiel, as well as Jeremiah). Locusts are a sign of judgment in the prophet Joel (1:4, 2:25), and in the account of the ten plagues in Egypt they are connected with the judgment of God (Exod. 10:1–20).

Unlike the men of Qumran, John apparently lived alone (thus providing a model for the later Christian hermits). This circumstance must not be construed, however, to suggest that there was not a close relationship between John and Qumran. Rather, John appears to be a type of *shaliach*, an apostle of the sect of Qumran, who pursued an inner mission even as he directed his service to those outside the community. Whereas the Qumran people form a holy brotherhood among themselves, John goes away into the wilderness where the Qumranians themselves have their center. He calls the masses into the wilderness for repentance and an immersion bath. This wilderness must be understood as a *wilderness of stones*. Thus John chooses his famous metaphor according to which the new children of Abraham awaken from the stones of the wilderness (Luke 3:8). It is probably not wrong to see here an allusion to the legend of Lot's wife, who was turned to stone (the so-called pillar of salt is in fact a great stone) in the wilderness because of her disobedience (Gen. 19:26; cf. Luke 17:32). Disobedience leads to petrifaction of the heart, which is precisely what the legend means to express in symbolic language. If the judgment of God makes stones out of men, the grace of God can make men out of stones, an image also found in the prophets in the form of a conversion of the heart of stone into a heart of flesh (Ezek. 36:26).

The immersion or baptism ritual of John represents nothing unique to his time. Indeed it is documented with frequency among the Essenes—so frequently, in fact, that a later scoffer, Adolf von Harnack, once opined that the "little folks" never made it out of the bathtub.

Still, the immersion bath is not known to the old prophets in this form. Ezekiel speaks only of a sprinkling with pure water (36:25), which was probably not the same thing, since it recalls the purification ritual in which the ashes of a red heifer are dissolved in water (Num. 19:17–22).

Although water is known to be John's element, fire too was undeniably an element of this zealous preacher. It burns through the few words of John that have been transmitted to us: "Every tree therefore that does not bear good fruit is cut down and thrown into the *fire*" (Luke 3:9), and following this threat, the promise, "I baptize you with water; but one who is more powerful than I is coming. . . . He will baptize you with the Holy Spirit and *fire*. His winnowing fork is in his hand . . . and [he will] gather the wheat into his granary; but the chaff he will burn with unquenchable *fire*" (vv. 16–17). In Matthew 3:10–12 these three sentences follow one another in immediate succession.

The water of the immersion bath in the Jordan precedes the fire of the revelation (the Holy Ghost) and of judgment, just as in the Old Testament the water of the flood precedes the fire of revelation (that of the burning bush and Mount Sinai).

Among the many Jews who underwent the ritual immersion bath of John was Jesus of Nazareth. Naturally, a later time must have found it particularly objectionable that Jesus allowed himself to be baptized by John or, better stated, that he undertook the ritual bath of immersion under John's direction, for the meaning of this immersion was in fact the purification from sins. Since the transfigured master appeared later on to the circle of Jesus' disciples as without sin, the purification by John seems meaningless. Matthew, a later version than Mark, reports accordingly that John at first declines to do the baptism, stressing that *he himself* is in need of baptism by Jesus and not the other way around (3:14). Jesus commands him, however, to complete the ritual, and the Jesus who comes forth from the waves of the Jordan is proclaimed by a heavenly voice to be the son of God.

Compared with John's own self-proclamation as a "voice of one crying out in the wilderness," the words of the heavenly voice are analogous to the Consolation Scripture in the second half of the book of Isaiah. Here too there is an allusion to the servant of God (Isa. 42:1), upon whom the *ruach,* the spirit of God, rests.

It is obvious that this story involves a later addition. If John in fact had been convinced that Jesus was the expected Messiah; if John truly had been witness to this *bath-kol,* this heavenly voice; if John had in fact said that he was unworthy to untie Jesus' sandals (Mark 1:7), then the later question he sends to Jesus while imprisoned in the Machaerus fortress would make no sense.[23]

Herod Antipas had the revivalist arrested and later beheaded (Matt. 14:3–12). But now, from his prison cell, John charges a disciple to ask Jesus whether he is the expected Messiah or whether they should be waiting for another.

In this we can clearly discern that Jesus was a disciple of John but that after the incarceration of the master a certain element from the band of John's disciples acknowledged Jesus as the leader—perhaps even already as the messianic claimant. Some even considered him to be the reincarnation of John (Matt. 16:13–14).

That led to a rupture with John and his disciples, especially when Jesus broke openly with the ascetic ideals and practices of John. The Gospels report that the fast observed by John's circle and the Pharisees (twice weekly, on Monday and Thursday, a devout custom practiced to this day in ascetic circles of Judaism) was not taken over by Jesus and his disciples (Mark 2:18). That is apparently only a detail to suggest that the practice of Jesus and his disciples was undertaken more in keeping with Psalm 100:2: "Worship the Lord with gladness." At first, however, Jesus remained very much a follower of John. After his rebirth in the Jordan, Jesus, like his master John, betakes himself *alone* into the *desert.* Here he clearly identifies with the *succession of John.* Only thus can we understand the statement that Jesus, after his baptism, was led, or driven, into the wilderness by the spirit. And now the New Testament interprets the purpose of his going-out into the desert as the temptation by Satan. This places Jesus naturally in the company of Moses and Elijah—who experienced their revelations in the solitude of the wilderness—as well as directly in the succession of John.

Jesus dwells in the wilderness for forty days (Mark 1:12–13). These forty days strike a clear parallel with the forty days spent by Moses on Mount Sinai, the forty years of Israel's wandering in the wilderness, and the forty days of Elijah's pilgrimage through the wilderness to the sacred mountain of Horeb. The number forty simply means, in biblical usage, a long time, and we are not obliged to attach numerical precision to it.

Satan's first temptation says, "If you are the Son of God, command these stones to become loaves of bread" (Matt. 4:3). Does the undertone here not contain a rejection of John? According to John (Matt. 3:9), God can cause children to rise up to Abraham from stones, a motif that is heard again in the epistle to the Romans and in the Gospel of John. Here it is Satan that commands Jesus to transform stones into bread. The bread and the true children of Abraham are probably to be closely associated, since later, in the kerygmatic version of the Last Supper, Jesus calls himself the "bread of life" (John 6:48). At any rate, a miracle related by John is modified here so that Satan commands it of Jesus. This motif is sounded again in Jesus' parable of a father who will not give a stone to the child that begs bread of him (Matt. 7:9). In Jesus' refusal to transform the stones, one may perceive a first breach with the conceptual world of the Baptist.

After the temptation in the wilderness—a period of meditation and self-abnegation, as we might call it—Jesus detaches himself internally from John. Thus the text continues (Matt. 4:12; cf. Mark 1:14; Luke 4:14–15): "Now when Jesus heard that John had been arrested, he withdrew to Galilee. He left Nazareth and made his home in Capernaum [Kefar-Nachum] by the sea [Gennesaret], in the territory [of the tribes] of Zebulun and Naphtali." Thus only after Jesus hears of John's incarceration does he leave the wilderness—which is to say, the way of life and tradition of his master—to set out on his own unique path.

The Jordan baptism is the rebirth of Jesus. Here he steps into the light of history. And yet he continues to stand in the shadow of John until he separates himself internally by the forty days of solitude. After John is taken prisoner, Jesus assumes the leadership of the circles of disciples prepared by John for an eschatological awakening.

Now at last Jesus becomes himself; the process of individuation appears to be complete. It is only natural that Jesus, following this extended period in the wilderness, should return immediately to his hometown, Nazareth, presumably in order to recuperate from the rigors of his wilderness stay. It is probable that he could not at first appear in Nazareth as the Transformed One, the One Reborn. We know that he was unable to accomplish any miracle in Nazareth, since, as the original Hebrew proverb says, *'Ein navi' be'iro*, 'a prophet is not accepted in his native town' (Luke 4:24). Nevertheless, he chooses the more intimate environs of his hometown as the place to begin his public ministry, to raise on his own the call of the imminently expected kingdom of God.

We must not forget that John, the ascetic, lets this call go forth from the burning, stony wilderness of Judea, whereas Jesus raises his call from the gentler, pleasant landscape around Lake Kinnereth, the loveliest area in the country. At first hearing, his call sounds like John's: "Repent, for the kingdom of heaven [the dominion of God upon earth] has come near" (Matt. 3:2, 4:17). In the Greek text we have the word *metanoia*, 'change of mind,' for the concept of repentance. But we must penetrate further behind the text to the Hebrew notion of *teshuva*, which is intended here. This Hebraic concept means simultaneously 'return' and 'answer' and is central to rabbinic ethics. The gates of return stand always open, and one hour of complete return is better than a lifetime in the world to come. The rabbis outdid each other in their praise of return, which represents a person's greatest possibility: namely, to correct an erroneous direction and return to the origin, to God. In its simple language use, however, the word *teshuva* also means 'answer.' *Teshuva:* the return is the answer to God's call to mankind, "Where are you?" (Gen. 3:9), which had already been posed to Adam. Man, in returning, answers as Abraham did: "*Hinneni*, here I am" (Gen. 22:1).

John was not the first or only person to raise the ringing call for *teshuva. Teshuva* is a basic motif of Judaism. Nor was his follower

Jesus the last to direct to Israel the call of repentant return. And yet it seems to me that the very same call as raised by John, who scolds even the repentant with insults such as "you brood of vipers!" (Matt. 3:7), is ruder in tone than that of Jesus. It is not possible to imagine John speaking Jesus' words "Come to me, all you that are weary and are carrying heavy burdens, and I will give you rest. Take my yoke upon you, and learn from me; for I am gentle and humble in heart, and you will find rest for your souls. For *my yoke is easy, and my burden is light*" (Matt. 11:28–30).

I find a difference here similar to that between the schools of the brusque Shammai and the gentle Hillel. The same psychological contrast is discernible between John and Jesus.

3 *Physician and Teacher*

According to the tradition of the Gospels, Jesus begins his teaching activities in his immediate homeland of Galilee. He finds himself on the Sabbath in the synagogue of Nazareth; the text expressly states, "as was his custom" (Luke 4:16). This must be understood to mean that Jesus, from the time of his youth, had been accustomed to taking part in the divine service in the synagogue on the Sabbath.

At the time of Jesus this service was already well defined and represented an important complement to the sacramental prayer service in the Jerusalem temple. Following the destruction of the temple, the synagogue service became the central prayer rite of Judaism. But even in Jesus' day the synagogue had already so thoroughly established itself as a house of assembly (Hebrew, *beth-hakeneseth*), a place of "prayer in spirit and in truth," a place of the proclamation of the word of God, that there was even a synagogue in the temple at Jerusalem.

Whereas the temple was the seat of a sacred hierarchic divine service carried out by priests and Levites, the synagogue represented the democratic element in Judaism. Here the divine service was and still is carried out by laity, in contrast to the Aaronic priests and the

Levites related to them; here in the synagogue, those learned in scripture were the leaders, the precursors of the rabbis. In the temple the bloody animal sacrifice formed the focal point of the sacred activities, enveloped by the aromas of incense (the *ketoreth*) and by songs, especially psalms accompanied by various musical instruments; in the synagogue the divine service had always had a much simpler character and was by its very nature founded entirely upon the *word*.

Clearly, from the time of his childhood, Jesus had been familiar with the ritual in his local synagogue. He surely must not have been considered unlearned even in his local community, for otherwise he would not have been entrusted with the recitation of the *haftara* (lit. 'conclusion'), the prophetic sections.

The synagogue year is divided into Sabbaths, on each of which a certain pericope is read from the Pentateuch (Torah), the Five Books of Moses.[24] In addition, a passage from the Prophets is read which is related thematically to the Torah reading. At the time of Jesus, differentiation was probably already made between the Babylonian cycle and the one in common use in the land of Israel. The Babylonian cycle completes the reading of the Pentateuch within one year; the Palestinian cycle encompasses three years.[25] We may assume that the Palestinian cycle was the one followed in the synagogue at Nazareth in Galilee.

Just as today, the pericope from the Pentateuch was read from a Torah scroll, whereas the prophetic passages were contained in separate scrolls. A remarkable talmudic prescription notes that touching the scrolls of Holy Scripture defiles one's hands and that after handling the scrolls, it is therefore necessary to wash one's hands.[26] The scrolls were looked upon as taboo.

When and how the recitation of the pericopes arose is not clear. The Jewish tradition traces the recitation of the Torah portions on the Sabbath back to Moses; the recitation of shorter sections on Monday and Thursday (the traditional market days) is thought to go back to the learned scribe Ezra: that is, to the time following the return from the Babylonian exile. These details cannot be historically validated, however. Even less certain is the question of the reading of the prophetic pericopes. A completely unauthenticated tradition locates the institution of these readings in the time of the Maccabean persecutions, when the Syrian successor king Antiochus Epiphanes forbade recitations from the Torah; the recitations from the Prophets are said to have been inserted in their place.[27] It certainly is doubtful that the inquisition of Antiochus Epiphanes could have distinguished so finely between the Law (the Torah proper) and the Prophets, but apparently the dissemination of the sacred scriptures of Israel was forbidden, just as it was during the later Hadrianic persecutions.

Evidence from within pharisaic Judaism, however, readily demonstrates that the recitations from the Five Books of Moses were complemented by corresponding pericopes from the Prophets, since the Pharisees, unlike the Sadducees, valued the prophetic writings highly.

On this occasion Jesus is bidden to approach the Torah, obviously as a *maftir*—that is, as the last and concluding person among those called up.[28] After completing the recitation he is handed the prophet scroll for the recitation of the *haftara*. He reads from Isaiah 61:1–2, which speaks of the calling of God's servant:

> The Spirit of the Lord God is upon me,
> because the Lord has anointed me;
> he has sent me to bring good news to the oppressed,
> to bind up the brokenhearted,
> to proclaim liberty to the captives,
> and release to the prisoners;
> to proclaim the year of the Lord's favor,
> and the day of vengeance of our God;
> to comfort all who mourn.

He then returns the scroll to the *shamash,* the synagogue ministrant.

We can assume with relative certainty that this first appearance of Jesus in his hometown synagogue—following his rebirth through the immersion bath in the Jordan under John's direction—happened in the summer, for the sixty-first chapter of Isaiah, which we have just cited, is adjoined to the Torah double-portion *Ki-thavo'* and *Nitsavim* (Deut. 26–29). These portions belong to the fiftieth and/or fifty-first week of the Torah cycle, a period that in the Jewish calendar falls in the summer or early autumn.[29]

Up through the conclusion of the prophetic reading, the appearance of Jesus in the synagogue is basically uneventful, though people have now heard from him and are eager to know what he will say. To the recitation from the Law and the Prophets there was adjoined, just as today, the *derasha,* or exegetical sermon, whose classical compilation is preserved in the great literature of the Midrash. Jesus relates the prophecies of Deutero-Isaiah to himself, personally. Remarkably, this allusion to his messianic calling—more than an allusion it is not—remains at first uncontradicted. Just as Jesus had already found public approbation as a preacher in the smaller areas around Galilee, so here in Nazareth too, people are deeply impressed by his scriptural interpretation. They are astonished at how the son of Joseph—whom they knew as a child and whose mother Miriam may be present in the synagogue in the women's section—can preach like a learned rabbi. Matthew 13:54–56 presents the entire family of Jesus: his brothers James and Joseph and Simon and Judas, along with his sisters. The number and names of the sisters, as was typical, remain unmentioned, since girls and women did not appear actively in the life of the community.

The Jewish-Christian Matthew remarks, however, that the community was struck with awe at the bold authority with which the young man set forth his teaching. This emotional response apparently did not register with the pagan-Christian Luke, and he accordingly attributes the reason for the scandal, the anger that Jesus' sermon occasions, to an entirely different cause. According to Luke, the anger is sparked by Jesus' denigration of the community's consciousness of being the chosen community. Luke refers to passages in 1 Kings and 2 Kings which indicate that the God of Israel is especially accepting of foreigners who do not belong to his own proprietary people.

Jesus' words (Luke 4:25–26) regarding the widow in the Sidonean Zarephath (Sarepta), for whom the prophet Elijah worked his oil miracle (1 Kings 17:8–24), and the reference to the Syrian Naaman, whom the prophet Elisha healed of leprosy (2 Kings 5:1–19), bespeak a sympathy for the non-Jew that is not matched by his later brusque behavior in his discussion with the Canaanite woman from the area of Tyre and Sidon who asks for his help (Matt. 15:21–28). First, he refuses to answer her at all, a gesture entirely in keeping with those learned in the law, who refused extended conversations with women. He answers his disciples, who beg him simply to ignore the woman, with the words, "I was sent only to the lost sheep of the house of Israel" (v. 24). He thereby restricts his mission in narrowly nationalistic terms.

When the woman refuses to be dismissed, Jesus goes so far as to let her know in a very offensive metaphor that the food he has to give is not meant for her: "It is not fair to take the children's food and throw it to the dogs" (v. 26).

Only after this mother, whose concern is for her sick child, humbles herself to the extent that she actually joins in the metaphor, saying, "Yes, Lord, yet even the dogs eat the crumbs that fall from their masters' table" (v. 27), is Jesus overpowered by her exhibition of faith. He says, "Woman, great is your faith! Let it be done for you as you wish" (v. 28). This statement is of a similar nature to what he said in Kefar-Nachum (Capernaum) to a Roman centurion: "Truly I tell you, in no one in Israel have I found such faith" (Matt. 8:10; Luke 7:9).

It is surely no accident that the haughty parable of the lords and the dogs is found in Mark (7:27) and Matthew (15:26) but not in the pagan-Christian Luke or in the Hellenistic Gospel of John.

But back now to Nazareth. Here Jesus fails to win the people's trust because he is too close to the community itself. In this situation he himself cites two sayings, which are ironically meant to express his view of the community's reaction to him: "Doctor, cure yourself!" (Luke 4:23), an obvious allusion to the community's familiarity with the humble circumstances of his birth; and *'Ein navi' be'iro,* 'a prophet is not accepted in his native town.'

Occasionally, the conclusion has been drawn from these and similar sayings that Jesus considered himself a *prophet,* and there are in fact a few passages in the New Testament that depict Jesus as a prophet. But these cannot be understood in the stricter sense of the old, especially pre-Exile, prophets. The saying that a prophet is not accepted in his own hometown is hardly proof of any prophetic messianic consciousness in Jesus.

Jesus legitimates himself not through prophecies but primarily through his miraculous healings. In fact, he begins his activities as a physician; he is probably alluding to this in the first saying quoted above. As Stefan Zweig puts it, Jésus is a "mental healer." He casts out demons, unclean spirits, known in Hebraic literature as *shedim.*

This concerns the ritual of exorcism as it is understood today not only in Christian circles but throughout chasidic Judaism as well. The authority of a chasidic rabbi, or *tsaddik*—Jesus bears great similarity to this type of rabbi—is particularly manifest in his power over the *dibbukim,* the incubi and succubi, which he is able to expel by virtue of his (magical) authority.[30]

The rationalistic explanation for such healings strikes me as weak. The New Testament itself repeatedly refers to the suggestive and autosuggestive power of these "miracles" with the formula "Your faith has made you well" (e.g., Matt. 9:22). A holy healing power emanates from Jesus. The fame of the miracle worker immediately permeates the land of Galilee, drawing suffering people to him, so that Jesus the physician is scarcely able to rescue himself from the masses of his patients. A roof is even broken open in order to lower a paralyzed man into the room where Jesus happens to be found, surrounded by the troop of those seeking his healing (Mark 2:1–12).

A mere rationalism that seeks to explain the "miracles" simply within the framework of the gospel completely misses the reality of Jesus and his contemporaries. That which is holy and that which is healing at the time of Jesus are not yet separable from each other. One need think only of the instructions regarding lepers (Lev. 13–14), who are required to show themselves before the priest, an ordinance with which Jesus expressly complies. Nor are physician, priest, prophet, and one learned in scriptural law to be separated from one another in a cognitive hierarchical division. We frequently observe even today in Israel, especially among the Oriental circles of Jews and Arabs, that people go not to a physician but to a miracle worker—or rather, *also* to a miracle worker. The psychic ailments, which are clearly at the center of the healing activity of Jesus, are by their very nature controllable by charismatics. Sickness of the spirit or mind, mental illness, is in turn healed through the spirit or mind. We have arrived at this knowledge again today through psychoanalysis and psychotherapy.

A relationship of trust between the physician and his patient is the precondition for these healings. It is therefore understandable that in Nazareth, where people knew him and his family too well—where the aura was missing—Jesus could accomplish no miracles. On the other hand, wherever he appeared as a stranger, but one whose reputation had preceded him, he was able to accomplish miracles.

Nothing connects people so much as suffering and sorrow. It is for this reason that Jesus as physician immediately reaches *all* quarters of the population: not only pious Jews but the less observant as well, who stand in Herod's royal service or are engaged as tax collectors for the Roman authorities and enjoy therefore, as collaborators, no particular love among their own folk. From the Canaanite woman all the way to the centurion of a Roman cohort (Matt. 8:5–13), each looks for healing either for him- or herself, for children, for a mother-in-law (e.g., of Peter: Mark 1:30–31), or for other associates and servants. The power of Jesus extends so far, according to the reports of the Gospels, that even revivals from the dead are possible (based on the precedents of Elijah and Elisha). The tradition of the New Testament lays particular value on the implicit point that Jesus does not pray at these revivals from the dead but rather *commands* upon his own authority that the dead, such as the daughter of Jairus (Luke 8:40–56), the young man at Nain (Luke 7:11–17), and Lazarus (John 11:1–44) should come forth.

All these stories should be taken just as they are, as testimony to an ineradicable impression that Jesus made on his world. To the unfettered reader of the Gospels it must be clear that the healings through the spirit, with which the public course of Jesus begins and which stretch throughout his entire period of activity, are for Jesus himself of only secondary significance, though they serve to legitimate him to the outer world.

In this antagonism is to be found Jesus' deepest tragedy, which is understood by neither his disciples nor his community. It is in fact probably understood more readily by his opponents, who attack not so much the physician as the *teacher,* one who interprets the law in a way that they cannot accept. Accordingly, they attack the miraculous healings of Jesus only insofar as they occur on the Sabbath. Jesus' saying "so the Son of Man is lord even of the sabbath" (Mark 2:28; Luke 6:5) and his admonition that the notion of Sabbath rest should not be carried to an extreme—"The sabbath was made for humankind, and not humankind for the sabbath" (Mark 2:27)—are not without parallel in rabbinic writings. A statement to this effect made by Rabbi Yonathan, a contemporary of Jesus, is preserved in the Talmud (BT, Yoma 85b): "The sabbath is in your hands, for it is written, 'The sabbath is for you'" (cf. Exod. 16:29; Ezek. 20:12). To see these statements primarily as an expression of the messianic authority of Jesus would be wrong. The Son of Man, who is the subject here, is simply man, to whom the Sabbath is given for pleasure and joy and not as a legal straitjacket.

Jesus makes use of the powers awakened in him in the act of his rebirth to heal the sick, especially the demon-possessed, but for him this is only the point of departure for his activity. Once having claimed authority for himself, he proceeds to select his disciples. In doing so, it is not incidental that he looks to his own people in Galilee, unschooled fishermen, who have no interest in *pilpul:* that is, the hair-splitting arguments of those learned in the law.

The opposition between the learned, known as the *chaverim* or *talmidei-chakhamim,* and the simple folk, collectively the *'am-ha'arets,* was no less than tragic. We have a statement from Rabbi 'Akiva, who remained an unschooled shepherd until his fortieth year, in which he admits that his hatred of those who were learned in scriptural law had formerly been so great that he once swore to tear one of them apart if he ever met him (BT, Pesachim 49b). The learned ones themselves even extended the biblical prohibition against sexual unchastity with animals to those of their own companions who married the daughter of an *'am-ha'arets,* a common person.

One must imagine this hostile opposition in order to appreciate the revolutionary act of Jesus of Nazareth as he now proceeds, with full cognizance, to select the band of his disciples from the population group of the *'am-ha'arets.*

The concept of *'am-ha'arets* has gone through a long evolution. Originally, it connoted the autochthonous population of Canaanites. The expression is used thus in the Abraham story in Genesis, in the episode of the property sale at Hebron, where the patriarch acquires the burial place in the Cave of Machpelah (49:30). We later encounter the expression *'am-ha'arets* as a designation for the landed gentry. At the time of Jesus, however, the concept, which literally translated means "the people of the land," signified the unlearned masses.

The Pharisees, or *Perushim,* clearly were the ones who had separated themselves (thus the word *perushim*) from the masses. A rift was thereby created in the united people, since the Pharisees constituted, as it were, the caste of the elect from within the ranks of the chosen people themselves.

Jesus breaks through the wall erected by the legal piety of those learned in the law. Examples of this sort appear again and again throughout the history of Judaism. Similarly, the chasidic movement of the eighteenth century represents the revolt of popular piety against the institution of scriptural legal experts.

We should not, however, imagine that Jesus himself belonged to the *'am-ha'arets;* quite to the contrary. He shows himself, in his disputes with the learned in the law, to be their full equal. Indeed, numerous passages in the New Testament demonstrate that Jesus' disciples, who did belong to the *'am-ha'arets,* did not understand their rabbi.

Those whom Jesus wished to make into fishers of men were predominantly fishermen from Lake Kinnereth. This figure is not merely taken from social reality but also alludes to the statement of the prophet Jeremiah (16:16), "I am now sending for many fishermen, says the Lord, and they shall catch them; and afterward I will send for many hunters, and they shall hunt them from every mountain and every hill, and out of the clefts of the rocks." What surely qualifies as a threatening statement in Jeremiah is transformed in Jesus' call into something positive. Still, in the call to become fishers of men we hear an echo of the consciousness of martyrdom connected with the apostolate, those succeeding generations that followed in the footsteps of the apostles. Jesus, in calling his followers, knows well that he is leading his disciples down a dangerous path, though he cannot yet predict, in this first phase of his activity, its tragic end; his assumption is that the kingdom of God is at hand.

The disciples themselves, simple Galilean fishermen, exist in the narrative of the Gospels in a relatively pale light. We know very little about them as individuals; they are seen primarily as a group that constitutes the foil for the figure of the Master.

The person of Simon Peter, however, stands out somewhat from the group, thus allowing us to discern his emotional ambivalence. Jesus' thrice-repeated question of whether Peter loves him (John 21:

15–17) is to be understood in these terms, for Jesus, of whom it is said that he knew what was in man (John 2:25), senses the unreliability of this unfinished character. It is therefore not surprising that Peter will betray his lord in the hour of danger.

The figure of Yochanan, the favorite disciple, is painted in softer colors. Fanciful scholars like Hans Blüher (*Aristie*, 43–45) have gone so far as to assume a homoerotic relationship between Jesus and John. I cannot agree with him, for the implied Greek master-disciple relationship (as in Socrates) is completely incompatible with the Jewish milieu in which Jesus operated. Had even the slightest suspicion of such a relationship been present, Jesus' enemies would have seized upon it at once, since in the Torah homosexuality is worthy of capital punishment (Lev. 18:22, 20:13).

The disciples of Jesus, as we said, were mostly fishermen, and for that reason the fish symbol had an important function within the primitive Christian community. The fish is older than the cross as a Christian symbol.

My guess is that a later pagan-Christian misinterpretation of this symbol enters into the equation. The church father Eusebius explained the Greek word for fish, *ichthus,* by an acrostic:

I = Jesous
Ch = Christos
Th = Theou (God's)
Y = Yios (Son)
S = Soter (Savior)

The church father Tertullian (*De Bapt.,* 1) designated Jesus as a great fish. The spokesmen of the early pagan-Christian church thought in Greek, whereas in the original Jewish community the fish symbol was probably associated more strongly with Jacob's blessing of Ephraim and Manasseh (Gen. 48:16), in which occurs the remarkable expression *veyidgu larov bekerev ha'arets,* 'let them grow into a multitude amid the earth.' Luther translates here, *daß sie wachsen und viel werden auf Erden,* 'that they should grow and become many on earth.' The remarkable word *veyidgu* derives, however, from *dag,* 'fish.' Buber and Rosenzweig, in their German translation of the Bible, accordingly translate this passage as *Fischgleich mögen sie wachsen zur Menge im Inneren des Landes,* 'May they grow fishlike into a multitude in the midst of the land.' This is the proper sense, it seems to me, of the fish symbol. The fish is the sign of fruitfulness, and the community of Jesus is supposed to multiply fishlike on earth.

The fish symbol was also associated with the sign of Jonah. According to Matthew 12:40, Jesus compared his three-day burial with the stay of the prophet Jonah in the belly of the fish (Jon. 1:17).[31] But all this comes from a later community tradition, and we can assume that "the sign of Jonah" penetrated into early Christian eschatology on the basis of the fish symbol. Because the fish was the sign, and probably originally the secret sign, of the Jesuan community, it was connected with the legendary giant fish of Jonah. In fact, the symbol comes, on the one hand, from the real world of the fishermen from Kinnereth and, on the other, from Jacob's blessing of Ephraim and Manasseh (Gen. 48).

As we noted, Jesus selected his first disciples from a group of fishermen and proved his lordship to them by assisting them in a miraculous fish haul. The Gospel of Luke presents a particularly lengthy version of this story (5:1–11) and implies that fishing on Lake Kinnereth usually took place at night, as is still the case today. At Jesus' word, however, the nets are cast in daylight, and with extraordinary success. Here too the question of historical content is incidental. The church father Chrysostom recognized the sense and intent of these stories when he noted that Luke's Gospel shows how Jesus reveals himself to people in a manner that is understandable to them: to the astrologers from the Orient he speaks through the star of Bethlehem; to the fishermen from Kinnereth, through a fish haul. What Chrysostom, a sworn enemy of Judaism, did not recognize is that the tradition of the Gospels actually employs the talmudic principle here, according to which the Torah speaks *kileshon benei-'adam,* 'according to the language of men.' That means that the Divine avails itself of plain and simple symbols of earthly material in order to be understood.

Among the disciples called from the group of fishermen it is striking that pairs of brothers are selected (Matt. 4:18–21): Simon (Peter) and Andrew, and James and John, the sons of Zebediah. In this process it is no wonder that besides the pure Hebrew names like Shim'on, Ya'akov, and Yochanan, we also find non-Jewish names such as Andrew. The influence of the Greco-Roman world was strong enough, particularly in Galilee, for such names to become indigenous. Significantly, the region was called *Galil hagoyim,* 'Galilee of the nations.'

Whereas Matthew adduces only the few disciples named here, in Luke (6:13–16) we have the twelve disciples. They are always named in pairs; even the dark disciple Judas Iscariot is named together with that Judas who was the son of Jacob, apparently with the purpose of juxtaposing the two Judases—the one positive, the other negative.

The number twelve of disciples derives from the twelve tribes, and to the disciples it is promised that they will judge the tribes of Israel at the end of time. The community of disciples is to represent as a microcosm, so to speak, the entire people of God. In this regard it is significant that a tax collector, Levi, is also included.

We will deal more with the figure of the betrayer Judas later on. For now, let us note only in passing that his name could also be read as *'Ish krayoth,* 'a man from the cities' (or of the area) along the seacoast where the callings took place. The name could also, however, be associated with the Sicarians, the dagger-bearing Zealots, to whom this activist may well have belonged.

After the first disciples have been chosen—the witnesses of the narrower circle, as it were—the strategic dissemination of Jesus' message begins. Matthew's Gospel leads immediately, following the calling of the disciples, to the high point of the Sermon on the Mount. We may assume, however, that it was preceded by the sermon on the sea mentioned in Luke 5:3, the episode in which Jesus speaks from a fishing boat to the multitude gathered on the banks. The content of the sermon on the sea is not known, but the narrator's intent lies probably on a different level. Magical notions were still rife among the people. One was that a magician, or a god, could work his wonders on either sea or land, on the mountains or the plains. Just as the book of Jonah, which Jesus uses as a sign, acknowledges God as lord over sea and land (1:9), the Gospel narrative seeks to present Jesus too as powerful on sea (the Lake of Gennesaret is called in Hebrew *Yam Kinnereth,* Sea of Kinnereth—the Gospels also use the expression "Sea of Galilee") and land and plain. Jesus commands the waters in a storm (Luke 8:22–25); he is transfigured on a mountain (Mark 9:2); and he teaches in the cities along the coastal plain. This motif must not be overlooked. That the sermon on the sea (though it is not narrated) precedes the one on the mountain must be viewed in the symbolic sense of the statement in Psalm 29:3: "The voice of the Lord is over the waters."

The Sermon on the Mount, on the other hand, offers in condensed form not only Jesus' doctrine but his method as well.

The Sermon on the Mount

The Sermon on the Mount, as it is transmitted to us in the Gospel of Matthew (5–7) and in the corresponding text in Luke (6:20–49), has often been viewed as a battle cry—that great "But I say to you" (e.g., Matt. 5:22)—of Christianity against Judaism. This view mistakes the tenor and intent of the speech on the mountain. We have here a piece of Jewish doctrine that fits organically into the tradition of rabbinic Judaism, notwithstanding the fact that certain individual traits of the preacher, Jesus, are visible. He teaches entirely in the manner of the Tannaim; he espouses his doctrine, but it remains Jewish doctrine from beginning to end. The School of Jesus, the *Beth-Midrash Yeshu'*, is founded, so to speak, on the occasion of the Sermon on the Mount.

It is not easy to determine where this sermon was held. The geographical data of the Gospels are not precise, for it did not occur to the Evangelists to indicate specific places. It strikes me as essential, however, that this decisive sermon was delivered on a mountain. This mountain, somewhere on the shores of the Sea of Kinnereth, stands, as it were, in the shadow of Mount Sinai. Revelation happens on mountains. As the Psalmist confesses in prayer, "I lift up my eyes to the hills—from where will my help come?" (Ps. 121:1).

Mount Sinai itself cannot be precisely located. Even this peak, so important to the history of salvation, remains clouded in uncertainty, since different traditions give it different names: Sinai, Horeb, or simply Mountain of God.

The mountain as a *site of God* is an ancient conception. Accordingly, it is fitting that the introductory sentences to the Sermon on the Mount begin as they do: "When Jesus saw the crowds, he went up the mountain; and after he sat down, his disciples came to him. Then he began to speak, and taught them, saying . . ." (Matt. 5:1–2).

This does not mean that Jesus was seen here as the "true God," as later dogma has it. The same may be said for all of the New Testament, and such a conception would be totally unthinkable for a Jewish audience. But the teacher does allege to present God's word (even if not in the form of a prophetic speech), though this does not accord any special advantage to his opinion in controversial questions. In the rabbinic tradition, even contradictory doctrines and opinions can be taken as God's word: "These and also those are words of the living God" (BT, 'Eruvin 13b). The speaker and the saying can be seen as one; "And the Word became flesh" (John 1:14) is probably best interpreted in this way. The teacher himself, the conveyer of the message, becomes identical with it. Such an interpretation of this famous passage in John is not understandable from the Greek, which says that the *logos*, 'the word,' has become *sarx*, 'flesh.' If, however, we translate this back into the corresponding Hebrew, a wordplay results: *besora lebasar*, 'the message, the gospel, becomes flesh'—and precisely that occurs in the hour of the Sermon on the Mount.

Naturally, it is difficult to reconstruct the Sermon on the Mount in its original form, though in fact there is no reason to do so. The extended version in Matthew contains a good deal of kerygmatic material, and yet it seems to me that it is precisely here in Matthew that we can ascertain the real voice of the speaker. Martin Buber's comment that exegesis is the art of hearing was made in just this context. It is here, if anywhere, that the voice of Jesus is audible as that of a Jewish brother—a Jewish voice whose very inflections we are able to discern. As far as I know, Alfred Kerr was the first to make note of this, in his poetic essay of 1903, "Jeruschalajim" (sec. 39). He rightly corrects Oscar Wilde, who had his Christ speak Greek. Kerr remarks intuitively that Jesus "spoke discriminatingly in the manner of lightning."

The Sermon on the Mount begins powerfully with the Beatitudes. The first Beatitude reads, "Blessed are the poor in spirit, for theirs is the kingdom of heaven."

Who are the poor in spirit, or the spiritually poor? Are they intellectually stunted people? Is this a praise of simplicity, of naiveté, or even of stupidity? Is it a consolation for the unschooled over against the scholars of the law? One could perhaps make that assumption. But a look into the papyrus rolls from the Dead Sea provides us with different and better information. Here, in the sect of Qumran, we find the concept of 'aniyei-haruach, those who have remained poor for the sake of the spirit. These are people who were already living the Franciscan ideal of poverty centuries before Francis of Assisi, rejecting possessions in order to devote themselves fully to the spirit. From the parables of Jesus it becomes clear that he, who probably came into association with Qumran through John or as a result of his own stay in the wilderness, shared the Qumranians' scorn for earthly goods: "For what will it profit them if they gain the whole world but forfeit their life?" (Matt. 16:26); "It is easier for a camel to go through the eye of a needle than for someone who is rich to enter the kingdom of God" (Matt. 19:24); "Do not store up for yourselves treasures on earth, where moth and rust consume . . . ; but store up for yourselves treasures in heaven" (Matt. 6:19–20). Many other words ascribed to Jesus could be cited in this regard. The spiritually poor, with whose blessing the Sermon on the Mount begins, are therefore the people who intentionally remain poor in order to prepare themselves for the spirit, the spirit of God, in the recognition that all sins are forgiven except those against this spirit (Matt. 12:31).

The second Beatitude (v. 4) relates to those who suffer: "Blessed are those who mourn, for they will be comforted." Jesus here draws on a motif, found in Isaiah (57:18, 60:20, 61:1–2) and in the Psalms (94:19, 126:5), doubtless familiar to his listeners. We do find a rejection of this conception in the Talmud, "Not sufferings and not their reward" (BT, Berakhoth 5b), but Jesus sees suffering in the present in light of the future consolation inherent in the prophetic proclamation.

"Blessed are the meek, for they will inherit [or, possess] the earth" (v. 5). This saying borrows a basic motif from Psalm 37:11: "But the meek shall inherit the land, and delight themselves in abundant prosperity."

This motif sounds again in Psalm 37, verses 9, 22, 29, and 34. We may therefore presume in the Sermon on the Mount a deliberate allusion to a conceptual corpus familiar to the listeners. Jesus' admonition contradicts the activist Zealots, typified by the disciple Judas Iscariot, who violently opposed the idea of foreign Roman domination. Jesus preaches passive resistance. The meek, who with their unwavering trust in God's promise credulously expect to take possession of the land as the holy property vouchsafed to them, will be the victors. The same thought is uttered by Rav[32] in the Talmud:

> On account of four things, landowners' property can be confiscated by the state treasury: on account of those who withhold wages from their laborers; those who defraud laborers of their wages; those who cast off the yoke from their own neck and place it as a burden upon their neighbor; and those who are arrogant. Arrogance outweighs them all. Of modest folk, however, it is written, "The modest (meek) will inherit the land."
> (BT, Sukka 29b)

"Blessed are those who hunger and thirst for righteousness, for they will be filled" (v. 6). Is there not an echo here of Amos's prophecy? Hunger and thirst are to be sent into the land—not hunger for bread and not thirst for water, but for the word of God, which is the guarantor of justice (Amos 8:11).

"Blessed are the merciful, for they will receive [or, find] mercy" (v. 7). Here the *lex talionis* of the Torah, "an eye for an eye, a tooth for a tooth," is turned in a positive direction: mercy for mercy. The idea that mercy should find mercy is also contained in the Talmud: "Rabbi Gamaliel said in the name of Rabbi,[33] 'Whoever has mercy on his fellowman will find mercy in heaven; whoever does not have mercy on his fellow man will not find mercy in heaven'" (BT, Shabbath 151b).

"Blessed are the pure in heart, for they will see God" (v. 8). This thought is often expressed in the Psalms and is elucidated in the midrashic commentary Shocher Tov on Psalm 11:7: "For the Lord is righteous; he loves righteous deeds; the upright shall behold his face." The Jewish tradition emphasizes here that only the pure of heart are able to witness the pure light of God.

"Blessed are the peacemakers, for they will be called children of God" (v. 9). Here again is a prophetic idea (Isa. 52:7–10, 57:19). Va-yikra' Rabba 9 expounds the thought of how the *rodefei-shalom*, 'those who pursue peace,' represent an ideal in the rabbinic view of man.[34] Peace is considered the seal of God. The peaceful Hillel, who has many character traits in common with Jesus, teaches in Pirkei-'

Avoth 1.12, "Belong to the students of Aaron, who love peace and strive for peace."

"Blessed are those who are persecuted for righteousness' sake, for theirs is the kingdom of heaven" (v. 10). Again, prophetic material (Isa. 50:4–9, 51:7–11). The thought is found in rabbinic literature, for example in the Mekhilta to Exodus 22:20[35] and the Babylonian Talmud (Shabbath 88b), where the rabbis taught, "Regarding those who are humbled without humbling others, who accept slanderous words without rejoining, who serve out of love and accept chastisements happily, the Scripture says, 'But may your friends be like the sun as it rises in its might'" (Judg. 5:31). Who would not be reminded here of Jesus' saying that one should offer the left cheek if one is smitten upon the right, or that one should not resist an evildoer (Luke 6:29; Matt. 5:39)? Those who follow his instruction are the true children of God, in the sense expounded in the Sermon on the Mount and Judaism alike.

The Beatitudes close then with "Blessed are you when people revile you and persecute you and utter all kinds of evil against you falsely on my account. Rejoice and be glad, for your reward is great in heaven, for in the same way they persecuted the prophets who were before you" (vv. 11–12).

The thought expressed at the conclusion of the Beatitudes, that the reviled will achieve the crown of martyrdom, is nothing unique to listeners who, exposed as they were to the insensitivity of a foreign, Roman dominion, already knew this very well. The traditional Jewish literature offers many examples in this regard, time and again bringing up the motif that Israel, out of obedience, will be "like a lamb that is led to the slaughter" (Isa. 53:7).

Nor does this inward turn violate the framework of the tradition. The boiling blood[36] of Zechariah, which was poured out on the altar, returns again and again as a motivation for the destruction of the temple. The persecution of the prophets was recognized by the teachers of Judaism as Israel's guilt. The only thing that is genuinely new here is the idea of persecution for the sake of Jesus, but this also is probably a later kerygmatic interpretation. The loyalty of disciples to their master, however, was often extolled in Judaism at the time of

Jesus. One particularly recalls the account of the apostate 'Elisha' Ben-'Avuya, to whom his pupil Rabbi Me'ir remained loyal even after his teacher had been placed under the ban. Although the rabbis made 'Elisha' Ben-'Avuya into a heretic, they praised the loyalty of his pupil Rabbi Me'ir (BT, Chagiga 15b).

The Beatitudes function as a kind of prelude to the Sermon on the Mount; the radical ethical demands of Jesus constitute its actual core. In his now classic book on Jesus, written in 1926, Rudolf Bultmann remarks, "The demands of the Sermon on the Mount have always been regarded as particularly characteristic of the preaching of Jesus. Here we find at the beginning the new set over against the old in strong antitheses, in a peculiar interpretation of the Old Testament which evidently aims to establish its true meaning as against the scribal interpretation, thus completely destroying . . . the formal authority of Scripture" (*Jesus and the Word*, 89).

I cannot subscribe to Bultmann's view here. He himself stressed a few sentences earlier that Jesus makes in fact no new demands and that his concrete instructions have rich parallels in the Jewish tradition.

The authority of scripture is not shaken by the Sermon on the Mount. Quite the contrary: "Do not think that I have come to abolish the law or the prophets; I have come not to abolish but to fulfill. For truly I tell you, until heaven and earth pass away, not one letter, not one stroke of a letter, will pass from the law until all is accomplished" (Matt. 5:17–18).

In light of these words, how can one say that Jesus shakes the authority of the Torah?

What is meant here by "letter" (or jot) and "stroke of a letter" (or tittle)? Clearly, the Hebrew letter *yod*, which can be omitted in abbreviated writing; by the tittle (or dot), we must understand both the later pointing of the Masoretic text, which adds the vowels sublinearly to the consonant text, and the marks of cantillation (*ta'amei-hamikra'*, or *neginoth*) of the traditional Torah recitation. Rabbi 'Akiva also stresses the importance of these dots and adds to them the little crowns on certain letters. Pointing can be decisive for the meaning of a word. Let us take, for example, the root consisting of the consonants *chlv*, which can be read as *chalav*, 'milk,' or *chelev*, 'animal fat.' The tonal indications, which appear in place of our punctuation marks, can convey a variety of meanings. Let us again recall the famous passage about the "voice in the wilderness" (Isa. 40:3). We can read it as the Septuagint does: "The voice of him that crieth in the wilderness," or according to the intonation marks:

A voice cries out:
"In the wilderness prepare the
way of the Lord . . . ."

Jesus therefore holds to the Masoretic text.[37] He holds also to the rabbinic principle that in the Torah there are no great and small laws, for even the seemingly smallest law is inviolable.

It was only after Christian theology had separated itself from its Jewish roots that an antagonism was read into the Sermon on the Mount: "Jesus sets the demand of law over against the demand of God" (Bultmann, *Jesus and the Word*, 91). No! Jesus is opposing the original intent of the law to the casuistic leveling of the law by certain schools of the Pharisees. The radicalness of Jesus, which always interprets *lechumra*, 'in the strictest manner,' again separates him from Hillel, to whom so much binds him with respect to the love of peace. Beyond that we also discern a certain inward turn of the law in Jesus. Not only the completed action but the intention, *kavvana*, is decisive. But this, again, is by no means unique to Jesus.

If, as Bultmann insists, we focus on what Jesus *wanted* (not on who he was), we clearly see this radicalness as the total fulfillment of the law, the manifest will and commandment of *God*.

Jesus' harsh preaching is first of all directed at his circle of disciples. From a spatial perspective, we must imagine the disciples sitting in the most intimate circle around the Master and, in a wider circle, the randomly scattered masses of people. In the number twelve of disciples, as we noted earlier, we have a reconstructed ideal model of Israel (the federation of twelve tribes). Therefore, for these chosen ones from the chosen people, the proclamation has *new* validity: "I will give you as a light to the nations" (Isa. 49:6). They, the disciples, are now *'or lagoyim*, "as a light to the nations, that my salvation may reach to the end of the earth." What Deutero-Isaiah promised to all of Israel, Jesus promises in the Sermon on the Mount to his band of disciples. This promise surely came to pass in time, even if the light has been darkened repeatedly throughout the history of the church.

The promise to the disciples follows their calling. After the radical turning to the law, to *mitsva,* the principle is applied in concrete terms: murder (not killing) and adultery are interpreted in the strictest fashion, so that the very inclination—the desire for murder, even hatred of one's neighbor, or sexually coveting the wife of one's neighbor—weighs before God as heavily as the perpetrated deed itself. Even an oath, as sacred expression, is rejected as a profanation of God, and in its place simple speech is advised: "Let your word be 'Yes, Yes' or 'No, No'; anything more than this comes from the evil one" (Matt. 5:37).

We have here the clear rejection by Jesus of *pilpul,* the disputational habit of the experts in scriptural law to twist the meaning of words, particularly the words of Scripture, often into their exact opposite. But in truth, Jesus himself does not hold to the maxim of simple speech. His own speech is very often ambiguous, or enveloped in an opacity that neither the disciples nor his enemies are able to understand. To the statement from the Sermon on the Mount ("Let your word be 'Yes, Yes' or 'No, No'"), we may contrast what Jesus says in Matthew 10:16: "Be wise as serpents and innocent as doves."

Jesus was in fact no dogmatic or systematic thinker, for he was—a Jew. He spoke and behaved as dictated by circumstances, and to absolutize individual sentences of Jesus would do violence to him.

The most difficult passages in the Sermon on the Mount, both exegetically and ethically, are those having to do with the love of peace:

> "You have heard that it was said, 'An eye for an eye and a tooth for a tooth' [Exod. 21:24]. But I say to you, Do not resist an evildoer. But if anyone strikes you on the right cheek, turn the other also; and if anyone wants to sue you and take your coat, give your cloak as well; and if anyone forces you to go one mile, go also the second mile. Give to everyone who begs from you, and do not refuse anyone who wants to borrow from you." (Matt. 5:38–42)

If Jesus is here citing the *lex talionis,* both he and his listeners know that no one took this law in a literal sense; quite to the contrary, a person was subjected only to a monetary indemnification handed down by the court (BT, Baba Kama 83b ff.). As Achad Haʻam writes:

> The judges were therefore required to clarify whether, according to the Torah, one is allowed to act in such a way, and they came to an explicit determination: Take no expiatory money for the life of a murderer (Num. 35:31), from which they rightly concluded that one must take no expiatory money for the *life* of a murderer, but one may indeed take expiatory money for the maiming of limbs (Baba Kama 83b). Thus the law's harshness was reduced. ("Worte des Friedens," 229)

Just as the experts in scriptural law interpreted the *lex talionis* in a human sense, Jesus interprets the law of recompense in his own way: "But I say to you . . . ." But this way is so radical that it exceeds human capacity to uphold it. Nevertheless, I cannot agree with Bultmann when he comments,

> Whoever appealing to a word of Jesus . . . offers the other cheek to one who strikes him, *because* Jesus said so, would not understand Jesus. For he would have missed exactly the obedience which Jesus desires; he would imagine that he could achieve and present an act of obedience when obedience is not really present as the determining factor of his life. (*Jesus and the Word,* 92)

This is no longer Jesus speaking through Bultmann but Paul, even Heidegger. According to Pauline theology, natural man is incapable of good; only Christ effects the good in him. Heidegger goes so far as to say that our being, abased to nothingness, is utterly damaged. Jesus of Nazareth has nothing to do with any of this. He means simply what he says: if you are struck on the right cheek, then hold out the left cheek as well. Jesus himself, however, does not always behave consistently with this principle. When at the hearing before the high priest he is slapped on the cheek by a guard enraged over what he takes to be an unfitting response, Jesus does not hold out the other cheek to his tormentor but answers logically, "If I have spoken wrongly, testify to the wrong. But if I have spoken rightly, why do you strike me?" (John 18:23).

The idea that one should not strive against evil is also found in the rabbis. Still, I think that Jesus' radical behavior in this context is understandable only in light of his imminent eschatological expectations. Along with John the Baptist and many of his contemporaries, Jesus expected the kingdom of God, the messianic kingdom or the "coming world," to arrive soon; consequently, the struggle against evil—in principle already conquered—did not pay, so to speak.

The most astonishing statement in this passage is "You have heard that it was said, 'You shall love your neighbor and hate your enemy'" (Matt. 5:43). The commandment to love one's neighbor is clearly ordained in the Torah: "You shall love your neighbor as yourself" (Lev. 19:18; cf. v. 34). Jesus cites this commandment, together with the love of God, as the highest one (Matt. 22:36–40), thereby continuing directly in the tradition of Hillel. What is problematical outside of the Sermon on the Mount is not so much where the love of one's enemies is commanded but where hatred of enemies is expressly commanded. The law requires, as we recall, "When you come upon your enemy's ox or donkey going astray, you shall bring it back. When you see the donkey of one who hates you lying under its burden and you would hold back from setting it free, you must help to set it free" (Exod. 23:4–5).

Only a look at the papyrus rolls at Qumran makes the thought "you shall hate your enemies" understandable to us, for in the "War Roll of the Battle of the Sons of Light" of the sects of the Dead Sea, there is an explicit command to hate the sons of Belial, the sons of darkness. One must hate them.[38] Jesus thus distinguishes himself from Qumran, whereas he identified himself with Qumran in the first beatitude. It is obvious that among his audience, presumably within the inner circle of disciples, one or more Qumranians were present.

Only by loving one's enemies can a person truly act in the *imitatio Dei*, the imitation of God, an ideal within the doctrinal tradition of the synagogue. Jesus concludes this section with "Be perfect, therefore, as your heavenly Father is perfect" (Matt. 5:48), in a conscious variation on Leviticus 19:2: "You shall be holy, for I the Lord your God am holy." Israel as "a royal priesthood, a holy nation" (1 Peter 2:9), was the principal goal of pharisaic Judaism and remained the ever unfulfilled ideal of Judaism. That goes as much for the community of Jesus as for, in greater measure, the later church.

Although we have been primarily following Matthew's version of the Sermon on the Mount, we must make note of the very important supplement in Luke (6:31): "Do to others as you would have them do to you." This is nothing other than the Golden Rule of Hillel: *De'alakh sani lechavrakh la ta'avid*, 'Whatever you find hateful, do not do to your neighbor' (BT, Shabbath 31a). According to Hillel, this injunction encompasses the entire substance of the Torah. This wisdom dates even prior to Hillel, presumably from the first pre-Christian century in the apocryphal book of Tobit (4:15): "And what you hate, do not do to anyone." One would not be wrong to take these words as an interpretation of the love commandment (Lev. 19:18). In Matthew's Gospel we have the sentence a little later, with an addendum, "In everything do to others as you would have them do to you; for this is the law and the prophets" (7:12), which essentially completes the citation of Hillel. We adduced the Luke text specifically, since that is where the sentence properly belongs.

The Targum of Jonathan, an early Aramaic translation of the Pentateuch and of a portion of the Prophets and the Writings,[39] which is mentioned in the Babylonian Talmud, Megilla 3a, extends the translation of the love commandment into the sense of the Golden Rule, so that here again we see Jesus as a teacher in the synagogue. In this instance we do agree with Bultmann's contention that there are in fact no new "ethical" requirements in Jesus (*Jesus and the Word*, 88). That does not denigrate Jesus' sermon but simply places it in its proper context.

The conclusion of the Sermon on the Mount constitutes the admonition on proper almsgiving. The concept of alms, or welfare, is not stated as such in Hebrew. Remarkably, this concept is paraphrased by *tsedaka*, which in fact means 'justice' and is etymologically derived from the word *tsedek*. The welfare that I provide to the needy is an act of justice, because it is owing to the recipient. *Tsedaka* is treated in rabbinic scripture exactly in the same sense as in the Sermon on the Mount. It supersedes every commandment (BT, Baba Bathra 9a); it goes beyond any sacrifice (BT, Sukka 49b); but only in love does it receive its full worth (BT, Sukka 49b).[40] The rejection of hypocrites, whom the Talmud calls "colored Pharisees," who do their good works publicly, represents the true spirit of the Jewish *tsedaka*. *Tsedaka*, 'alms,' is at the same time something sacred, for the second tithe belongs to the poor; the temple and its priesthood receive the first tithe. It is in this sense that we understand Matthew 7:6: "Do not give what is holy to dogs; and do not throw your pearls before swine, or they will trample them under foot and turn and maul you."

This admonition is understandable in terms of Deuteronomy 23: 18:[41] "You shall not bring the fee of a prostitute or the wages of a male prostitute [Hebrew text: 'dog'] into the house of the Lord your God in payment for any vow, for both of these are abhorrent to the Lord your God." The male temple prostitutes of the pagan Canaanite cult were called dogs (among the Babylonians they even wore dog masks) because they were exploited sexually in canine fashion in the temple orgies. Therefore, the dog money is named in conjunction with the harlot money. The harlots are clearly, in the hardly less crude phraseology of Jesus, the "swine," which are on the same level as the dogs. Jesus here attacks the perversion and travesty of *tsedaka,* which obtains when the money owing to the poor is cast at the feet of harlots and male prostitutes.

The impression could arise here, as a result of this listing of parallels and the interpolation of the Sermon on the Mount into the doctrinal material of Judaism, that I am attempting to relativize or diminish Jesus' sermon. That is by no means the case. The Sermon on the Mount remains what it is even when we see it in light of the Jewish tradition to which it belongs, just as the Ten Commandments remain what they are even when we examine them in the historical light of the Code of Hammurabi and other precedents. The concept of originality was foreign to antiquity. That is difficult for the modern mind to understand. Modern literature suffers under the danger of plagiarism, whereas ancient literature suffered under the danger of pseudepigraphy, which is exactly the opposite of plagiarism. The plagiarist copies the intellectual property of another under his own name. The rabbis cautioned against this practice and stressed the importance of documenting sources: "Whoever utters a statement in the name of another who has said it redeems the world" (Pirkei-'Avoth 6.6). The teachers of the Talmud go so far as to cite numerous sources for a given remark. It is striking that Jesus never mentions an author (his appeal to the written word exists on another level), but we have reason to assume that the Evangelists, who propagate the undiluted authority of Jesus, consciously or unconsciously repress such references.

Pseudepigraphy represents a type of ancient literature that is no longer conceivable. Unknown authors wrote their works under the name of venerable, usually biblical, personages. The author wished in fact not to be original but to validate his thoughts by the conveyance of a well-known name. Thus the objection that the Sermon on the Mount contains nothing "original" would appear to Jesus and his contemporaries only as a justification. Jesus did say, to be sure, "But I say to you," but these words themselves belong to a recognized tradition of teaching. What is scattered throughout the Talmud and Midrash is rolled together in the words of Jesus in rhapsodic blocks. That is what gives his words their eternal power.

4   *The Wedding at Cana*

The first miracle of Jesus, the first act to give credibility to his mission, was the transformation of water into wine at the wedding at Cana (John 2:1–11). The episode occurs only in John.

The report begins, "On the third day there was a wedding in Cana of Galilee, and the mother of Jesus was there." The phrase "on the third day" has puzzled many interpreters, for it does not fit meaningfully into the narrative. After all, we know nothing of any event on the first or the second day—that is, of the public activity of Jesus. The rationalist Heinrich Schmidt, who offered a new German translation of the Gospels in 1910, escaped the dilemma simply by deleting the remark "on the third day" and beginning in commonsense fashion: "There was a wedding at Cana in Galilee." A more recent translator, Helmut Riethmüller, in seeking to transpose the New Testament into more accessible language, began with the distasteful heading "At a wedding, of all places," and then continued: "Three days later a wedding feast took place in Cana, a place in Galilee." The phrase "three days later" is awkward, for we do not know precisely from what point it is calculated.

A number of interpreters understand this "third day," a wedding day, as a *semeion,* one of the (pre)figurations in John's Gospel. Accordingly, the first miracle "on the third day" is to signify the resurrection of Christ "on the third day," and the wedding scene is to signify the bridegroom, whose voice (*kol chathan*) resounds "in the towns of Judah and the streets of Jerusalem" (Jer. 33:10). John the Baptist hears this voice as "the friend" of the bridegroom, whom he identifies as Jesus (John 3:29).

If we translate the phrase "and on the third day" back into Hebrew—into the atmosphere, the milieu, in which it belongs—it reads *Uvayom hashelishi.* Franz Delitzsch (translator of *Evangelien*) and Isaac Salkinson, independently of each other, have frequently applied this method of back-translation in rendering the New Testament into Hebrew. Although no original Hebrew text exists, of course, the Greek-writing authors of the synoptic Gospels thought in Hebrew-Aramaic; even the author of the later Gospel of John worked within a non-Greek linguistic tradition.

Yom hashelishi, 'the third day,' simply means Tuesday, for the Jewish week begins with Sunday and ends with the seventh day, the Sabbath. The individual days have no names, with the exception of the Sabbath, which means 'day of rest'; they are only numbered: the first, the second, the third day, and so on. The third day, Tuesday, was the chief Jewish wedding day, for it is the *kefel ki tov,* the day of the repeated "it was good" in the creation story (Gen. 1:10, 12).

The Talmud specifies Wednesday as the wedding day of virgins (BT, Kethuvoth 2a). But among the commoners, the *'am-ha'arets* (these are the people with whom we are dealing here in Galilee), Tuesday, the third day, was and still is preferred as the wedding day.

The phrase *ki tov,* 'for it was good,' which occurs two times in reference to the acts of creation performed on the third day, was symbolically transferred to the two participants in the marriage ceremony: one *ki tov* for the bridegroom and one *ki tov* for the bride. In this symbolic interpretation the bride and groom may look forward to double happiness in marriage.

The puzzle in the reported date of the wedding at Cana is solved just that simply. Too much has been read into this third day; in fact, the simple reality about this Jewish peasant wedding in Galilee has gone unnoticed.

The mother of Jesus was also at the wedding. She was probably already a widow, for it was not common for a married woman to attend a wedding alone without her husband.

Jesus and his disciples were likewise personally invited, an honor that Jesus' mother can appreciate. Her son has been invited to the wedding as a rabbi with his disciples. She has confidence in her son and turns to him with the request that he do something about the lack of wine at the celebration. It is precisely to *him* that she says, "They have no wine" (v. 3).

And it is at this point that we have Jesus' rude reply to his mother: "Woman, what concern is that to you and to me? My hour has not yet come" (v. 4). However we translate this reply—whether in the usual manner: "Woman, what have I to do with you?" or in the literal manner: "What to me and to thee, Woman?" (*ti emoi kai soi, gunai?*)—the reply is shocking. It amounts to a blatant violation of the commandment to honor one's parents, "Honor your father and your mother" (Exod. 20:12), which was always treated with the highest reverence in Judaism.

Indeed, a son is to honor his mother even over his father; furthermore, honoring one's parents was considered equal to honoring God (BT, Kiddushin 30b). Dishonoring one's parents was considered blasphemy: "At the moment that a man insults his father and his mother, the Holy One, blessed be He, says, 'I have done well that I do not dwell among them. For if I dwelt among them, they would also insult me'" (BT, Kiddushin 31a).

If any statement of Jesus is genuine, then surely it is this hard and completely unjustified rebuke of his mother, spoken publicly. For what writer would have made up such a statement?

An abyss is opened here that later Mariology could never bridge. This Mother-of-God cult probably originated in Ephesus, the legendary death place of Mary, not in Galilee, where people were aware of the uneasy relationship between the young itinerant preacher and his poor mother.

The so-called Thomas Gospel (a collection of apocryphal sayings of Jesus from the papyrus finds in Nag Hammadi in Egypt, discovered in the mid-1940s), in an intensified variation on Matthew 10:37 and

12:49–50, states, "Whoever will not hate his father and his mother, as I do, will not be my disciple" (Saying 101a).

Thus a harsh word to his mother is pronounced at the beginning of Jesus' career. Another is uttered at its tragic end, when he calls out to the grieving woman beneath his cross, who is being supported by his beloved disciple John, "Woman, here is your son" (John 19:26). Once again, this cold, distanced address—even now in the unspeakably painful hour of death: "Woman!" What other man ever spoke to his mother so? And now he points to John and commands him to take the bereaved mother as his own. Jesus himself has nothing to do with her; she remains emotionally alien to him. Jesus seems to have identified as a son so thoroughly with his heavenly father that he never speaks of love for one's mother even in his parables. That may well have something to do with the masculine conception of God in Judaism (God as father and king); still, we do have that lovely image of the comforting God who promises Israel, "As a mother comforts her child, so I will comfort you" (Isa. 66:13). These words are unthinkable in the mouth of Jesus.

And yet Mary proves to be the stronger of the two here in Cana. Despite the callous address and despite his feeling that his hour has not yet arrived, at his mother's request Jesus undertakes the miracle of transforming the water into wine.

There is nothing to be gained by looking for some historical basis in miracle stories of this kind. This is obviously an etiological saga connected with a specific place: namely, the village of Cana (fourteen kilometers north of Nazareth), which was also the home of the disciple Nathanael (John 21:2). The miracles of the wine and the multiplication of the bread, localized in Nazareth, Jesus' place of origin, function at the beginning of his public career as a means of anticipating its high point, the sacramental words of the Last Supper, where the transubstantiation of wine and bread is proclaimed. It is apparent that this involved a later kerygma, in which Hellenistic mystery-cult elements, alien to Judaism, were integrated. Nor is it surprising that such prefigurations occur precisely in John's Gospel, with its exclusive focus on the mystery of Christ.

Let it suffice for now to establish that Jesus—at the beginning of his brief public activity, even before he himself became aware that his hour had come—meets his mother at a wedding in the environs of his home and, as a consequence of his strange behavior, calls public attention to himself. In the tradition of the Christian community, in the kerygma, this event was transformed into a miracle of turning water into wine.

It is important to note the significance of wine in Jewish tradition. Wine is absolutely essential to Jewish ritual. At a wedding it is of course offered to the guests as a drink of celebration, but the wedding ceremony itself begins with a blessing over the fruit of the vine, the cup offered to the bride and bridegroom. It is not only in the Seder ritual of the Passover festival that wine plays a dominant role, as it has since at least the time of the second temple; every Sabbath is likewise ushered in with the *kiddush* blessing over the cup filled with wine and concluded with the pouring-out of a few drops of wine. This custom, too, was doubtless known at the time of Jesus. The Psalter sings of "wine to gladden the human heart" (104:15). And because the Lord is to be served "with gladness" (Ps. 100:2), wine belonged in the divine service, both in the Levitical worship cult in the temple in Jerusalem and in the laical cult of the rabbis in synagogues and houses. The cultivation of wine goes back to the patriarch Noah, with whom God, according to a talmudic tradition, concluded a pact that encompassed seven commandments valid not only for Israel but for all people (BT, Sanhedrin 56a–b).

The sects of the Essenes and Rechabites refused the enjoyment of wine. Likewise, the consecrated group of Nazirites—to which, for example, the judge Samson belonged—did not touch wine and grapes (Judg. 13:7).

Jesus certainly did not belong to these sectarians; in fact, his enemies accused him of being a drunkard (Matt. 11:19; Luke 7:34). In this regard he stood closer to the rabbis, who taught that one should give one's last shekel for noble wine. The rabbinic tradition does, however, recommend thinning strong wine with water: either one-third wine and two-thirds water or one-quarter wine and three-quarters water (BT, Shabbath 77a).

Thus we understand very well the indication that there were six stone water jugs at the wedding at Cana to be used for mixing the noble wine into a *mezeg,* 'mixed drink,' which is mentioned as early as the Song of Solomon (7:2). We know from an admonishing statement of Rabbi 'Akiva that this song was sung in wine houses as a profane love and drinking song (Tosefta, Sanhedrin 12.10; cf. BT, Sanhedrin 101a); as a wedding song it may well have been sung here at Cana. (John's remark that the water in the jugs was intended for the "Jewish rites of purification" (v. 6) suggests to me that he did not understand the custom.)

The water is drawn out from the jugs at Jesus' command and presented to the *architriklinos,* 'chamberlain,' for his approval. This chamberlain, who tests the transformed water and pronounces it noble wine, is known to us today as the *marshalik,* 'marshal,' at Jewish weddings. He is simultaneously master of ceremonies and *maître de plaisir* at every wedding. He presents the gifts, praising them elaborately, to the bridal couple and is generally responsible for maintaining the proper mood at the feast. This *architriklinos* enunciates the wine rule: "Everyone serves the good wine first, and then the inferior wine after the guests have become drunk" (v. 10). Regarding the Johannine wine rule, which is attested nowhere else, many complicated opinions have been voiced. They all overlook the simple fact, however, that it is a *joke,* which the professional comedian (our *architriklinos*) tells at a Jewish wedding. In the Cana story he is made the first witness to the miraculous power of Jesus, introduced here as a magician—in other words, in that dubious role found in the medieval Jewish anti-gospel, the *Toledoth Yeshu*ʿ.[42] In John, of course, it is (harmless) white magic. The folk book *Toledoth Yeshu*ʿ presents Jesus as a black magician who, through misuse of the tetragram (YHWH = Yahweh), yields to supernatural forces by sewing into his flesh a parchment with this sign. Thus the same folk fantasy responsible for the story of the wine miracle at Cana—altered by the opponents who hated him—also accounts for the narration of negative acts of enchantment by Jesus as magician. This Jesus, of course, is far removed from the teacher of inner piety in the Sermon on the Mount and the parables. Legend also ascribed magic to the great lawgiver of Israel, Moses, who changed his staff into a serpent and entered into a magical contest with Pharaoh's magicians. A miracle is the dearest child not only of belief but of superstition as well, which does not ascribe essential importance to the pure announcement of the word, or the life-giving exposition of Torah, the simple power of prayer. Instead, superstition seeks legitimacy through magical wonders and exorcisms—through the signs and miracles that Jesus himself rejected in the strongest terms (Matt. 12:39, 16:4; Mark 8:12; Luke 11:16, 29).

5 *The Parables*

Jesus of Nazareth taught not only through the sermon but especially through parables, to which he alluded in asking, "Do you have eyes, and fail to see? Do you have ears, and fail to hear?" (Mark 8:18).

That did not surprise his disciples, since at the time of Jesus the form of the parable enjoyed great popularity among those learned in the law. But the disciples were astonished that he spoke to the broad masses in parables, which often were not readily comprehensible: "Why do you speak to them in parables?" (Matt. 13:10), they asked. He answered,

> "To you it has been given to know the secrets of the kingdom of heaven, but to them it has not been given. For to those who have, more will be given, and they will have an abundance; but from those who have nothing, even what they have will be taken away. The reason I speak to them in parables is that 'seeing they do not perceive, and hearing they do not listen, nor do they understand' [Isa. 6:9]." (vv. 11–13)

Thus he answers figuratively in his characteristically paradoxical manner, which embraces the paradox of human existence. To the person who already has something, more will be given, so that this person should have fullness. What that means is that whoever already has the proper spirit and faith will receive, through parables, the message of the kingdom of God—Jesus' purpose—even more completely and clearly, as a deeply intimate possession. Whoever lacks this spirit and this faith, however, as well as this inner preparedness, will be even more confused, and the last remains of faith in God will be erased by the paradoxical nature of the parables. Thus the parables function like a distilling element.

The disciples therefore ask Jesus why he teaches in parables. He answers them after his manner, but his answer (Matt. 13:11–17) resonates with the words of the rabbis (Song of Sol. Rabba 1.1.3; cf. BT, 'Eruvin 21b):

> Let not the parable be lightly esteemed in your eyes, since by means of the
> parable a man can master the words of the Torah. If a king loses gold
> from his house or a precious pearl, does he not find it by means of a wick
> worth a farthing [lit. an *as,* the least valuable coin]? So . . . by means of
> the parable a man arrives at the true meaning of the words of the Torah.

This basic position of the rabbis relative to the parable reminds one immediately of Jesus' manner of teaching; the justification of parabolic speech is itself delivered through a parable, one indeed in which the motif of the pearl is taken up (Matt. 13:45–46).

The parable, called *mashal* in Hebrew, belongs to the most essential constituents of the Midrash, the legendary exposition of Torah. There is hardly a religious or ethical thought that the wise men of the Talmud did not attempt to clarify through parables. It is especially remarkable that it was the Palestinian rabbis in particular who cultivated the parable, whereas the Babylonian rabbis applied it much more rarely. Jesus, who was a Jew entirely in the tradition of the Jewish homeland, in this respect too remained true to a culture alien to diaspora Judaism; this is readily borne out by comparing Paul's manner of teaching. It is therefore no coincidence that the parables appear predominantly in the synoptic writers but recede in the Gospel of John, which is, despite Qumran, more strongly informed by Greek thought.

Just how highly the parable was valued can be gathered from a comment of the Mekhilta [see note 34] on the weekly section Beshal-lach (Exod. 13:17–17:16): "'What is right in their own eyes'—those are the parables spoken before the ears of all the people." Here too we have the motif of the hearing ear, for the parables were *spoken,* not written. They represent the original state of the oral, improvised in-terpretation of the written word; the exegetical connection to it is of-ten quite loose. The parables of Jesus do not always spring from a directly recognizable written word but circle around basic concepts of Judaism; most important, however, they are spoken from within the context of an imminent expectation of the kingdom of God.

One of the most insightful modern explicators of the parables of Jesus, Leonhard Ragaz, has stressed the revolutionary meaning of these parables. He correctly remarks,

> They signify an upheaval of thought and being of the world as nothing else has done since the speeches of the prophets and besides the Sermon on the Mount of Jesus himself. . . . This character of Jesus' parables has further been misunderstood, because their relationship to the prophets of Israel has been overlooked. They must be integrated within this context. (*Gleichnisse,* 8)

I can agree with Ragaz here only conditionally. Parables are rela-tively uncommon among the prophets, and by the time of Jesus they lay far in the past. The parables of Jesus need to be directly integrated with the Haggada, the *meshalim* of the contemporary Tannaim, with which they are equatable in the history of narrative form. It is unfor-tunate that Christian theology is incapable of seeing Jesus and his message in this natural context, and the consequence is that an inter-preter as impartial even as Ragaz can fall into error. This only hinders our understanding of the parables of Jesus.

Joseph Klausner, the Hebrew investigator of the life of Jesus, views Jesus' position within the literature of the *meshalim* very differently (*Jesus,* 264–65). He concurs with the former chief rabbi of Vienna, H. P. Chajes, who believes (*Markus-Studien,* 10–12) that Jesus was known as a *moshel,* a speaker of parables (cf. Num. 21:27). The word *moshel* was later misunderstood in the sense of 'ruler,' as it is used in Micah 5:2, the famous "Christological" passage: "But you, O Bethlehem of Ephrathah, who are one of the little clans of Judah, from you shall come forth for me one who is to rule in Israel, whose origin is from of old, from ancient days." *Moshel* can mean both 'speaker of parables' and 'ruler.'

Klausner rightly remarks concerning the parables of Jesus,

> His parables had a double object. In the first place, he wished to interest the simpler-minded folk who formed his usual audience. . . . Jesus was a poet and skillful story-teller and, therefore, he made use of poetical descriptions drawn from every-day life. . . . In the second place, he often endeavored, by these parables and metaphorical sayings, to wrap up an esoteric significance which could not yet be openly proclaimed or which men could not yet comprehend, and which he revealed only to the more discreet. (*Jesus*, 265)

To speak here of "poetical descriptions," however, and to claim that Jesus was a poet, appears misguided to me. The images of Jesus are not poetic but entirely realistic. They are culled from the landscape and daily life of his environment—with perhaps the exception of the parable of the wise and foolish virgins (Matt. 25:1–13), where it is not understandable how *one* bridegroom should celebrate a wedding with several virgins at the same time. (In Israel at the time of Jesus, polygamy was still entirely customary. We recall the humorous anecdote of the man who has a younger and an older wife. The young wife plucks out the white hairs of his beard and the old wife the black ones, so that eventually he is completely bald. Despite the existence of polygamy, however, there was no such thing as marriage to multiple brides at the same time.)

About the parables of Jesus, Ragaz says, "They are understandable to any child; indeed they are easiest for a child" (*Gleichnisse*, 7). I can agree with this conception only in part, even though Jesus himself says, "Let the little children come to me, and do not stop them; for it is to such as these that the kingdom of heaven belongs" (Matt. 19:14). Obviously, certain parables are understandable to children but by no means all of them.

The parables of Jesus are not systematically arranged in the Gospels, but each is inserted into the conversations of Jesus with his disciples or opponents relative to the situation. If we attempt to arrange them systematically, what results is a threefold division corresponding to rabbinic hermeneutics. The rabbis divided obligations into two categories: obligations between man and God (*beyn 'adam lamakom*) and obligations between man and his fellowman (*beyn 'adam lechavero*). The parables of Jesus hold precisely to this twofold division but are preceded by a third group of parables that speak directly of the kingdom of God and of the judgment prior to it; we may call these eschatological parables.

It is not possible, but neither is it necessary, to discuss all the parables of Jesus here, for they are among the best-known portions of the Gospels. They have been called "the picture book of the New Testament." This all too often hid their purely Jewish character, however, because the observers were ignorant of the parallels in the Haggada, the corpus of Jewish sagas and legends. Viewed within this literature, the parables of Jesus represent a high point in paradoxical dialectic.

From the first of the three groups of parables I should like to select the parable of the vineyard (Matt. 21:33–41; Mark 12:1–11), whose opening section is so reminiscent of the one in Isaiah (5:1–7):

> "There was a landowner who planted a vineyard, put a fence around it, dug a wine press in it, and built a watchtower. Then he leased it to tenants and went to another country. When the harvest time had come, he sent his slaves to the tenants to collect his produce. But the tenants seized his slaves and beat one, killed another, and stoned another. Again he sent other slaves, more than the first; and they treated them in the same way. Finally he sent his son to them, saying, 'They will respect my son.' But when the tenants saw the son, they said to themselves, 'This is the heir; come, let us kill him and get his inheritance.' So they seized him, threw him out of the vineyard, and killed him. Now when the owner of the vineyard comes, what will he do to those tenants?" [The chief priests and elders] said to him, "He will put those wretches to a miserable death, and lease the vineyard to other tenants who will give him the produce at the harvest time."

This parable is totally concerned with the message of the kingdom of God. Israel as the vineyard of God is depicted in the sense of Isaiah.

Then, however, the parable turns to the messengers sent by the lord of the vineyard: none is accepted, not even the son. Jesus thereby alludes to his own mission.

It would be erroneous, however, to assume that Jesus is saying that the guardians of Israel were deluding themselves and that consequently God would choose another Israel from the nations. Rather, the parable means to say that the leadership among the people will be taken from the Pharisees and priests and given to the disciples of Jesus, who are more faithful guardians of the vineyard of God.

In his commentary on Matthew 21:28 ff., Leo Baeck points out that to the parable of the two sons in the vineyard (vv. 28–32), the second vineyard parable (that dealing with the wicked tenants, quoted above) was later attached as a means of foretelling the death of Jesus and the scattering of the Jewish people ("Gospel," 134). I do not agree that the second parable in its *entirety* came later; I think rather that what we have here is a later kerygmatic revision (the version that has come down to us), in which particularly the passage about the son was added after the death of Jesus. This probably has nothing to do with the scattering of the entire Jewish people but rather with a change in the spiritual leadership.

Viewed somewhat differently, this parable is also typical of another category, which we may designate as the kingly parable. In Jesus' improvisational style, the king is variously called lord, house lord, or house father, and *within* a given parable this designation can change. Rabbinic literature contains hundreds of *meshalim* of this type, which tell of a certain *melekh basar vadam,* 'king of flesh and blood,' who is regularly substituted for the "king of kings, the Holy One, blessed be he." The usual formula "king of flesh and blood" is lacking in the Gospels, however, owing to the fact that the Gospels exist only in a Greek version. Hearing the word *melekh,* the Hebrew speaker thought first of God; if one meant an earthly king, it was necessary to say so specifically in order to establish the parabolic intent of the narrative. For the Greeks, this specification was unnecessary. We may confidently assume, however, that Jesus originally began his kingly parables with the formula *melekh basar vadam.*

Another corpus of parables has as its object to demonstrate the relationship between man and God. One of these is the parable of the lost or prodigal son:

Then Jesus said, "There was a man who had two sons. The younger of them said to his father, 'Father, give me the share of the property that will belong to me.' So he divided his property between them. A few days later the younger son gathered all he had and traveled to a distant country, and there he squandered his property in dissolute living. When he had spent everything, a severe famine took place throughout that country, and he began to be in need. So he went and hired himself out to one of the citizens of that country, who sent him to his fields to feed the pigs. He would gladly have filled himself with the pods that the pigs were eating; and no one gave him anything. But when he came to himself he said, 'How many of my father's hired hands have bread enough and to spare, but here I am dying of hunger! I will get up and go to my father, and I will say to him, "Father, I have sinned against heaven and before you; I am no longer worthy to be called your son; treat me like one of your hired hands."' So he set off and went to his father. But while he was still far off, his father saw him and was filled with compassion; he ran and put his arms around him and kissed him. Then the son said to him, 'Father, I have sinned against heaven and before you; I am no longer worthy to be called your son.' But the father said to his slaves, 'Quickly, bring out a robe—the best one—and put it on him; put a ring on his finger and sandals on his feet. And get the fatted calf and kill it, and let us eat and celebrate; for this son of mine was dead and is alive again; he was lost and is found!' And they began to celebrate.

"Now his elder son was in the field; and when he came and approached the house, he heard music and dancing. He called one of the slaves and asked what was going on. He replied, 'Your brother has come, and your father has killed the fatted calf, because he has got him back safe and sound.' Then he became angry and refused to go in. His father came out and began to plead with him. But he answered his father, 'Listen! For all these years I have been working like a slave for you, and I have never disobeyed your command; yet you have never given me even a young goat so that I might celebrate with my friends. But when this son of yours came back, who has devoured your property with prostitutes, you killed the fatted calf for him!' Then the father said to him, 'Son, you are always with me, and all that is mine is yours. But we had to celebrate and rejoice, because this brother of yours was dead and has come to life; he was lost and has been found.'" (Luke 15:11–32)

The parables in this group have to do with the rediscovery of something that has been lost. The parable of the lost sheep and the parable of the lost penny precede the parable of the lost son. They create three variations on the central theme of *teshuva,* the return of the sinner. The gates of repentance are always open, according to the saying of the rabbis, and nothing is greater than repentance. That is the idea with which these *teshuva* parables are concerned. In the parable of the lost son, God's mercy appears to the older brother as injustice. This sovereign grace of God, however, is not something similar to revelation or knowledge in Jesus but has already been clearly established in the Old Testament: "I will be gracious to whom I will be gracious, and will show mercy on whom I will show mercy" (Exod. 33:19), as God says at the moment in which he causes his *kavod,* 'manifestation of glory,' to pass before Moses. But an additional feature also occurs here: the favoring of the younger person with respect to the inheritance. This motif also can be followed throughout the Old Testament: Isaac is younger than Ishmael (Gen. 16:15, 21:2–3); Jacob is younger than Esau (Gen. 25:24–25); Joseph was the second youngest of Jacob's sons (Gen. 30:24, 35:17–18); Moses is younger than Aaron (Exod. 6:20); David is the youngest brother (1 Sam. 17:14). The intent of Jesus' narrative is clearly to establish the primacy of grace over the law. But the love of the father is bestowed precisely upon the prodigal child who recognizes his guilt.

That the younger, prodigal son becomes a swineherd shows that he has departed from the Jewish people, for whom the cultivation of pigs was anathema.

The older brother is not, as many Christian interpreters presume, a kind of representative of the synagogue; nor does the younger brother represent the pagan-Christian church that found its way out of squalor to the God of Israel. Such an interpretation would mean that this parable belongs to a much later kerygma and therefore lacks authenticity. I believe instead that it entails a variation on a rabbinical principle: "In the place where those returning (*ba'alei-teshuva*) are standing, even the completely righteous (*tsaddikim gemurim*) cannot stand" (BT, Berakhoth 34b).

But the parable also received another, much later, interpretation that lay well beyond Jesus' intention. He himself, the narrator of the parable, entirely against his own will became the "lost son of Israel." For almost two thousand years he dwelt in a foreign land, while the older brother, the Jewish people, remained under the strict discipline of the Father. But now a process to fetch Jesus home to the Jewish people has begun. He is returning to his Father's house, and there his older brother will rejoice with him. For our brother Jesus was dead for us but now lives again. He was lost to us and has been found again.

The third group of parables deals with the obligations between individuals. Let us look at the parable of the merciful Samarite, the Good Samaritan, related by Jesus in response to the question "And who is my neighbor?" posed by an expert in the law:

> Jesus replied, "A man was going down from Jerusalem to Jericho, and fell into the hands of robbers, who stripped him, beat him, and went away, leaving him half dead. Now by chance a priest was going down that road; and when he saw him, he passed by on the other side. So likewise a Levite, when he came to the place and saw him, passed by on the other side. But a Samaritan while traveling came near him; and when he saw him, he was moved with pity. He went to him and bandaged his wounds, having poured oil and wine on them. Then he put him on his own animal, brought him to an inn, and took care of him. The next day he took out two denarii, gave them to the innkeeper, and said, 'Take care of him; and when I come back, I will repay you whatever more you spend.' Which of these three, do you think, was a neighbor to the man who fell into the hands of the robbers?" He said, "The one who showed him mercy." Jesus said to him, "Go and do likewise." (Luke 10:30–37)

The parable of the merciful Samaritan arises out of a dialogue with a teacher of the law, a *talmid chakham,* who had previously asked Jesus what he must do to inherit eternal life. Jesus answered that question with another question, in a manner entirely typical of Jewish dialogues: "What is written in the law? What do you read [or learn] there?" (Luke 10:26). The teacher of the law, who apparently belonged to the school of Hillel, later carried on by Rabbi 'Akiva, responded with the commandment to love God (Deut. 6:5) and the commandment to love one's neighbor (Lev. 19:18). His method here is similar to that of Jesus, who elsewhere gives the same answer (Matt. 22:37–40; Mark 12:29–31) and who views the synthesis of love for God and for one's fellowman as the summation of all laws. The love of one's neighbor, as ordained in the third book of Moses, is declared by Rabbi 'Akiva to be a Great General Rule (*kelal*) in the Torah (JT, Nedarim 9.4); Rashi emphatically cites it in his own commentary on the Leviticus passage.

But now the learned man raises the question "And who is my neighbor?" (Luke 10:29), which implicitly broaches the problem of a Jew's relationship to non-Jews. The intended question here is probably whether the concept *re'a*, 'fellowman' or, better, 'companion,' as Buber and Rosenzweig translate it (i.e., *Genosse*), connotes only one's ethnic companion or every person.

Jesus' answer clearly implies that the commandments between man and his fellowman (*beyn 'adam lechavero*) are not to be limited by national boundaries. He therefore adduces as an example the Samaritan, who, without halakhic (religio-legal) reflection, enacts the commandment of love spontaneously, over and above the boundaries of nationalistic caste-thinking.

The commandment of love in the third book of Moses is not isolated but forms the next to last part of a complex formation (Lev. 19:17–18):

> You shall not hate in your heart anyone of your kin;
> you shall reprove your neighbor,
> or you will incur guilt yourself.
> You shall not take vengeance or bear a grudge against any of your people,
> but you shall love your neighbor
> as yourself:
> I am the Lord.

It is clear from this passage that the commandment of love applies to deportment toward one's own people, with whom one shares a collective bond. This is implicit in the Hebrew phrase *benei-'amekha,* 'the sons of your people' (i.e., ethnic companions). The preceding sentence speaks of the brother, against whom one should not bear anger. Thus we have different expressions here: brother, son of your people, and neighbor (companion). It thereby becomes apparent that the intended object was the person belonging to the actual Hebrew people. Jesus goes beyond this initial sense, but it is characteristic of him that he does not choose a Jew to perform an act of love toward a Samaritan but rather the reverse: a Samaritan performs an act of love simply toward a "man" whose identity is not narrowly specified as Jewish, Samaritan, Greek, or Roman. Thus the parable begins, "A *man* was going down from Jerusalem to Jericho, and fell into the hands of robbers" (v. 30). Toward this man the Samaritan shows himself to be a true fellowman, who does not stand idly by at the sight of his neighbor's blood (cf. Lev. 19:16).

The relationship of Jesus to the Samaritans is not consistent, however, a fact that gives us a certain insight into the role of this parable within the unfolding of Jesus' life and work.

In commissioning his disciples, Jesus expressly says, "Enter no town of the Samaritans" (Matt. 10:5). He himself, after all, formerly had had a negative experience with them: they once refused lodging to him and his disciples (Luke 9:52–56).

Nevertheless, Jesus and his disciples do not hesitate to continue through Samaritan territory on their way from Galilee to Jerusalem, the destination of their pilgrimage. In the fourth chapter of John's Gospel (v. 5) we find Jesus again in their area, in the city of Sychar, which is probably identical with the Old Testament Shechem (today Nablus). There, at the well of Jacob, Jesus enters into a discussion with a Samaritan woman (John 4:1–30), to whom he recapitulates in clairvoyant fashion—off the top of his head, as it were—her past and present: "You have had five husbands, and the one you have now is not your husband" (v. 18). In this conversation Jesus requests a drink of water—as a rule, Jews did not accept food or drink from Samaritans (that may not have applied specifically to water, however)—and reveals himself as the fountain of the living water. Here we can discern a sharp rejection of the Samaritans: Samaritans pray for what they do not understand (that is, for what they do not *properly* understand, for Samaritans also had the five books of Moses and the book of Joshua as revelation documents), whereas he, as a Jew, belongs to those who pray for what they do understand. He arrogantly concludes that "salvation is from the Jews" (v. 22). The discussion then takes a positive turn. Many Samaritans have begun to believe in Jesus, which prompts him to remain in their city for two days. This conversion of the Samaritans, who were said to be acknowledging Jesus as "the Savior of the world" (v. 42), is doubtless unhistorical; in the Samaritan communities that exist today in Cholon in Israel and in Nablus there is no evidence of a once vital Jesus tradition whatsoever. Even the parable of the Good Samaritan is unknown among them. The Samaritans never extended their tradition beyond the Pentateuch and Joshua and still today celebrate their Passover sacrifice in an archaic fashion on Mount Gerizim above Nablus. I myself have participated in this sacrificial ritual and discovered in conversations with Samaritan priests that they either never knew the New Testament at all or, if so, only indirectly through English missionaries.

Jesus' conversation with the Samaritan woman at Jacob's well bears an unmistakable similarity to his conversation with the Canaanite woman (Matt. 15:21–28; Mark 7:24–30). In the region of Tyre and Sidon a Canaanite, or Syrophoenician, woman comes to him and begs for the healing of her daughter. He rejects her, saying that he has been sent only to the lost sheep of the house of Israel. When she refuses to take no for an answer, he remarks coarsely that one should not take bread from children only to cast it before dogs. And yet he gives in after she replies with quick wit that even dogs eat the crumbs that fall from the table of their masters. These two conversations with *women*, particularly *non-Jewish* women—conversations the disciples find so offensive—call forth a change in Jesus, loosening his stiff nationalistic attitude into one of simple human concern. There is nothing coincidental about this; it is a clear rejection—in story form, of course—of two blessings that go together in the liturgy of the morning prayer: "Blessed art thou, Lord our God, King of the Universe, who has not made me a heathen," and "Blessed art thou, Lord our God, King of the Universe, who has not made me a woman."[43]

The parable of the Good Samaritan is spoken to the experts in scriptural law as an example of a just fulfillment of the law. That would have been nothing short of scandalous for them, since the Sa-

maritans (or Kutim, as they are called in the Talmud after their Babylonian city of origin, Kuta) had the reputation of being untrustworthy
and were suspected of practicing idolatry in secret; they were accused
even of having secretly buried idolatrous images on the holy mountain of Gerizim. This may allude to Genesis 35:4, where it is reported
that Jacob buried the idols of his clan under an oak in Shechem.

The chief topic of contention between Jews and Samaritans, which
comes out in Jesus' conversation with the Samaritan woman, concerned the two holy places: the Jewish temple in Jerusalem and the
Samaritan temple on Mount Gerizim above Shechem. Of the seven
small Talmud tractates (*massekhtoth ketanoth*), the sixth is dedicated
to the Kutim, the Samaritans. The Kutim were settled in Samaria by
the Assyrian King Sennacherib or his son following the destruction of
the kingdom of Israel in 721 B.C.E. They were later called Samarites,
or Samaritans, after the region in which they had been settled. They
reerected the old Israelite temple at Beth-El, the traditional site of
Jacob's dream. Since the colonists were threatened by wild lions, they
found it necessary to institute the autochthonous cult of Yahweh in
order to receive protection from the god of the land. An Israelite
priest was sent to them from Babylon for the purpose of establishing
this cult (2 Kings 17:24–41).

In the wake of the later reform undertaken by King Josiah of Judea,
all priests of Israelite provenance were killed (cf. 2 Kings 24). The
Samaritans in fact sought affiliation with the Jerusalem temple but
were repeatedly rejected. Following the return of a portion of the Jews
from their Babylonian captivity, the Samaritans also negotiated to
participate in the rebuilding of the temple in Jerusalem under the
condition that they be recognized as belonging to the federated community; the returned Israelites refused. Zerubbabel, leader of the returned Israelites, excluded them from the construction of the temple
(Ezra 4:1–3), thus provoking open enmity between Jews and Samaritans and leading in turn to the construction of a competing temple
on Mount Gerizim.[44] This temple existed as a provocation to Jews at
the time of Jesus, and the relationship between the Jews and the Samaritans was extremely tense, as we can gather from the sixth small
Talmud tractate. Intermarriage with Samaritans was proscribed. It
was also forbidden to sell religious objects to Samaritans for fear they

might desecrate them. On the other hand, purely monetary transactions between Jews and Samaritans were permitted, as was mutual participation in almsgiving.

Jesus himself was originally not without prejudice against the Samaritans, and he soon enough experienced rejection at their hands, as well. But he must have revised his prejudices, and we may assume that his parable of the Good Samaritan was spoken *after* the encounter at Jacob's well.

We notice right from the opening sentence the striking realism of the parables of Jesus. The man going from Jerusalem to Jericho falls into the hands of robbers. The road from Jerusalem to Jericho was, until very recent times, an area threatened by thieving bedouins. I myself remember reluctantly having to travel the road without police escort. The British Mandate Authority provided chauffeurs who drove this route with a license to carry guns. The road leads through a desert region, the very one into which the scapegoat was sent on the Great Day of Atonement to be cast down from the 'Azazel rock (Lev. 16:8–22). It is along this road that the man falls victim to an attack by highway robbers, who leave him lying there half dead.

A priest now passes by on his way from Jericho to Jerusalem, apparently in order to perform service in the temple. He presumes the man dead and therefore goes around him to avoid being defiled by him—for a priest who has touched a corpse can no longer participate in the temple service. That is to say, the conscientious *kohen*, 'priest,' holds a ritual commandment higher than the commandment to love one's neighbor. Exactly the same is true for a Levite who, had he touched a corpse, likewise could not have participated in the temple service as a choir singer, for example, or even have entered the temple. Both priest and Levite would have been required to undergo a purification ritual, which would have made it impossible for them to arrive at their service on time. That is doubtless the intention of the parable; otherwise, it would make no sense to mention a priest and a Levite instead of, say, a Pharisee and an expert in scriptural law. The latter two would in fact have corresponded directly to the dialogical context, since the parable is told to a pharisaic expert in scriptural law. The latter immediately understands the point: *ritual versus duty of the heart.*[45]

The sequence in our parable—priest, then Levite—reflects a descending honorific scale within Judaism.[46]

The Samaritan, however, who is free of such ritualistic scruples, takes compassion on the poor man and does everything for him that can be done. Consequently, he fulfills the commandment of love in its true sense, and Jesus concludes the parable with an exhortation to the expert in scriptural law: "Go and do likewise" (Luke 10:37). The unprecedented provocation that this exhortation represents becomes clear only when one grasps that an expert in scriptural law is being challenged to take a Samaritan as his model and to behave accordingly—in other words, to learn from *him* the proper meaning of Torah.

The parable of the Good Samaritan certainly is one of Jesus' most beautiful and profound parables and never loses its relevance. We have attempted to place it in the historical and cultural context necessary to its being properly understood. Beyond that, however, its eternal validity surely applies in the human realm of every time and every culture.

The significance of this parable came home to me in a profound way on 16 May 1961 at the forty-first session of the Eichmann trial in Jerusalem. Provost Dr. Heinrich Grüber of Berlin, a German official who had selflessly aided persecuted Jews and paid for it in a concentration camp, related the following conversation: "Eichmann said to me, 'What do you care, after all, about the Jews? They won't be grateful for your effort. Why, then, all this activity on behalf of the Jews?' Since I figured that he, as a former Templar, was familiar with this country (Israel), I replied, 'You know the road that leads from Jerusalem to Jericho?' Then I said, 'A Jew who had fallen among thieves once lay along this road. Someone who was not a Jew came by and helped. The Lord, whom alone I listen to, said to me, *Go and do likewise.* That is my answer.'"

The quintessence of this parable is that we see our neighbor in whatever person we encounter in daily life. We are not to question whether that person is an ethnic companion or a member of the same faith. The parable speaks only of a "man" who fell among robbers. It does not say that he was a Jew, even if that is assumed from the context. The suffering man rather is our neighbor whom we must help, and one can learn that even from a Samaritan. *Whoever saves a soul in Israel is as a person who has saved an entire world,* so the rabbis teach. In the parable of the Good Samaritan the ethnic boundary is consciously removed: whoever saves a soul, whoever saves a human life, saves an entire world. That is the fulfillment of the commandment of love.

Hermann Cohen once said that brotherly love is otherly love. The other person, who does not belong to my people or to my religion or to my language group, can be my brother in a certain situation: namely, when that person has need of me. That too is contained in our parable. Brotherly love is not meant as a Schillerian *Seid umschlungen, Millionen* (Be embraced, O Millions), which lumps all people together in a nonbinding fashion. What is meant is taking people individually—an actual person in an actual situation that is given to me to resolve. Thus Jesus replies to the legal expert's question "And who is my neighbor?" with the parable of the Good Samaritan. Jesus does not conclude with an answer to the question, only with the imperative to act.

6 *Teach Us to Pray*

According to the Gospel of Luke (11:1), it is one of the disciples of Jesus, not mentioned by name, who turns to him with the request "Lord, teach us to pray, as John taught his disciples." This request means not that the disciples of Jesus previously knew no prayers but that in addition to the usual prayer of the daily and Sabbath service the various masters commonly recommended other private prayers, *tachanunim,* to their disciples. We are reminded here of a statement in the Babylonian Talmud (Berakhoth 29b): "Whoever views his prayer as something obligatory does not offer a fervent prayer." What does it mean that something is (only) obligatory? Rabbi Yosef explains, "When one does not know how to insert anything new into it."

It is in this sense that we understand the disciple's wish to be taught to pray; Jesus' answer, the "Our Father," is directed to that purpose. One misunderstands the nature of this prayer if one conceives of it as a liturgical formula or, worse, as the only acceptable liturgical prayer. It is precisely not that; rather, it is a model for the art of praying in complete simplicity of heart.

Prayer is not an end in itself; praying is not a duty or good deed but a conversation with God. The eminent orthodox Jewish exegete of the nineteenth century Samson Raphael Hirsch[47] had a similar opinion of prayer: "The inner Divine service (prayer) should serve as a preparation for the outer (active) one and should realize, in it, its main purpose" (*Chorev*, para. 616). Nevertheless, we can agree with Adolf von Harnack's observation in his fourth Berlin lecture of 1899–1900: "It is by their prayers that the character of the higher religions is determined" (69). Harnack intended this statement to refer to Christianity (and possibly to Islam) but not to Judaism, which he, like so many of his theological colleagues, viewed as a religion based on justification by works. This view is belied, however, by what Rabbi 'El'azar says in the Babylonian Talmud (Berakhoth 32b): "Prayer is better than good works."

The degree to which Judaism conceives of prayer as something beyond a routine activity can be gathered from a passage in Berakhoth 30b: "Earlier pious people used to wait silently for one hour in order to direct their hearts to the Omnipresent."

Rabbi 'El'azar's statement that prayer is better than good works could be seen as diametrically opposed to Jesus' conception, since for Jesus prayer is not something meritorious but a bestowed favor that allows us to call upon God. Yet I see no conflict here, for Rabbi 'El'azar probably means to say that the effect of prayer is greater than the effect of good works. And here Rabbi 'El'azar and Rabbi Jesus meet, for Jesus was deeply convinced of the direct efficacy of prayer. "Ask, and it will be given you," he says; "search, and you will find; knock, and the door will be opened for you. For everyone who asks receives, and everyone who searches finds, and for everyone who knocks, the door will be opened" (Matt. 7:7–8). Now, it is typical of Jesus' faith that he continues by saying, "Is there anyone among you who, if your child asks for bread, will give a stone? Or if the child asks for a fish, will give a snake? If you then, who are evil, know how to give good gifts to your children, how much more will your Father in heaven give good things to those who ask him" (vv. 9–11).

For Jesus, prayer is a conversation with the Father in heaven, during which we are made conscious of our childlike position. Three prayers are proper for a human being: the prayer for daily bread, the prayer for forgiveness of sins, and the prayer for the kingdom of God.

In all of this, Jesus operates within the Jewish tradition of his day, as Bultmann rightly recognizes: "The unique character of the Lord's prayer as contrasted with Jewish prayers does not consist in any special originality of formulation or content. On the contrary, all petitions have parallels in Jewish prayers" (*Jesus and the Word*, 181).

Not only do they have parallels in Jewish prayers, but the prayer that Jesus teaches his disciples *is* a Jewish prayer from the first word to the last. On a personal note, whenever I am present when the Our Father is recited, I always pray along, without feeling that I am abandoning or violating my own Jewish faith in the slightest.

The prayer that Jesus teaches his disciples (Matt. 6:9–13) begins with the invocation "Our Father in heaven." If we translate this invocation back into Hebrew—and we may assume that Jesus taught his disciples to pray in Hebrew, even though they spoke Aramaic among themselves, since at the time of Jesus, at least in the land of Israel, prayers were still spoken predominantly in Hebrew—what results is *'Avinu shebashamayim,* 'Our Father in heaven.' We know this invocation from other contemporary prayers. The designation of God as "Our Father in heaven" is found, for example, at the end of two Mishna tractates. At the end of the tractate Yoma (8.9), Rabbi 'Akiva intones, "Happy are you, O Israel. Before whom do you purify yourselves? And who purifies you? It is your Father in heaven." And at the end of the tractate Sota (9.15), we find a description of the fearful time of the messianic woes and the accompanying remark "On whom can we rely? On our Father in heaven." [48]

"Our Father in heaven" is therefore less a Christian conception than a genuinely Jewish one. Had Jesus been conscious in any way of the divine nature that later dogma conferred upon him, this would have been the place to express it. But it never occurred to him to urge the disciples to pray to him. Indeed, he even rejects being addressed as "Good Teacher," explaining, "No one is good but God alone" (Mark 10:17–18).

Nor does he imagine himself to be *the* mediator between God and man; had he done so, he would have taught the disciples to call in his name upon the Father in heaven. That is by no means the case. Rather, the person who prays is a child of God and is, as are all who call upon God, justified in saying the words "Our Father."

Although Jesus recommends private prayer—"Go into your room and shut the door and pray to your Father who is in secret" (Matt. 6:6)—he chooses the plural form for the invocation, and this is typical of Jewish prayer. To be sure, Jesus recommends praying not (only) in the synagogue but at home, and yet for the individual the invocation "*Our* Father" is still proper, for no individual in prayer is alone. And the Jewish individual, as a member of a distinctive union of people, is particularly cognizant of this bond with God and therefore rightly utters the words "Our Father."

The idea that God dwells in a secret place derives from the prayer of Solomon, who imagines God as dwelling in the darkness (1 Kings 8:12). The passage in Isaiah (45:15) that speaks of the hidden God is also echoed here. The hiddenness of God corresponds to that same basic sentiment in the Jewish soul that was expressed in the construction of the temple, where God was depicted as enthroned in the Holy of Holies. At the time of Jesus, the Holy of Holies was an empty room. In this emptiness, incomprehensibly hidden, God was localized, as it were—although here also, in a paradoxical sort of recognition by faith, Jews of the time were conscious that the heavens of the heavens cannot encompass God.

In both the prayer invocation and the parables, in the sermons and the conversations of Jesus, the name of God, the tetragram YHWH, is never spoken. In the mid-twentieth century, David Horowitz—a Jewish fantasist and adherent of the sect of one Moses Gibori in the United States—sought to prove that since Jesus did not speak the name of God, Jesus was a magician in union with the powers of darkness, much as Faust was unable to utter the name of God once he had concluded his pact with Mephistopheles.

This is nothing but malicious fantasy. The simple truth is that even Jesus' contemporaries, the Tannaim, whether out of reverence or magical fear, avoided mentioning the name of God. The name was reserved for the canonical biblical writings of the time; out of holy fear one paraphrased the name, thereby literally fulfilling the commandment "You shall not make wrongful use of the name of the Lord your God" (Exod. 20:7). In place of the name of God we find such circumlocutions as "the Holy One, blessed be he"; "the All-merciful"; "the blessed name"; even "the Place" (for God is the place of the world; the world is not the place of God); and, last but not least, the invocation "Our Father." Thus Rabbi 'Akiva opens his famous litany with the words *'Avinu malkenu,* 'Our Father, our King.'

The intimate father-child relationship that characterizes the faith of Jesus, who cries out "Abba" (Mark 14:36) in childlike despair, also allows God to appear metaphorically as a king, as was common in the Hebrew Haggada; in the language of prayer, however, God is only the Father for Jesus. The distinction becomes palpable in two final utterances of Jesus on the cross that have been handed down. Turning to God at the moment of death, he addresses him again as Father: "Father, into your hands I commend my spirit" (Luke 23:46). He expresses his despair, however, with the question from Psalm 22:1: "My God, my God, why have you forsaken me?" (Matt. 27:46). In this tragic climax the father-child relationship is shattered.

The prayer that Jesus teaches his disciples is recorded in Matthew 6:9–13 and in Luke 11:1–4. Scholars are uncertain whether both versions originated with Jesus himself; however that may be, they are an expression of his faith, which lived on in the community. Nor can we be certain which text is older, that of Matthew or that of Luke. There are variants in the manuscripts, particularly for the Luke text. These questions, however, are best left to philologists. In both versions the brotherly voice of a praying Jew can be heard.

The prayer begins (in Matthew) with the sanctification of the name:

Our Father in heaven,
hallowed be your name.

The formula "hallowed be your name" corresponds to the Kaddish prayer in the synagogue. The Kaddish is an old prayer. Although predominantly Aramaic, it also displays Hebrew components that may well derive from the time of Jesus. The Kaddish begins with the formula "Glorified and sanctified be his great name in the world which he has created according to his will. And may he establish his kingdom in your lifetime and in your days, and in the lifetime of the entire house of Israel, speedily and soon; and say, Amen."

The congregation then responds, "May his great name be blessed forever and to all eternity."

The reciter continues, "Blessed and praised, and glorified and

exalted, and extolled and favored, and adored and lauded be the name
of the Holy One, blessed be he, beyond all the blessings and hymns,
praises and consolations that are ever spoken in the world; and say,
Amen."

My sense is that a certain polemic against the Kaddish may be present in the Our Father. In the injunctions that precede the prayer, it is
true, Jesus turns on the Gentiles, who think they are being heard because they speak with many words, formulating his criticism with the
admonition "When you are praying, do not heap up empty phrases
as the Gentiles do" (Matt. 6:7). The praise of the Name in the Kaddish is indeed fulsomely baroque, whereas Jesus restricts his prayer to
a simple, direct appeal to God: "hallowed be your name."

In its original form the Kaddish was a hymn with a prospective
view of the kingdom of God; the experts in scriptural law used it to
conclude their exegeses (*derashoth*). This form is still known today in
the synagogue as *Kaddish derabbanan* and is recited after an instructional reading. This helps to explain why the Our Father is adjoined
(in Matthew) to the Sermon on the Mount.

> *Your kingdom come.*
> *Your will be done,*
> > *on earth as it is in heaven.*

The positioning of the request for the kingdom of God at the beginning of the prayer is owing to Jesus' expectation of an imminent es-
chaton, the doctrine of messianic expectation, which he took from his
teacher John and which was widely shared in this tension-filled time.
The Kaddish too begins with the request for the kingdom of God. In
the prayer of Rav (early third century), after the messianic expectation
had subsided, the same hope is central: "Therefore we wait on you,
Lord our God, to show us quickly the glory of your victory, to expel
and exterminate the godless from the earth, to order the world for the
kingdom of the Mighty One." Even today the holy service in the synagogue ends with this prayer, known as the '*Aleinu.*

Jesus' prayer is connected to the sanctification of the name and
request for the kingdom, begging that the will of God be done on
earth as in heaven. Transcendence was not merely a devout wish; in
fact, Jesus expected it to occur in this mortal world as a concrete

event. Judaism has never set its hopes on an afterworld. Hebrew does not even have an expression for it, speaking instead of the world to come, the 'olam haba'. First let the kingdom of heaven come to this earth; then the will of God can be done here as already in heaven. The will of God—that is Peace. Thus the Kaddish ends, "He who creates peace in his celestial heights, may he create peace for us and for all Israel; and say, Amen."

Despite the high level of congruence between the Our Father and other Jewish prayers, it is striking that Jesus does not mention Israel— or make any national reference at all. This is surprising, given that Jesus' consciousness of his mission was limited primarily to the lost sheep from the house of Israel. Presuming that the mention of Israel was not simply deleted, then it would appear that we are dealing with a *tachanun*, a private prayer, which involves a pouring out of the in-dividual heart and therefore often ignores the national component.

Give us this day our daily bread.

It is right that people, even while expecting the kingdom of God, should pray for daily bread. In Hebrew we would probably read this as *lechem chukenu*, 'the bread due to us.' But to pray for more does not seem right to Jesus. We must especially recall that Jesus rejected the accumulation of material goods, an attitude consistent with the pharisaical ideal of his time. Many experts in the law went so far as to assert that bread, water, and salt sufficed for human nourishment.

And forgive us our debts,
as we also have forgiven our debtors.

We have adduced talmudic passages above, according to which only those people will be forgiven in heaven who themselves forgave on earth. Jesus elaborates on this thought in the parable of the unforgiv-ing servant (Matt. 18:23–35).

Jesus, who deeply understands human nature, knows that people are exposed to temptation daily. He thus concludes his prayer with this request:

And do not bring us to the time of trial,
but rescue us from evil.[49]

"And do not bring us to the time of trial" has an almost literal parallel in the daily morning prayer in the synagogue: *Velo liydei-nissayon*, 'and not into the hands of trial.' Deliverance from trial can also be conceived of as deliverance from evil, though not in the sense of *the* evil one, the Devil. In Jesus' language use, the Devil is simply called Satan, whom he had seen fall from heaven in the form of lightning (Luke 10:18).

The concluding formula

> *For yours is the kingdom and the power*
>   *and the glory forever*

is appended to some early versions of the prayer, along with the liturgical conclusion formula "Amen." This kind of praise is like that found in 1 Chronicles 29:11. When one observes the similar formulation in the liturgy of the synagogue before the recitation from the Torah, it seems quite possible that this sentence was meant to occur *before* the Beatitudes: in other words, at the beginning of the Sermon on the Mount. It does not belong to the text proper of the Our Father. Rather, as many scholars have rightly noted and as we want to emphasize once again, this prayer must be conceived of not as a closed liturgical unit but as a model for how one should pray in all simplicity of heart. Sentences may therefore be added or modified, as one sees fit.

In its simplicity and completeness, however, this prayer is indeed classical. It is timeless, even as it exudes the spirit of its time. From the imminent expectation of the kingdom, of course, a distant expectation arose, but faith always exists in the condition of expectation—the expectation of the unknown, the entirely other. And that is in fact the kingdom of God. Franz Rosenzweig spoke of the possibility of praying for the kingdom (*Star of Redemption*, 185). However far away the kingdom of God may be, for the person in prayer—if it is the right kind of prayer—the kingdom in that moment is intimately near. The presence of the kingdom is indeed presupposed within the praying community. As Jesus said, "The kingdom of God is among you" (Luke 17:21).

7 Jesus and the Women

In a subchapter titled "Jesus as Rabbi," Rudolf Bultmann remarks, "One may . . . note that among his adherents were women, who are elsewhere never included among the followers of a rabbi" (*Jesus and the Word,* 61). Bultmann's remark is obviously based on the well-known report in Luke 8:1–3:

> Soon afterwards he went on through cities and villages, proclaiming and bringing the good news of the kingdom of God. The twelve were with him, as well as some women who had been cured of evil spirits and infirmities: Mary, called Magdalene, from whom seven demons had gone out, and Joanna, the wife of Herod's steward Chuza, and Susanna, and many others, who provided for them out of their resources.

This is not an isolated report, for the role of women around Jesus is more strongly emphasized in Luke than in the other three Gospels. The other Gospels make no similar reference to the female disciples in the circle of Jesus. The second sentence indicates that the women joined the band of disciples at the time when Jesus undertook his activity as an itinerant preacher. These were obviously affluent women who served their revered rabbi not only with moral support but with corresponding material assets as well.

Bultmann's supposition that women were not to be found around a rabbi or that those learned in the law always kept their distance from women is not entirely accurate. One need only think, for example, of the remarks in the Babylonian Talmud's tractate Shabbath 13a: "When 'Ula returned from the house of instruction he was wont to kiss his sisters on their breasts, some say on their hands." It is reported of another rabbi that he observed the beautiful women and maidens at the entrance to the bath houses and offered blessings over their beauty.[50] We must not therefore assume that the ascetic ideal of Christian anchorites and monks was also typical for rabbis at the time of Jesus. Unlike the (other) disciples of John, Jesus himself was no ascetic, indeed, he was thoroughly devoted to the joys of life.

The women in the entourage of Jesus bear the character of female disciples, even if for the most part they had serving functions. In fact, the condition of this new community—which must have seemed very strange, especially to the male disciples—is suggested by the statement in the epistle to the Galatians that "there is no longer male and female; for all of you are *one* in Christ Jesus" (3:28). Paul's statement no doubt represents a later dogmatization of the spontaneous behavior of the early Christian community, whose living center must have been Jesus.

The three most prominent women figures in the life of Jesus remarkably all bear the same name: Mary, that is, Miriam. Thus we speak of the three Marys: Mary the mother, Mary the disciple, and Mary the courtesan.

Regarding Jesus' relationship to his mother, we need only recall our earlier remarks to be reminded that it was obviously a disturbed relationship. Mary did not understand her son, and his attitude toward her was always emotionally charged and lacking in the respect due the mother in a Jewish family. We cannot think of this Miriam, wife of the simple Galilean carpenter Joseph, as anything but a good Jewish mother and incapable of looking beyond her immediate family, a mother who could follow the curious paths of her son only from a distance. That she did nevertheless follow him is not a contradiction but rather fills out her image as a concerned mother who stood up for her son even when she did not understand him. He was still her son, after all, and she was proud of his accomplishments, even if she would rather have seen him doing something different. We have already surmised that the darkness surrounding the birth of Jesus may relate to the strained relationship between mother and son; that is only a supposition, of course. There is no question but that the mother of Jesus joined with the disciple community in some form or fashion. We may assume that Miriam-Mary was already a widow at the outset of her son's public career and could therefore easily have gotten out of the house. In fact, it was probably unbearable for her to remain any longer in Nazareth, to be subjected to attacks from her son's enemies; within the community of disciples she could feel more secure. The Magnificat (Luke 1:46–55), Mary's song of praise, is obviously incompatible with the simple, compelling image of this Jewish mother. This marvelous song is essentially a New Testament psalm, artfully constructed from elements of the Hebrew Bible: that is, from the thanksgiving prayer of Hannah (1 Sam. 2:1–10) as well as various passages from the Psalms and Genesis. One cannot accept that a simple Jewish woman from Nazareth could have composed this learned lyric.

Mary the disciple is one of the sisters of Lazarus (John 11:1–2), whom Jesus called back to life from the grave. The sister pair, Mary and Martha, has often been viewed typologically: Mary the contemplative one, Martha the active one. It is the contemplative one for whom Jesus has greater fondness, a fact that probably constitutes the new element in the relationship between Jesus and the women around him. The serving woman is not unusual in contemporary Judaism. Up to this day in observant Jewish circles the idea continues to exist that a woman who truly serves a man learned in the Scriptures (Hebrew *'esheth-chayil*, 'woman of valor') will share eternally in the merits that he gains for himself through study. But a female disciple who only listens to the words of the master is unusual, if not entirely without parallel. One thinks of Beruria, the learned wife of Rabbi Me'ir.[51] Such women are exceptions, however, and that is true also in the circle of Jesus.

Finally, we have Mary the courtesan, Mary Magdalene—that is, Miriam of Migdal on the west bank of the Sea of Kinnereth—the Mary from whom Jesus is said to have driven out seven evil spirits (Luke 8:2), which later came to be associated with the seven deadly sins. This Mary is the prototype of the female sinner whom Jesus accepts into his circle. How could it be otherwise? As a physician of the soul, who said regarding himself that it is not the healthy who need a physician but the sick, Jesus does not turn away from sinful women any more than he does from the hated "tax collectors" who collaborate with the Romans, or indeed from sinners of any kind. In his turning to sinners or, perhaps better said, in his readiness not to reject them, we see the latent messianic impulse in Jesus: the attempt, expressed in many parables, to redeem what has been lost, and the readiness to take seriously the rabbinic wisdom that the gates of return stand open always and to everyone.

In Luke's version of the anointment of Jesus by the sinful woman of Bethany (7:36–50), we find the key comment that expresses Jesus' attitude toward courtesans: "Therefore, I tell you, her sins, which were many, have been forgiven; hence she has shown great love" (v. 47). Even in the perverted form of love for hire, Jesus recognizes the germ of love.

Nor is he alone in this; one should not imagine that those learned in scripture at his time or, for that matter, the later Christian ascetic preachers of repentance had nothing but words of anger and scorn for courtesans. In the Talmud we find respectful words for courtesans as far back as the patriarchal story concerning Judah and Tamar (Gen. 38:13–26). Still, I can think of no other words that express greater depth and kindness than those spoken by Jesus to the sinful woman anointing him.

The story of the anointing in Bethany (Beth-Heni or Beth-'Aniya) is reported variously in the Gospels. On one occasion the scene is played in the house of Simon the leper, another time in the house of Lazarus. It is also unclear whether the woman who anoints Jesus, moistening his feet with tears and drying them with her hair—what an incomparable image, one that has repeatedly inspired the fantasy of painters!—is Mary Magdalene or another female sinner. That is of no particular concern, however. The scene itself speaks to us, and in it Jesus' relationship to women is illuminated. But it appears to me that the Evangelists misunderstood something here. The anointment by a female sinner, which the disciples, particularly the treasurer Judas, feel to be both scandalous and extravagant, is taken in the Gospels simply to foreshadow the coming anointment of Jesus' corpse. I believe, however, that the Evangelists were unaware of the presence of another motif here: in the New Testament, Jesus is seen as the new Adam, the new Moses, and the legitimate successor to David—but in this anointing scene he also becomes the new Abraham, the new father of faith, or the father of the new faith. This motif becomes visible when we view the anointment with precious spikenard within the context of a certain midrash (Genesis Rabba 39:2) in which Abraham is compared to a bottle of precious perfume that has been standing closed in a corner. The bottle is now to be opened and carried from place to place in order to disseminate a lovely aroma. God says to Abraham, "Go from your country. . . . I will make of you a great nation" (Gen. 12:1–2). Thus Abraham is to spread the "aroma of holiness" through his wanderings. Jesus too, in his own wandering—his pilgrimage to Jerusalem, where he wins many disciples—is anointed with a bottle of precious spikenard in the symbolic act of establishing a great new nation of faith. One must recognize this combination of motifs in order to grasp the anointment scene completely. It seems to me important and typical that gentle female hands should anoint this new Abraham, much as the earlier Abraham was pictured in the company of his exquisitely beautiful wife and half-sister Sarah.

The other memorable encounter of Jesus with a female sinner is reported to us in the eighth chapter of the Gospel of John (3–11): Jesus and the adulteress.

> The scribes and the Pharisees brought a woman who had been caught
> in adultery; and making her stand before all of them, they said to him,
> "Teacher, this woman was caught in the very act of committing adultery.
> Now in the law Moses commanded us to stone such women. Now what
> do you say?" They said this to test him, so that they might have some
> charge to bring against him. Jesus bent down and wrote with his finger on
> the ground. When they kept on questioning him, he straightened up and
> said to them, "Let anyone among you who is without sin be the first to
> throw a stone at her." And once again he bent down and wrote on the
> ground. When they heard it, they went away, one by one, beginning with
> the elders; and Jesus was left alone with the woman standing before him.
> Jesus straightened up and said to her, "Woman, where are they? Has no
> one condemned you?" She said, "No one, sir." And Jesus said, "Neither
> do I condemn you. Go your way, and from now on do not sin again."

The entire scene is properly an illustration both of Jesus' saying "Do not judge, so that you may not be judged" (Matt. 7:1) and of his assertion that he has not come in order to judge others (John 3:17).

The indication that Jesus twice writes on the ground in the court of the temple is peculiar to this narrative (John 8:6–8). It is doubtful that this means writing in the usual sense, since no one attempts to read what he has written. Instead, Jesus probably draws a circle around the woman, thereby evoking a tradition from the first pre-Christian century, known to us through the personality of Choni the Circle Drawer, *Choni Hame'aggel*. This Choni, who is mentioned in the Talmud tractate Ta'anith, draws a circle on the ground and places himself within it, praying for rain. The "men of the Hall of Hewn Stones"—the members of the High Council of the Sanhedrin, which assembled daily in the Hewn Hall—say to this Choni, "You will also decree a thing, and it shall be established unto you" (BT, Ta'anith 23a).[52] The contextual association with Choni imposes itself here, since the scene takes place in the shadow of the Hall of Hewn Stones in the temple, and Jesus, like Choni, draws signs in the dust. He places not himself but rather the female sinner in this circle, thus protecting her (magically, as it were) from her accusers. The Jerusalem Talmud version of the tractate Ta'anith (3.9) says of Choni, "When he entered the hall of the temple it became light." Something of this light of Choni falls here upon the later Jesus.

In thinking about Jesus' relationship to women, we should also recall his two conversations with non-Jewish women: the Syrophoenician woman (Mark 7:24–30) and the Samaritan woman in Sychar at Jacob's well (John 4:1–30). As we noted in chapter 5, these conversations are decisive for Jesus' inner development, for these women rid him of his nationalistic prejudices. Is that mere coincidence? Or is there not something here that we often observe in human behavior—that national walls fall in the encounter between the sexes?

But let us now turn to the key question: was Jesus married? I am quite aware that even posing this question will shock many readers. To Christian thinking the question is objectionable and senseless, for how could the God-Man, the only begotten Son of God, have found a wife equal to him? Furthermore, later Christian thought turned everything having to do with sex and the libido into something sinful and disreputable. The concept of *agape,* Christian love, repressed sexual love. Only an enlightened cynic of the eighteenth century such as Casanova (as in the episode of the lady theologian) dared to pose salacious questions concerning the sexual union of a woman and God.

Our intention in raising the question here is far from such frivolity. The question arises naturally out of the cultural-historical context. Jesus was addressed by his disciples and the larger community of his followers as "Rabbi." An unmarried rabbi is hardly imaginable. The Talmud sharply condemns celibacy: "Whoever has no wife is without joy, without blessing, . . . without *Torah,* without walls (against sexual promiscuity), . . . without peace; . . . a man without a wife is no man" (BT, Yevamoth 62b).

We must now ask, if Jesus had been unmarried, would his disciples not have questioned him about this fault? Even more, would his opponents not have used against him the fact that in his own life he had left unfulfilled the first of the obligations, or *mitsvoth,* in the Torah: "Be fruitful and multiply" (Gen. 1:22)? The opponents of Jesus were ready and eager to accuse him and his disciples of being too lax in their handling of the law. Thus it was objected that his disciples did not always wash their hands before they ate; that they plucked ears of corn on the Sabbath; that Jesus healed on the Sabbath, even when it was not a matter of life and death; that he sat at table with tax collectors, sinners, and harlots. Would these accusers of Jesus not have exploited the fact of his celibacy against him if he had been unmarried? We read not one word to this effect.

Now one may argue that we also read no word about Jesus' wife or children. That is true. Yet neither do we read anything about the wives of the disciples. Can they all, entirely against Jewish custom of the time and all times, have been unmarried? That is patently unacceptable. We do learn indirectly, for example, that Peter was married, since Jesus cures Peter's "mother-in-law" (Mark 1:30). About Peter's wife we learn nothing.

Indeed, we know virtually nothing about the wives of the great teachers of the law and wise men in Israel at the time of Jesus. Nothing is known about Mrs. Hillel or Mrs. Shammai. We hear of only two wives: Beruria, wife of Rabbi Me'ir, a learned woman who is held up as both a model and a cautionary figure,[53] and 'Akiva's wife, daughter of the rich Kalba-Savua', who married the poor cowherd and assisted him in his studies. These are two *exceptions*. Hundreds of names of wise men are transmitted to us in the Talmud, and we know nothing about their wives. Can they all have been unmarried? That is out of the question.[54]

Why then should anything be reported about the wife of Rabbi Jesus of Nazareth if she did not appear during the brief period of his public ministry? Obviously she did not, and we can easily understand that a young wife would have to remain at home with the children, whereas her widowed mother-in-law could join her son's band of disciples. Thus we do not find a wife of Jesus beneath the cross, which should not surprise us.

I am therefore of the opinion that Jesus of Nazareth, just like every rabbi in Israel, was married. His disciples and his opponents would have questioned him if he had deviated from this universal custom.

Beyond that, however, Jesus himself employs such touchingly profound words about marriage. In reference to Genesis 2:24, "Therefore a man leaves his father and his mother and clings to his wife, and they become *one* flesh," he adds, "So they are no longer two, but *one* flesh. Therefore what God has joined together, let no one separate" (Matt. 19:6). Are these the words of a man for whom celibacy is the ideal?

Jesus goes so far as to allow divorce only in the case of hard-heartedness, emphatically stating, "It was because you were so hard-hearted that Moses allowed you to divorce your wives, but from the beginning it was not so. And I say to you, whoever divorces his wife, except for unchastity, and marries another commits adultery" (Matt. 19:8–9).

In the conversation about marriage, divorce, and celibacy (Matt. 19 and Mark 10), Jesus concedes only that there are some who forgo marriage because they are incapable (impotent, that is). He mentions eunuchs in this regard, but his remark "Let anyone accept this who can" (Matt. 19:12) distances him from any notion that the failure to marry was acceptable.

By contrast, Jesus frequently chooses the bridegroom as the active figure in his parables, which again suggests that he had experienced a wedding hour. He himself is the bridegroom (Matt. 9:15; Mark 2:19; Luke 5:34). The final book of the New Testament, John's Revelation, speaks about the marriage of the Lamb and concludes, "The Spirit and the bride say, 'Come'" (22:17), to which the eschatological Christ answers, "Surely I am coming soon" (v. 20). Even here in the hour of fulfillment he is the bridegroom for whom the bride fervently longs and who will go to her.

None of these images would be appropriate to an unmarried Jesus who knew nothing of a bridal night and matrimonial companionship.

Above all, we must free ourselves from the notion that a married Jesus would have been at all objectionable in his world. Precisely the opposite is the case. As Julius Wellhausen declared in 1905 in his introduction to the first three Gospels, "Jesus was not a Christian: he was a Jew. He did not preach a new faith, but taught men to do the will of God; and, in his opinion, as also in that of the Jews, the will of God was to be found in the Law of Moses and in the other books of Scripture" (113). To this we may add Joseph Klausner's comment on Wellhausen's statement: "How could it have been otherwise? Jesus derived his entire knowledge and point of view from the scriptures, and from a few, at most, of the Palestinian *apocryphal* and *pseudepigraphical* writings and from the Palestinian *Haggada* and *Midrash* in the primitive form in which they were then current among the Jews" (*Jesus*, 363). In none of the writings considered sacred within Judaism at the time of Jesus is celibacy idealized. That is significant.

8 Who Am I?

The synoptic Gospels report three versions of an episode in which Jesus poses the question "Who am I?" The question is not transmitted to us in this literal form, of course.

In Luke 9:18–21 we read the following:

Once when Jesus was praying alone, with only the disciples near him, he asked them, "Who do the crowds say that I am?" They answered, "John the Baptist; but others, Elijah; and still others, that one of the ancient prophets has arisen." He said to them, "But who do you say that I am?" Peter answered, "The Messiah of God." He sternly ordered and commanded them not to tell anyone.

In Luke's version of the episode no setting is indicated. According to Matthew and Mark, however, this questioning of the disciples took place in Caesarea Philippi, a place near the source of the Banias, one of the three source streams of the Jordan. The grotto from which the stream pours forth was sacred to the Greeks and dedicated to Pan (hence probably the name Banias, since the Arabic language does not possess the *p* sound). Herod erected a temple to Pan there with a statue of Caesar. The founding of the place itself goes back to the Tetrarch Philip, who died in 34 C.E., meaning that it was already known by the name Caesarea Philippi (rather than Caesarea) by the time of Jesus.

Whereas in Luke and Mark, Jesus asks, "Who do the crowds say that I am?" in Matthew 16:13–20 the concept of the *son of man* is introduced: "Who do people say that the Son of Man is?"

In any case, Jesus is not posing an exam question here, as Martin Buber once jokingly remarked. But, I should add, neither is he asking a sort of Gallup Poll question. It is most certainly not the case that Jesus wishes, on the one hand, only to investigate popular opinion while expecting, on the other, to receive a dogmatically correct, cate-chistic answer from his disciples. Rather, in this kind of questioning we perceive the confusion of a person who, deeply implicated in the adventure of faith, is inquiring about his own existence and its mystery.

In this exchange he is seeking to know himself. If one holds, how-ever, like Rudolf Bultmann, to the modern "dogma" that "we can now know almost nothing concerning the life and personality of Jesus" (*Jesus and the Word*, 8), then the profoundly human signifi-cance of the question remains closed to us. For my own part, I do not believe that agnosticism is called for; indeed, Jesus is closest to us pre-cisely in this moment in which he is no longer certain of himself and asks the question fundamental to all human existence, "Who am I?"

In the act of posing this question, Jesus truly becomes the son of man, for what he asks here is the question about man as such.

Like every utterance that Jesus makes, this one has not only a gen-eral human aspect but a specifically Jewish modality as well. Jesus uses the singular here for what occurs in the liturgy of the synagogue in the plural: "What are we, what is our life, what are our merits and our justice, what is our salvation, our power?" This amounts simultane-ously to a questioning of human existence.

As it is transmitted to us, Jesus' question to his disciples suggests his secret messiahship. Yet one may wonder whether the kerygmatic tradition has not added an overtone here that did not belong to the original question.

In Matthew's text (16:13) Jesus designates himself as the "Son of Man," but that naturally was later construed as an expression of Jesus' understanding of himself as the Messiah. The concept *son of man* was interpreted in a purely Christological manner with the help of the statement ascribed to Stephen (Acts 7:56): "Look, he said, I see the heavens opened and the Son of Man standing at the right hand of God!" A. J. B. Higgins remarks, "This sentence comprises the single example in the New Testament outside of the Gospels for the occurrence of the title 'son of man' in the mouth of someone other than Jesus himself" (*Menschensohn-Studien*, 11).

In asking this question, did Jesus in fact have this son-of-man concept in mind? I do not think so. I agree with Bultmann, who says, "I am personally of the opinion that Jesus did not believe himself to be the Messiah" (*Jesus and the Word*, 9). To this I should like to add what Higgins says: "Jesus did not pretend to be the son of man but simply announced the kingdom of God" (*Menschensohn-Studien*, 10).

In attempting to answer what the term *son of man* means, we need to keep three possibilities in mind: the eschatological, the prophetic, and the purely human. The dogmatic origin of the concept rests on Daniel 7:13–14, an Aramaic passage in the Old Testament, in which the expression *bar-'enosh* is used for 'son of man':

> As I watched in the night visions, I saw one like a human being [*bar-'enosh*] coming with the clouds of heaven. And he came to the Ancient One and was presented before him. To him was given dominion and glory and kingship, that all peoples, nations, and languages should serve him. His dominion is an everlasting dominion that shall not pass away, and his kingship is one that shall never be destroyed.

That is the eschatological son of man with whom Stephen and the primitive community identified their exalted lord. But was it not also inherent in Jesus' self-understanding when he explicitly applied the expression "Son of Man" to himself? Certain proclamations of suffering do in fact exist in which this name is sounded repeatedly, as in "the Son of Man must undergo great suffering" (Luke 9:22). There is also the famous saying about the vagabondage of man: "Foxes have holes, and birds of the air have nests; but the Son of Man has nowhere to lay his head" (Matt. 8:20). It is difficult to unify the all-too-human utterances concerning human existence, which encompasses suffering and vagabondage, with the image of the eschatological son of man in Daniel's night vision.

The second possibility is to translate, or back-translate, the concept *son of man* into the Hebrew prophetic concept *ben-'adam*, a key motif of the prophet Ezekiel, who in his visions is addressed by God as *ben-'adam*, 'son of man,' or 'mortal' (e.g., 2:1–8). While the *bar-'enosh* in Daniel represents an eschatological dimension, *ben-'adam* in Ezekiel represents a prophetic dimension, lower than the eschatological in rank. If Jesus had in fact intended to reveal himself as a prophet, would he have done so effectively in designating himself as the son of man?

We have noted that Jesus was no prophet in the Old Testament sense, no messenger of Yahweh's glory, of God's words of wisdom.

And yet it appears to me that the concept *son of man* does figure into Jesus' understanding of himself. It occurs too frequently for us to view it *only* kerygmatically, although, to be sure, in its eschatological and even its prophetic interpretation it is kerygmatic.

Thus, a third possibility presents itself if we identify the term *son of man* with the vulgar form *bar-'enosh*, or *barnash. Barnash* means 'everyman,' anyone at all, man as such, a man such as you and I, a typical human being in his or her lowliness. This is the kind of man Jesus understood himself to be: a man who lives, as a man, a typically human life, without possessions and subject to pain. In designating himself "Son of Man," Jesus does not stand before us as a prophet or the Messiah but as our brother. And since he is the son of man, the human question erupts within him, "Who am I?"

We have already suggested the answer in chapter 2, "Birth and Rebirth." The popular belief in rebirth made it possible for the folk to see in Jesus the personage of John the Baptist, since beheaded; or Elijah, caught up to heaven and now returned; or even the prophet Jeremiah or another prophet from the past. Matthew's specific mention (16:14) of Jeremiah may be explained by the announcements of judgment in the preaching of Jesus, which bring him into the proximity of his rabbi, John, as well as into the shadow of Jeremiah.

Jesus does not respond to these popular conjectures about reincarnation. The human being cannot experience the truth of being, even if previous forms of existence could be recollected. What is essential is the here and now.

Jesus therefore probes further, turning directly to his disciples, his narrowest circle, and asking, "But who do *you* say that I am?" (Matt. 16:15).

And now Peter becomes the spokesman for all the disciples and confesses, "You are the Messiah, the Son of the living God" (v. 16). According to the oldest source, the Gospel of Mark, Peter says only "You are the Messiah" (8:29); in Luke he says "the Messiah of God" (9:20). Hence we find the designation *son of God* only in Matthew, though here too it must not be misconstrued by reading it dogmatically. "Son of the living God" can be applied as a kingly title, as in the coronation Psalm 2, in which the king who has been crowned by God on Mount Zion receives the promise:

"You are my son;
today I have begotten you.
Ask of me, and I will make the
nations your heritage,
and the ends of the earth your possession." (vv. 7–8)

The disciple therefore proclaims the master as his messianic king.

And yet perhaps it is unnecessary to reach so high. One can also understand the statement ascribed to Peter as meaning that Jesus' life is exemplary of the divine sonship that is held out to all men and women, as in Hosea, where the children of men are called "Children of the living God" (1:10).[55]

The statement "You are the Christ," as it has often been translated,[56] must of course be interpreted as "You are the Messiah" (*Mashiach*). This concept itself contains the kingly title *Hamelekh Hamashiach,* 'the anointed king.' The confession of the community is spoken in the words of Peter. The situation in which a disciple proclaims the master to be the Messiah is known to us from later Jewish history as well. Gershom Scholem makes reference to it in his book on the pseudo-messiah Sabbatai Tzevi, whose disciple Nathan of Gaza hailed him as messianic king (*Sabbatai Sevi,* 275).[57]

According to the texts available to us, Jesus does not deny Peter's proclamation, but he does forbid him and the other disciples to make it known (Luke 9:21).

It is commonly accepted that Jesus believed that his hour had not yet come, and thus he waited expectantly for his passion, in which he would at last be transfigured and glorified.

But all of these are much later speculations.

The unprejudiced eye will see here a confused individual confronting the mystery of his own existence without finding the key to unlock it. Bewildered, Jesus senses that a charisma emanates from him, a power not of himself but one that nevertheless compels others to their knees. This forces him to ask not only "Who am I?" but also "Is that who I am?"

The suffering man, the man who suffers over the riddle of his own existence, will not dare to speak the self-confident *I* words of the Johannine Christ (e.g., John 10:24–30). These words belong to a much later community tradition under the influence of Hellenistic thought, which was foreign to the nature of the bewildered young Jew from Nazareth who himself now becomes the object of questioning. I am well aware that statements of this sort will be dismissed with a superior smile by many New Testament scholars. But no one who has experienced Jesus as his brother—as his human brother and as his Jewish brother—will be able to ignore this inside perspective, however distant it may be from an exact philological methodology.

In both Matthew and Luke the proclamation of the master by the disciple is followed by the naming of the disciple by the master. Shim'on Bar-Yona, to whom no "flesh and blood" (Matt. 16:17)—the common Hebrew term *basar vadam*—has revealed the messianic secret of his rabbi, is now called Peter, the rock, upon whom Jesus intends to establish his community, the *ecclesia*, "and the gates of Hades will not prevail against it" (v. 18). To this rock, upon which the community is to be established (an allusion to the parable of the house built on the rock, which storms cannot destroy), the keys to the kingdom of heaven are now also entrusted: "I will give you the keys of the kingdom of heaven, and whatever you bind on earth will be bound in heaven, and whatever you loose on earth will be loosed in heaven" (v. 19)—but all of this in deepest secrecy. The text of Mark has nothing to report about the naming of Peter.

If this episode of the keys—which stands between Jesus' question and the announcement of his coming passion—rested upon historical truth, then the act of naming the disciple would certainly confirm Jesus' understanding of himself as the messianic king. For how could he elevate his disciples to such heights without possessing the full authority befitting only Daniel's son of man? Too much speaks against this text, however: in the first place, the simple fact that a Greek pun could scarcely be used as a significant factor in a conversation between a carpenter from Nazareth and a fisherman from Capernaum (Kefar-Nachum). Jesus and his disciples spoke Aramaic with one another, not Greek.[58] Still, the idea of the power of the keys does not appear to me to lie outside the Jewish realm, for the rabbis have always considered themselves to be the overseers of the law of God in the sense of Deuteronomy 30:12: "[The Torah] is not in heaven." The pharisaic learned men were thoroughly convinced that they possessed the power of the keys and that their doctrinal teachings had legitimacy, since God did not merely give his law to his people Israel but gave it fully into their jurisdiction. Jesus' appointment of Peter would fit within the framework of these conceptions of the office of teaching and jurisdictional authority, of binding and loosening.

Today, however, we know that the oldest manuscripts speak of a transference of the power of the keys neither to Peter nor to *all* the disciples (Matt. 18:18). Assumptions to the contrary are based on later additions that serve to establish and enhance the authority of the popes as successors to Peter.

This passage has played a remarkable role in my own life. It led me to a revered teacher, Professor Joseph Schnitzer, who used to lecture at the University of Munich on comparative religion, especially early Christianity. He was originally a Catholic theologian and as such was called upon to defend the validity of this passage against the Protestant Adolf von Harnack. But being the honest scholar that he was, he concluded that Harnack's proofs could not be disputed: the oldest manuscripts do not contain the power-of-the-keys texts. For standing for the truth, Schnitzer was removed from his religious office and eventually excommunicated. But since the university could not take away his professorship, he was transferred from the theological to the philological faculty, where he lectured on early Christianity. Because Catholic students of theology were prohibited from attending the lectures of this heretic, and there were no evangelical students of theology in the 1930s at the University of Munich, I, the Jew, was one of a bare handful who attended the lectures of this noted scholar. The so-called appointment of Peter thus turned tragic in the case of one scholarly life, but for me it became a living symbol of the struggle for truth.

Just how unconvincing this enthronement of Peter is becomes obvious only a few sentences later when Jesus says to this same Peter, "Get behind me, Satan! For you are setting your mind not on divine things but on human things" (Mark 8:33). Such a contradiction would suggest an emotional ambivalence in Jesus that could only be characterized as pathological.

In this episode the only things that belong to the reality of human interaction are Jesus' anxious questioning of the meaning of his own existence, the trusting faces of the disciples, and Jesus' justifiable fear lest they proclaim him to be the returned Messiah—this man who could imagine himself being the son of man only in the sense of being man as such, one who stood before the darkness that lay over his destiny.

This questioning Jesus is our brother, not the exalted Christ who has exchanged the human realm for the heights and depths of myth.

We know nothing about the external appearance of Jesus. The earliest tradition, based on Isaiah 53:2, tended to depict him as ugly: "He had no form or majesty." The Hellenistic church fathers, such as Clemens of Alexandria, avowed on the basis of Psalm 45:3 his sublime beauty, his "glory and majesty," since divine perfection implies physical beauty as well.[59]

9 *On to Jerusalem: Victory Procession or Path of Martyrdom?*

"The decision to go to Jerusalem is undoubtedly the turning-point in Jesus' life." So Günther Bornkamm remarks in his scholarly work *Jesus of Nazareth* (154).

But what exactly was this "path" to Jerusalem? Based upon the reports (Mark 11; Matt. 21; Luke 19; John 12), we can characterize it according to three aspects. First, it was a pilgrimage to the central sanctuary, as commanded in Deuteronomy 16:16–17. According to the law, all males were to make a pilgrimage to Jerusalem three times each year—at Passover (*Pesach*) in the spring; at the Feast of Weeks (*Shavu'oth*), seven weeks after Passover, in the summer; and at the autumn Feast of Tabernacles (*Sukkoth*)—to pray in the temple and offer fitting sacrifices. This was, of course, an ideal law that probably could never be fully realized. If in fact all Jewish males from all over Palestine had gone to Jerusalem three times a year, the land would have been exposed to a constant flow of tourism; the farmers would scarcely have had time to cultivate their fields; and the borders of the land would have remained unguarded. Yet one can well imagine that the traffic in pilgrims at the three festivals must have been extraordinarily brisk. We have vivid accounts of this in the Mishna (Chagiga 1.1) and in Flavius Josephus (*Jewish War*, 6.9.3). It is also explicitly reported that the family of Jesus was in the habit of making a pilgrimage to Jerusalem at Passover (Luke 2:41). If one assumes, as some scholars do, that Joseph of Nazareth, the father of Jesus, was an itinerant artisan, then a regular pilgrimage by the family seems even more likely. A glimmer of probability shines on the story of the journey of Joseph and his wife Miriam to Bethlehem, even if little else speaks for the authenticity of this fulfillment legend.

But we must certainly imagine Jesus of Nazareth as an itinerant preacher, who had been moving about not far from his Galilean homeland for several months already, teaching by means of parable (*mashal*) and sermon (*derasha*), healing the sick, casting out demons (the cure of neurotics), and gathering about himself a more or less stable band of disciples.

For this man without permanent residence, the pilgrimage to Jerusalem presented no particular difficulty; it was indeed quite typical of Jesus' manner of operating. The pilgrimage to Jerusalem could therefore be conceived of by his adherents, and presumably by himself as well, as a decisive form of testing. As long as the proclamation of the kingdom of God—and that, in the final analysis, was what it was all about—took place only in the province, the Jesuan movement itself remained provincial, only a marginal phenomenon of public life. But in moving on to Jerusalem in order to proclaim his message in the temple, the national and intellectual center of the country, the master took his decisive step.

It remains unclear whether this procession to Jerusalem took place only once—namely, at the Passover Festival in the final year of Jesus' life—or whether we should not rather accept the Johannine tradition, which speaks of several visitations in the Jerusalem temple. The description of the circumstances at Jesus' entry into Jerusalem points unequivocally to Sukkoth, the Feast of Tabernacles. The residents of Jerusalem come out to meet the rabbi from Nazareth with branches in their hands and singing "hosanna." One must back-translate this description into Hebrew reality in order to understand it rightly. The branches referred to here can only be the palm branches, the *lulavim,* of the Feast of Tabernacles. Together with the *'ethrog,* 'the fruit of a beautiful tree' (a citrus fruit), the willow, and the myrtle, the *lulav* was waved about as a festive bouquet in the encirclement of the altar, following a ritual that continues to this day. During this ritual, Psalm 118:25 was and still is recited: "Save us, we beseech you, O Lord!" In Hebrew this "save us" is *hoshi'a na,* which became common outside of Judaism in its Grecized form *hosanna.* The "save us" formula of the Psalm underwent later mutations that may have been known by the time of Jesus. One thinks here of the curious formula *'Ani vehu hoshi'a na,* 'I and HE, save us,' attested in the Mishna tractate of the Feast of Tabernacles (Sukka 4.5).[60] Ethelbert Stauffer has called attention to the connection between this *'Ani vehu* and the revelatory phrase "It is I" from the Jesus sayings in the Gospels (*Jesus and His Story,* 124; cf. 226). Stauffer believes that it is a "secrecy formula" and assumes that it was already known in Jesus' day, well in advance of the destruction of the second temple in 70 C.E.

Jesus rides into Jerusalem on a donkey procured by the disciples at his request. This too belongs to a fulfillment legend from a special Zechariah tradition, which is discernible in the background of this entire narrative sequence. The passage alluded to reads as follows:

> Rejoice greatly, O daughter Zion!
> Shout aloud, O daughter Jerusalem!
> Lo, your king comes to you;
> triumphant and victorious is he,
> humble and riding on a donkey,
> on a colt, the foal of a donkey. (Zech. 9:9)

Matthew (21:5–7) attempts to represent the fulfillment of this prophecy literally, so that even the Hebrew parallelism "on a donkey, on a colt, the foal of a donkey" is taken over explicitly: "they brought the donkey and the colt, and put their cloaks on them, and he sat on them." The painstaking detail of the fulfillment here is forced beyond plausibility, however, for Jesus can hardly ride on two donkeys, and considering that the distance is very short, it would be senseless for him to change mounts. Nevertheless, the author's purpose is obviously to report the fulfillment of prophetic promise literally.

The special Zechariah tradition documented in the literal fulfillment of these messianic prophecies, as well as in the so-called expul-
sion of the money changers and merchants from the temple, may be
understood retrospectively from the culminating statement in Zechariah 12:10: "They look on the one whom they have pierced." [61] The
fulfillment of this prophecy (John 19:34–37) is clearly owing to a kerygma of the community, but in the shadow of this prophecy certain
parts of the book of Zechariah become prefigurative for Jesus' entry
into Jerusalem, interpreted in messianic terms.

The entire episode points not to Passover but to the Feast of Tabernacles (or Booths) spoken of in John's Gospel (7:2–9). We can
imagine, however, that Jesus undertook pilgrimages to Jerusalem on
the occasions of both the Feast of Tabernacles and Passover. It is also
possible that he spent the winter in the environs of Jerusalem, in
which case he may have arrived in the city in the autumn but did not
decide upon his fateful procession until spring. Matthew, Mark, and
Luke brought the entry at the Feast of Tabernacles and the decision at
Passover together into one report, since for their later synoptic reconstruction it was more important to establish an internal relationship
between the two events than to respect the temporal interval between
them. Moreover, by the time of the Evangelists the Jewish background
of particular rituals was no longer familiar. The results of a sensa-
tional find in the summer of 1966 support this thesis. Professor Pines
of the Hebrew University in Jerusalem discovered in Istanbul an old
Hebrew manuscript that cast new light on the first centuries of Christianity. The document came from a Judeo-Christian sect that believed
that the original gospel text had been composed in Hebrew and subsequently lost. We learn from this document that some eighty different versions of the gospel texts once existed (the large number of
apocryphal gospels in our possession have likewise been augmented
by recent finds in Egypt). One may therefore assume that in other
accounts the chronological course of the procession to Jerusalem—
more accurately stated, the processions of Jesus to Jerusalem—was
represented differently. For our Evangelists, however, these details
had no relevance, for they were concerned exclusively with announc-
ing specific doctrines of salvation. The Greek version of the Gospel
text was addressed primarily to Hellenistic pagans who no longer rec-

ognized the mingling of two different feasts, Passover and the Feast of Tabernacles.

Psalm 118, however, with its formulas "Save us, O Lord!" (v. 25) and "Blessed is the one who comes in the name of the Lord" (v. 26), belongs to the Hallel Psalms, which were, and still are, recited at all three pilgrimage feasts.[62] The greeting formula "Blessed is the one who comes in the name of the Lord" is applied meaningfully to Jesus in the gospel, whereas in fact it was simply the standard greeting for pilgrims arriving at the temple. The branches being waved at Jesus' entry identify the Feast of Tabernacles. The "save us" formula was more strongly expanded for the liturgy of the Feast of Tabernacles than for the liturgy of the Passover feast.[63]

It is therefore quite natural that the procession of Jesus into Jerusalem, whether it happened only once or was repeated, takes place within the framework of the pilgrimage, the 'aliyath-regel, to Jerusalem, though it was construed at the same time as a victory procession. And thus we recognize the second aspect, perhaps also the second phase of this decisive journey. One should not, however, imagine this victory procession as particularly impressive. To the eyes of the disciples, who were timorously awaiting a revelation from their master, the few dozen curiosity seekers[64] who gathered to greet an unfamiliar rabbi and his disciples may have appeared to be a reverential acknowledgment of the messianic king. In time, with increased distance of the Christian community from the event, it is likely that the number of people singing Jesus' praise also increased in the memory of chroniclers. Still, we should not underestimate the stir that Jesus caused in Jerusalem (Matt. 21:10). The talk was of course concerned not with any messianic proclamation but rather with some "prophet" from Nazareth. Thus the temple authorities were very much alert to this unknown itinerant preacher and kept a wary eye on him.

In his splendid but fanciful work *The Messiah Jesus and John the Baptist*, Robert Eisler hypothesizes that Jesus' procession to Jerusalem in fact constituted the preparatory stage for a planned departure into the wilderness, from which point he would launch a struggle against Rome and the Jewish collaborators of Caesar. As I see it, this thesis is anchored too little in the texts and in the character of Jesus as we know it.[65]

Nevertheless, we may concur with Eisler that it was the inner circle of the twelve disciples along with the wider one of the seventy who urged Jesus to make his appearance in Jerusalem as a means of accelerating the tempo of salvation history, as it were. Thus the group making its way to Jerusalem would have consisted of a relatively large company of pilgrims, with little provision having been made for whatever the next day might bring (in keeping with Matt. 6:25–34). Certain episodes of this pilgrimage do in fact indicate that no provision was taken for food, transportation, or lodging. Jesus' "little flock" put itself entirely in the hands of the Father. This little flock, however, did not constitute a homogeneous party. It included pacifists and Zealots, skeptics and female enthusiasts, Hebrew chauvinists and probably also Hellenistic proselytes at the margin. Whoever joined the little flock may well have had to break family ties. Jesus' remark that he came to bring not peace but the sword and to set mother against daughter (Matt. 10:34–38; cf. Micah 7:6) assumes special relevance now. The community doctrine of schism, which divided the young church from the older synagogue, is clearly heard here; I think, in fact, that in the procession to Jerusalem we can hear simultaneously an echo of the revolutionary spirit.

Eisler and those who agree with him seize on the single occurrence of the statement that the hour has finally come to take up the sword and that whoever does not have a sword should exchange his coat for one (Luke 22:36). And yet we know that only *two* swords in all were present at the arrest of Jesus. That is a bit meager for an armed insurrection against the Roman legions. Jesus' statement to Peter, "Put your sword back into its place; for all who take the sword will perish by the sword" (Matt. 26:52)—which so strikingly recalls Hillel's statement, "They who have drowned thee shall [themselves] be drowned" (Pirkei-'Avoth 2.6)[66]—has for me the unmistakable ring of authenticity. The ostensible contradiction is resolved in view of the heterogeneous character of the little flock. The Zealots, to whom Judas Iscariot doubtless belonged, were eager to burst loose with that desperate courage of the little flock that we came to know in more recent times during the active years of struggle of the underground resistance forces in British Mandatory Palestine: the Hagana, the Irgun Tsevai Leumi, and the Stern Gang.[67] It may be that Jesus occasionally fell under a similar influence in his brief career and considered armed resistance. But given the reality at Jerusalem, with the Roman legions in the Fortress of Antonia and the temple watch of the Sanhedrin, all he could say was "Put your sword back into its place."

Eisler's and Carmichael's theory that the temple was occupied by the followers of Jesus belongs to the realm of fantasy—the fantasy not only of these modern investigators but also of the activist adherents of Jesus (cf. Carmichael, *Death of Jesus,* 140).

On the other hand, it is clear that Jesus did provoke some kind of commotion in the temple, although that too we must be careful not to exaggerate. To me, the image of a cause-driven orator in London's Hyde Park comes closest to illustrating the reality here. Those orators are not just harmless fools but often people to be taken seriously, people who hold no office and therefore speak uninvited and freely to the public, who win followers, provoke heated discussions, and challenge opponents to debate. But I am particularly reminded of the fanatical preachers from Jerusalem's orthodox Me'a She'arim quarter, where a man such as Rabbi Amram Blau, the intellectual leader of a small group of extremists, constantly used to attack what he called the godless authority of the Zionists, challenge the official rabbinic authority, and heatedly justify his point of view with quotations from the Bible and the Talmud. We have here the image of an uncommissioned teacher who, obligated only to his own conscience, declares war on the establishment.

Jesus obviously resided not within Jerusalem but in small locales around the Mount of Olives, just outside the city, in such places as Bethany and Bethphage. In his article on the "unhistorical Jesus," Hermann Raschke persuasively emphasizes the significance of evangelical traditions that are bound to specific places. I am not able, however, to share his basic thesis about the unhistoricity of Jesus.

Jesus taught in the temple, which is to say, in the forecourt of the temple, an area accessible to the public. The contention that he first purified the temple before teaching probably belongs to the realm of fulfillment legends. What we do hear in these passages (Matt. 21:12–17; Mark 11:15–19; Luke 19:45–48; John 2:13–22) is the outrage of Jesus and his disciples over the condition of the temple, which was one of Herod's opulent Hellenistic buildings and far from being Isaiah's "house of prayer" for all the people (56:7)—the ideal that inspired Jesus and every devout Jew.

The so-called money changers and merchants in the temple have been historically attested—not *in* the temple, of course, but around it in the semisecular forecourts. The money changers had the primary task of exchanging the current coin that bore the imprint of Caesar (the one handed to Jesus in just such a forecourt) for the plain temple currency, with which sacrificial animals could then be purchased on the spot. The story that Jesus, armed with a whip of cords, overturned the tables of the money changers and drove out the clerks of the temple bench is too adventurous to be true. It is hard to believe that a disturbance of public order (or disorder) of this magnitude would not have provoked arrest. This is a fulfillment legend that goes back to the last words of the prophet Zechariah (14:21): "And there shall no longer be traders in the house of the Lord of hosts on that day." Actually, instead of "traders" one must read "Canaanites"—but the Canaanites *were* the traders, and thus Buber accurately captures the intent of the passage with his double translation: "And no longer will a Canaanite trader be in *his* house of the Lord of hosts on that day." [68]

Jesus affirms the idea of the temple but rejects it in its present form, which he considers a perversion of holiness. He is not alone in that opinion. In the Talmud there is an entire series of motifs that recount the causes leading up to the destruction of the temple. One repeatedly finds here the kind of criticism that took offense at an externalized service of God having nothing to do with brotherly love and justice but only with an unfounded hatred of everyone for everyone.

We sense something of this hateful atmosphere in the discussions of Jesus in the temple with his adversaries. The episode of the tribute coin (Matt. 22:15–22) is typical of these temple discussions; this episode, and not the alleged purification of the temple, proved decisive in the subsequent arrest of Jesus.

Martin Buber selected Jesus' statement regarding the coin of tribute as the point of departure for a speech in 1953 ("Geltung und Grenze") on the limits of political authority. He pointed out that although it is typical of great, unforgettable statements of religious mission to be bound to their situation and directed to a particular group, their effect transcends place, time, and audience. That may be true in general, but

Jesus' statement in this instance cannot be absolutized in such a way as to derive from it a double-edged doctrine—a division, that is, into a temporal and a spiritual realm. The debate over the tribute coin was elevated only in the later transmission (papyrus Egerton 2;[69] cf. Justin Martyr, *Apologies*, 1.17) to universal ethical status, probably in an attempt to illustrate the loyalty of Christians to the Roman state. In fact, however, the intent of the original narrative was to diminish the ethical question relative to the eschatological imperative of yielding to the will of God.

Jesus does not address others here but is himself addressed—not in candid conversation as with Nicodemus but as the target of malicious temptation. His opponents, the Pharisees and Herodians, hope to mislead Jesus into expressing treasonable thought in order thus to gain a legal hold against this bothersome truth fanatic. To that end they send several of their disciples to Jesus with the strategy of posing a question about religious law, a *she'ela*, to him: should a Jew pay taxes to a non-Jewish ruler? His interrogators have no interest in being instructed, only in entrapping him into a revolutionary statement in order then to denounce him to the Roman authorities.

Jesus would have to have been a poor psychologist not to recognize the trap set by his opponents. As it turned out, he was anything but an otherworldly dreamer; it is aptly written that "he himself knew what was in everyone" (John 2:25). Forced into this precarious situation, Jesus deports himself according to his own maxim to "be wise as serpents and innocent as doves" (Matt. 10:16). He is "innocent" in saying bluntly to his opponents, "Why are you putting me to the test, you hypocrites?" (Matt. 22:18). But he is also "wise" in having them hand the tribute coin (the denar) to him and, in uniquely Jewish fashion, answering the question with a question: "Whose head is this, and whose title?" (v. 20). Now he has *them!* Now they must answer *him*. He opts for attack as the best form of defense. His opponents can only reply, "The emperor's." Thereupon, Jesus answers with the famous statement, "Give therefore to the emperor the things that are the emperor's, and to God the things that are God's" (v. 21).

That is the situation, and it must not be separated from the words. To remove it from its historical ground and to place it in the atemporal realm of dogmatism would be to misunderstand the words.

We must therefore sharpen our hearing in order to discern the *niggun*, the inflection, with which this fateful statement is uttered.

The inflection emerges from the situation. The conversation, whose final point is made by this inflection, is *a conversation among Jews*— among Palestinian Jews. But the subject of the conversation is Caesar, the *non-Jewish* state power, the representative of foreign imperialism.

One must have lived among Palestinian Jews in order to appreciate fully the stormy atmosphere of such a conversation. Not so very long ago, in fact, the situation of Judaism in Palestine greatly resembled the situation at the time of Jesus. For us Jewish citizens of Palestine, a conversation like the one heard in Matthew's Gospel was not something historical; it was immensely relevant to us. In fact, a uniquely Jewish behavioral trait frequently reveals itself with respect to foreign power, especially in those Jews who are knowledgeable of Israel from everlasting to everlasting! A cool distance, an aloofness to the colossus of power, fixed on final things and uninterested in temporal power, distinguishes these truest of Jews. But their behavior changes when they are confronted with the kind of Jews who no longer care to know about Israel's commission, who betray Yahweh to Baal and want to be "like all nations." There is no cool distance with respect to these Jews; in this situation "an Israelite in whom there is no deceit" (cf. John 1:47) will speak the unvarnished truth. Thus Jesus' behavior with, respect to his Jewish land sovereign Herod displays no trace of the splendid isolation he displays toward Caesar. Jesus flatly calls the assimilationist and Roman puppet Herod a "fox" (Luke 13:32), which amounts to nothing less than lèse majesté.

We have to be aware of this fundamental spiritual disposition in order to hear the correct inflection in the statement about the coin of tribute. I would like to attempt to convey that inflection here by bracketing into Jesus' statement that which is not explicitly spoken:

"Give therefore (what's the big deal, after all?) to the emperor (that *goy*) the things that are the emperor's (he only wants money and more money from you!) and (or, but [the biblical 'and'—Hebrew *ve*—has multiple values; very often in the Old Testament it means 'but'], and now comes the big But, and this is the key!) to God the things that are God's."

It is the statement of a *galuth* Jew, a Jew of the diaspora, which is transmitted to us here. It does no good to object that Jesus in fact was a Palestinian Jew who lived embedded within his own culture, for this culture was no longer autonomous. The *galuth* had already entered Palestine through the imperial overlordship of the Romans, which created three groups of Jews: the assimilationists (Herod's party and the Sadducees); the Zealots, who sought to answer force with force; and finally the nonviolence group, the Pharisees and Essenes, who made up the majority of the disciples of Jesus and John. As Gandhi once said, "Nonviolence sets all of the soul's strength against the will of the tyrant." That was exactly what the Pharisees and Essenes—and with them Jesus—did with respect to Caesar. In doing so they remained cognizant of the relativity of power, which must eventually yield to a greater power, having not one ounce of eternity in itself.

Jesus' declaration concerning Caesar and God must therefore be understood on two levels: it displays both a personal and a national dimension.

The personal dimension makes it tactically advisable to answer elusively so as not to fall into the trap of his enemies. The national dimension causes the *foreign* ruler to appear to him from this great— and at the deepest level probably eschatological—distance as the antithesis of God; at the same time, however, it assigns him a lesser relevance.

The Gospels see in Jesus the fulfiller of the prophetic mission. But a Jesus who used the statement on Caesar and God in the absolute sense of church doctrine would have been the antithesis of the prophets. For the core of the prophetic mission is precisely the *indivisibility of the kingdom of God.* Yahweh is king over all. No area can exist outside his dominion.

The God of the prophets demands neither cult, sacrifice, temple, nor liturgy but a life of justice and love! But the God of the *nevi'im,* the prophets, does not demand of the individual alone this everlasting, indivisible responsibility to him. He demands it also of the entire people on whom he passes judgment when they wrong one another, either inwardly or outwardly. The Lord passes judgment on them not because they fail to participate in the Jerusalem temple cult but because they have not upheld the practice of *tsedek* and *mishpat* (righteousness and judgment), *chesed* and *rachamim* (loving-kindness and mercy) toward one another.

A Jesus who wished to limit the claim of God only to the temple, the liturgy, or even the life of the individual would stand outside the prophetic succession.

I can only conclude, then, that the statement on Caesar and God is not absolute but situationally bound. It cannot be applied mechanically to completely different situations.

Although Jesus shows himself here to be as wise as a serpent, the curtain of fate continues to close over him. And thus we come to the third aspect of the journey to Jerusalem, which turns it into a path of martyrdom. It is in this context that the son-of-man sayings belong: "How then is it written about the Son of Man, that he is to go through many sufferings?" (Mark 9:12). This motif sounds over and over again throughout the Gospels, as in Luke: "Thus it is written, that the Messiah is to suffer" (24:46). The expectation of suffering resides in the shadow of the sufferings of the servant of God (Isa. 52:13–53:12) and in the Psalms of suffering (22 and 34), as well as in the mysterious words concerning the just martyr (Zech. 12:10). The later Christian tradition, which views the sufferings and announcement of the sufferings of the son of man from the vantage point of Easter, can easily be illuminated psychologically without doing violence to the text. As a clairvoyant man—and that he surely was—Jesus had to have been conscious of the risk involved in his provocation. It was no small thing to challenge all earthly powers simultaneously: the sadducean priesthood, the pharisaic legal scholars, the Herodians, and the Roman occupational authority. That appeared to leave the possibility now only of a miraculous victory, which would require the direct intercession of God, or else defeat in an entirely unequal struggle. But a *third* possibility arose that could hardly have been envisioned at the time: *the possibility of victory in defeat.* This third possibility was in fact to become history, albeit outside the history of Jesus' own life. Jesus, so we may assume, experienced his path to Jerusalem as the obligatory Jewish pilgrimage; the enthusiastic entry that was prepared for him transformed this pilgrimage, if only for a moment, into a victory procession. In the same moment, however, opponents were called into action, and the man who could not avoid them could reckon only with a path of martyrdom. That possibility coalesced into reality for Jesus within a few short days. Thus Jesus' path to Jerusalem was a pilgrimage, a victory procession, and a path of martyrdom, all in one.

10 *Seder Night in Jerusalem*

The question of whether Jesus' first solemn entry into Jerusalem took place at the Feast of Tabernacles or at Passover, which we dealt with in the preceding chapter, is of secondary importance to the fact that the tragic moment of decision in the life of Jesus fell on the Seder night, the night of the Passover celebration. I cannot understand how serious scholars such as Günther Bornkamm can doubt that Jesus' Last Supper was a Passover meal, a Seder meal (the domestic celebration of the Passover night). Bornkamm writes, "It is very doubtful, however, that this supper was itself held as a Passover meal, although it certainly took place near the time of the Passover festival. What we do know for certain is only that the first three Evangelists wished to see and describe it as such" (*Jesus of Nazareth*, 161). For me it is enough that the synoptic writers present this supper unambiguously as a Seder meal; even John (chap. 13) presumes temporal contiguity with the Passover festival. The issue here, however, as we shall show, concerns not only temporal contiguity but also the content of the feast and its renewal by Jesus. I therefore question Hermann Strack's assumption as well, that "the Last Supper was instituted by the Lord during the festive gathering on the occasion of the enjoyment of the paschal lamb, but was not connected to any Passover ritual" (*Passafest,* 10). I think rather that the institution of the so-called Last Supper fits organically into the Seder celebration and should be viewed as Jesus' new interpretation of the ritual. On the basis of this new interpretation, which is situationally bound, the Seder celebration was reformed from within the circle of disciples, and from this reform the Christian Eucharist developed later (also influenced, presumably, by the Hellenistic mystery cults).

Scholars today who claim that Jesus' Last Supper is not unambiguously identifiable as a Seder celebration base their argument mainly on the fact that the New Testament reports no essential details of the Jewish Seder celebration. The Haggada, the broad narrative of the Exodus of the Children of Israel from Egypt, is missing.

The New Testament, however, as must be emphasized again and again, has no interest in offering either a biography of Jesus or a description of Jewish antiquities as, say, Flavius Josephus does. Its purpose is rather to proclaim the joyful message of Jesus, the Messiah of Israel and the nations of the world. For the Gospels as "missionary writings," details of the Seder ritual are not essential. We must also keep in mind the situational context of the Gospels: insofar as they addressed a Jewish audience, the Evangelists could presuppose knowledge of the Seder ritual; insofar as they addressed a Greek (Hellenistic) audience or readership, the original content of the Seder celebration was incidental to the "new covenant" established on this night.

But even if we disregard these further considerations, it is clear that in the reports of the Gospels it is not the general aspect of the Seder celebration but the particular aspect of the last Seder of Jesus of Nazareth that is being represented. Its particularity lies not in the fact that something completely new is presented here but rather in the fact that a renewal of the ancient tradition takes place. The leading motif of the Seder night is the *zikkaron,* 'remembrance,' specifically of the act of salvation by Yahweh in the Exodus from Egypt. The memory of this act of salvation lives on in Israel from generation to generation. Jesus now seizes upon this memory: "Do this in remembrance of me," he says (Luke 22:19). Now, in addition to God's act of salvation in Egypt, we have God's act of salvation through the painful "transfiguration" of Jesus, who in this night comes to full consciousness of his tragic mission as a suffering servant of God. There are again motifs from the book of Zechariah running through the presentation of Jesus' last Seder night. First, the passage Zechariah 13:7:

> "Awake, O sword, against my shepherd,
> against the man who is my associate,"
> says the Lord of hosts.
> Strike the shepherd, that the sheep may be scattered;
> I will turn my hand against the little ones.

The Gospels cite the second portion of this passage from Zechariah explicitly in connection with Jesus' presentiments of death at the last Seder celebration. Jesus now recognizes that the sword, the power, the destruction must be raised against him—something to be equated not with failure, to be sure, but with the inevitable path of martyrdom. We are to recall the suffering and defeated Messiah alluded to in the Babylonian Talmud, tractate Sukka 51b–52a:

> They found a verse of Scripture, which they expounded: "The land shall mourn, each family by itself . . ." (Zech. 12:12). What does this have to do with mourning? Rabbi Dosa and the rabbis argued over this. One says, with the *Messiah, the son of Joseph,* who is then killed. And one says, with the evil force, which is then killed. That one is revealing who says, "with the Messiah, the son of Joseph, who is then killed," for it is written, "they look on the one [Hebrew: me] whom they have pierced, they shall mourn for him, as one mourns for an only child" (Zech. 12:10). But why would they mourn according to that one who says, "with the evil force, which is then killed"? For in this instance one would rather have a celebration and not cry!

The German translator of the Talmud, Lazarus Goldschmidt, aptly says about this passage, "According to Jewish eschatology, the Messiah Ben-Yosef, who will die in battle, is the precursor of the Messiah from the House of David. This name, furthermore, is so striking that its derivation from primitive Christianity can hardly be overlooked" (*Der Babylonische Talmud,* 399).

Siegmund Hurwitz, in his book on the dying Messiah, has dealt extensively with this entire complex of questions, drawing on all available sources and applying Jungian analytical psychology as a means of understanding the complicated motifs and theological issues. The dating of the pertinent passages from the Talmud seems irrelevant to me, considering that their definitive written version often was not established until centuries later. Apparently, traditions about the suffering Messiah were in existence already by the time of Jesus, perhaps much earlier. One also thinks here of the teacher of righteousness in the Qumran texts. It is particularly significant that in the talmudic passage cited above, this suffering Messiah is designated as a "son of Joseph," by contrast to the triumphant "son of David." Jesus of Nazareth is at once a son of Joseph and a descendant of the house of David, thus integrating both roles in his person.

According to the testimony of the Gospels, at his festive entry Jesus is greeted by the crowd of people as a "Son of David" (Matt. 21:9). Within the most intimate circle of disciples, however, he identifies himself as the son of Joseph, the son of man who is destined for suffering, and the servant of God in the form of one singled out for martyrdom. We said earlier that Jesus presumably did not consider himself to be the Messiah, but that does not exclude the possibility that he began to sense that he was destined for a path of martyrdom, given his clear realization of his inescapable situation. The attachment of a *messianic* label to this path of martyrdom is owing probably to a later, broadened interpretation of the event.

It is impossible to ignore the repeated reference in this context to the fulfillment of prophecies from Zechariah. That goes also for the betrayal by Judas, a subject to which we shall return later. I therefore find it probable that, from Jesus' entry into Jerusalem to the Last Supper to the crucifixion, the source is a midrash to the book of Zechariah.

Of all the available reports about the Last Supper, that of Luke (22: 7–23) gives the clearest picture of the sequence of events. He avows in the preamble to his Gospel that he has "decided, after investigating everything carefully from the very first, to write an orderly account" (1:3). We shall therefore follow Luke's report, providing cross-references to the parallel texts in Matthew (26:17–30) and Mark (14:

12–25) but also to John (chaps. 13–17). First, of course, we must deal with the problem of dating: when did Jesus hold the Last Supper, the Seder celebration, with his disciples in Jerusalem? Even the very first indication given in the Gospels is imprecise on this count:

> On the first day of Unleavened Bread, when the Passover lamb is sacri-
> ficed, his disciples said to him, "Where do you want us to go and make
> the preparations for you to eat the Passover?" (Mark 14:12)

Matthew says the same thing:

> On the first day of Unleavened Bread the disciples came to Jesus, saying,
> "Where do you want us to make the preparations for you to eat the Pass-
> over?" (26:17)

Luke's report, which we shall otherwise follow, reads similarly:

> Then came the day of Unleavened Bread, on which the Passover lamb had
> to be sacrificed. (22:7)

John's account begins rather more plausibly:

> Now before the festival of the Passover, Jesus knew that his hour had
> come to depart from this world and go to the Father. (13:1)

Repeatedly in the synoptic texts the first day of the celebration is confused with the day of preparation ('Erev Pesach), whereas John explicitly notes that it was "before the festival of the Passover."

Many authors have wrestled in vain with this problem of dating.
Strack, for example, writes as follows:

> What is there to say about the explicit assertion of the synoptic writers
> that this meal was prepared "on the first day of Unleavened Bread" (that
> is, on 14 Nisan, when eating unleavened bread had to cease before noon
> [see here the Mishna tractate Pesachim 1.4]) and consumed on the eve-
> ning of the same day?
>
> The simplest answer would be to cut up the knot: namely, to assume
> an error in Mark repeated by both Matthew and Luke. Whether this
> answer is the correct one, however, seems very doubtful to me. One
> could rather assume that Jesus, who was also "lord even of the sabbath"

(Mark 2:28), celebrated the Passover supper a day earlier in anticipation of his imminent death. But to me the most likely explanation is the following: that at that time there was no consensus as to the beginning date of the month of Nisan, and many people, including Jesus, probably on the evidence of their own observations of the new moon, set 1 Nisan, and accordingly 14 Nisan, one day earlier than the sadducean high court and priests did. (As I have read somewhere, Jech. Lichtenstein of Leipzig expresses the same opinion that I hold to.) The reckoning of Jesus, that is, his determination of when the Passover meal should take place, was, of course, valid for his disciples. (*Passafest,* "Einleitung," *9–*10)

First of all, it must be made very clear that it cannot be the first day of the celebration in question here but the day of preparation; the celebration begins in the evening of the day of preparation, just as all Jewish holidays, including the Sabbath, begin at sundown of the previous evening. Not all the gospel reports are in agreement on this point. There is no doubt here that Jesus is celebrating the Seder night with his disciples. Even if he had been taken into custody this night by the Jewish authorities, it would be unthinkable on this high holy night for the judicial hearing to have taken place in the house of the high priest Caiaphas; for Jesus to have been transferred to Pilate the next morning; and for Jesus then to have been crucified on the first day of the Passover festival. Hence the constant implications in the report of the special haste that was necessary in view of the approaching Sabbath. But there is no inference that the festival day itself was desecrated by any judicial hearing, execution, or burial.

Anyone familiar with Jewish law and custom will realize immediately that all of this is simply impossible. Had Jesus been taken into custody on the Seder night, he would have been kept under watch until after the festival day, and everything else would have taken place later.

On the other hand, there is no question that we are witnessing the description of a Seder ritual as celebrated by Jesus with his disciples. The ostensible contradiction has been solved only in recent years; as Hermann Raschke has correctly noted ("Der ungeschichtliche Jesus," 391), everything is different since the discoveries at Qumran. We may assume that Jesus, who stood in open opposition to the Sadducees and Pharisees and, presumably through his rabbi John the Baptist, had contact with the sect of Qumran, used the solar Qumran calendar, according to which he would have celebrated the Seder one day earlier than the official circles in Jerusalem.[70] In support of Qumran's influence on the last Seder of Jesus is the fact that only the twelve disciples took part in the supper, in keeping with the meal regulation of Qumran. In principle, women also could take part in the Seder celebration, as is universally true today as well; in fact, the Mishna discusses the question of whether it is better for a woman to take part in the Passover celebration in the house of her father or in the house of her husband (Pesachim 8.1). And yet we hear nothing more about the women around Jesus, women who were his loyal companions—later named the first witnesses of the resurrection—and who therefore had accompanied him to Jerusalem. But women did not participate in a Seder meal that followed the ritual and calendar of Qumran.

Jesus and the disciples were dwelling outside of Jerusalem, near the Mount of Olives. Just as the rabbi sent his disciples out to procure a donkey for him, he now sends them out to seek a proper room for the celebration of the Seder. A lodging room, already furnished for a Seder celebration, is found in the house of a water bearer. Although Jesus celebrated the Seder in keeping with the date and restrictions of Qumran, the brief notice in Luke 22:12–13 shows that he nevertheless did celebrate it thoroughly in the style of his time. Formerly a quick meal, as prescribed in the second book of Moses (Exod. 12:11), to be taken probably while standing with loins girded, walking stick in hand, and shoes on one's feet, it had been transformed under Hellenistic influence into a *symposion*. One reclined at table, stretched out on pillows, leaning on the left side, so that the four prescribed cups could be grasped with the right hand. Long discussions, often lasting the entire night, intertwined with the story of the Exodus from Egypt. The description of the Seder celebration at the time of the second temple, as the Mishna presents it in the tractate Pesachim (10.1–8), is powerfully reminiscent of the banquet in Plato's *Symposion* and provides an example of the way in which Greek forms and Hebraic content melded into a unified whole, a process again encountered in the later Christian tradition of the Last Supper. Certain terminology of the Seder ritual was even borrowed from Greek. Thus the final matsa, which is so significant in Jesus' Last Supper, today is still called the *epikomion,* or *'afikoman,* which represents the conclusion of the holy meal.

Where in Jerusalem the Seder celebration took place we do not know. Tradition has it that the house, unspecified in the Gospels, was situated on Mount Zion in the immediate vicinity of the so-called Tomb of David. The Upper Room is revered to this day by Christians, the Tomb of David by Jews. Both places are equally unhistorical. If the Upper Room had been situated on Mount Zion (if in fact the mountain by that name is identical with that biblical mount known as Zion), the Gospels surely would not have failed to make the point. Likewise, the proximity of the Tomb of David would have been mentioned, since Jesus is apostrophized in the Gospels as the son of David. But there is not a word about any of that. We must therefore imagine just a normal house hidden away somewhere among the bustling streets of Herod's city. In the inns of Jerusalem countless rooms were prepared for the Seder celebration by pilgrims, exactly as today in Israel one finds all the preparations for the Seder celebration being made by tourists in countless hotels.

Jesus takes his place beside his twelve disciples at the Passover table. We do not know exactly how he recited the Haggada, the narrative of the Exodus from Egypt. We may assume that the traditional forms provided the general guidelines, though they probably incorporated specific regulations of the Qumran sect. The particular doctrine of Rabbi Jesus—overshadowed now by the presentiment of death, which had condensed into certainty—was also probably set forth in a conversational manner, establishing the content of the ritual. Not only the presentiment of the imminent bitter end, symbolized in the ritual's bitter herb, the *maror,* and the bread of affliction, the matsa, but the presentiment of the betrayal as well casts a shadow over this celebration. Once again we hear an echo of a motif from Zechariah (11:12). We will turn to the figure of Judas, the presumed betrayer, below.

After Jesus and his friends have finished the supper, he distributes the *'afikoman,* the final matsa among the participants, just as is still done today.

> Then he took a loaf of bread [the matsa], and when he had given thanks
> [said the grace after meal, the *birkath-hamazon*], he broke it and gave
> it to them, saying, "This is my body, which is given for you. Do this
> in remembrance of me." And he did the same with the cup after supper
> [the third prescribed cup of the Seder night], saying, "This cup that is
> poured out for you is the new covenant in my blood."

These institutional words of the Last Supper come from Luke (22:19–20). Instead of Luke's formula "for you," however, Mark records "for many" (14:24). Matthew adds, logically, "for the forgiveness of sins" (26:28). Luke's "for you" would apply only to the circle of disciples and preclude any broad application of the institutional words.

How are we to understand now the remarkable words through which Jesus identifies himself with the matsa, the unleavened bread of the Passover feast? An old folk custom, which Strack also mentions in his discussion of the modern Seder celebration (*Passafest,* 37), may point us in the right direction. Three matsoth (unleavened flat loaves), each having a different name, are draped with a cloth and laid under the Seder plate on which the courses of the feast are represented: "Israel" on the bottom, "Levi" in the middle, and "Kohen" (priest) on top. It is not possible to date this custom precisely. E. D. Goldschmidt notes that older authorities, such as Alfasi and Maimonides, with whom Rabbi Elijah of Vilna [71] agrees, require only two matsoth, whereas the northern French school of Rabbi 'Amram Ga'on [72] requires three matsoth, the custom that gained acceptance everywhere outside of Yemen (*Pessach-Haggadah,* 14). As this case shows, we often do not know exactly when folk customs arose. They could have been practiced in uncodified form for centuries, since they have no legal status. Thus the popular cup for the prophet Elijah, which is now felt to be an integral component of the Seder celebration, is anything but a legal prescription; it is rather a popular interpretation of a controversial point of religious law. [73] The identification of the three especially carefully baked matsoth of the Seder celebration with the priestly caste (Kohanim), the caste of temple ministrants and singers

(Leviyim), and finally the large group of the people conjures the real presence of all of Israel at every Seder celebration. According to a ritual that continues to be valid today, the middle matsa is then *broken* and distributed by the father of the house among the partakers of the meal. Jesus does that as well, emphasizing that he himself has now become a substitute for all of Israel. In this sense he proceeds to raise the cup and speak symbolical words over the wine: "This is my blood of the covenant, which is poured out for many for the forgiveness of sins" (Matt. 26:28).

Here I follow Hans Kosmala, the head of the Swedish Theological Institute in Jerusalem, who has convincingly shown that Jesus speaks the institutional words "for many" as a conscious rejection of a problematical, negative portion of the Seder ritual (*Hebräer*, 186). In that portion the formula *shefokh chamathekha 'al hagoyim,* 'pour out your anger upon the nations,' is spoken over the fourth cup following the grace; this is the cup of anger, which provides the transition to the concluding Hallel Psalms.

Goldschmidt (*Pessach-Haggadah,* 78) argues that this utterance results from an integration of Psalms 79:6–7, 69:25, and Lamentations 3:66, forged in the Middle Ages under the pressure of persecutions; in some rituals it is expanded by additional Bible verses.

Kosmala makes the revealing observation that Psalm 79:6—"Pour out your anger on the nations that do not know you, and on the kingdoms that do not call on your name"—was definitely known in this context by the time of Jesus. He remarks,

> At the spot where the request has been made since time immemorial for God to pour out his anger upon the nations, Jesus adds his own words over the after-meal cup: "This cup and the new covenant in my blood— these are poured out for many." . . .[74] It is not the anger of God that is poured out here; no cup of anger is given "for many" to drink. The cup that is poured out is the new covenant in which God's love and mercy are revealed. (*Hebräer,* 186)

Here we need to consider the image of "pouring out." God's anger is poured out, an image that we encounter in John's Apocalypse, where the cup of anger is poured out by the angels of judgment (Rev. 16). But the blood of redemption is poured out here. This blood, as Kosmala emphasizes in his refutation of Joachim Jeremias, is in no way to be identified with the blood of the paschal lamb, which has no redemptive power (*Hebräer*, 174). In the description of the Last Supper the paschal lamb fades completely into the background, and the accent is on the bread (matsa) and the wine, whereas in other contexts Jesus is designated the lamb of God, the righteous paschal lamb, whose bones are not to be broken.

As I see it, the reason the central feature of the sacrificial ritual is relegated to the background is that the *descriptions* derive from the period *after* the destruction of the temple, at which point in time only the matsa and the wine (along with the bitter herbs) remained present, the paschal lamb having virtually disappeared by then.

The mystery of the number four pervades the Passover celebration. The number four is sacred in Judaism, and I am inclined to say that it is *the* holy number universally. In Christianity this knowledge was obscured by a fascination with the number three, the dogma of the Trinity, the Triune God, which is foreign to Judaism and, accordingly, to Jesus' own faith.

As a sacred number, four appears first of all in the tetragram (YHWH). In the vision of the prophet Ezekiel (chap. 1), in which he sees the divine chariot throne, we again encounter the sacred number four. The chariot of God is borne by angelic creatures with four faces: human, lion, ox, and eagle (v. 10). Later ecclesiastical tradition associated this vision with the four Evangelists, who exploit the symbols to their own ends.

In his book *Answer to Job*, C. G. Jung talks about the archetypal and psychological necessity of the number four to the human comprehension of God. As the All-Encompassing One who embraces all four directions, the four zones of the earth, God must be represented in the number four (141).

Something of this mystery is reflected in the role of the number four in the Passover celebration. The festival itself has four names: first, *Pesach*, which celebrates the passing-over by the angel of death (liberation from Egyptian bondage); second, *Chag Hamatsoth*, the festival of unleavened bread; third, *Chag Ha'aviv*, the celebration of spring; fourth, *Zeman Cheruthenu*, the time of our liberation.

For the celebration of the Seder meal on Passover night, four cups of wine were already prescribed in the Mishna in connection with Exodus 6:6–7:

> "I am the Lord, and I will *free* you from the burdens of the Egyptians and *deliver* you from slavery to them. I will *redeem* you with an outstretched arm and with mighty acts of judgment. I will *take* you as my people, and I will be your God. You shall know that I am the Lord your God, who has freed you from the burdens of the Egyptians."

The four proofs of grace are, then: freedom, deliverance, redemption, and taking (choosing).

In the ritual of the Seder night the narrative of the Exodus from Egypt begins with four questions,[75] asked by the youngest participant, and then proceeds to introduce the midrash of the four sons: the wise son, the evil son, the simple son, and the son who does not (yet) know how to ask. Each of these four sons, or characters, asks questions suitable to his particular nature about the meaning of the celebration, and in this way the midrash develops a variety of approaches to understanding the celebration, each in accordance with the understanding of the particular son.[76]

We meet these four sons now at the Last Supper of Jesus, at the Seder celebration in Jerusalem. In this regard it is necessary to consult John's Gospel. Although John does not speak of a Seder celebration as such, the Hebraic ritual, as described in the Mishna and as it continues to be observed in its essentials, becomes visible under a Greek disguise, as it were. The description of the supper in John 13 keeps the disciples in the background, though four personalities do stand out: the four sons of the Haggada. First, there is the wise son, Jesus himself, the son of man, who asks concerning the meaning of the hour (v. 12) and who himself provides the answer of transfiguration through suffering. Then there is the clearly recognizable evil one, Judas Iscariot, the "betrayer" (v. 2). The figure of the simple, straightforward son is embodied in Peter, who asks simply and straightforwardly, "Lord, where are you going?" and follows that with another question, "Lord, why can I not follow you now?" (vv. 36–37).

And finally, the figure of the son who does not yet know how to ask. That is the disciple whom Jesus loves, the one who leans on his breast. Through him Peter fulfills the command "You shall reveal it to him"[77] by encouraging him, prodding him, to ask the question: "One of his disciples—the one whom Jesus loved—was reclining next to him; Simon Peter therefore motioned to him to ask Jesus of whom he was speaking. So while reclining next to Jesus, he asked him, 'Lord, who is it [who will betray you]?'" (vv. 23–25).

One gets the sense that a ritualistic game is being played here in which the traditional four sons of the Haggada are asking their questions in terms of a different liturgy.

The youngest, whose role is to ask the questions, even though he does not yet rightly know how to do so and must therefore be prompted to ask, is presumably John. I say "presumably," since it is not explicitly stated that the favorite disciple—the one who leans on Jesus' breast at the Seder celebration, who later is the only one of the disciples standing beneath the cross, who at his master's bidding (John 19:27) takes the mother of Jesus to his own home after the crucifixion, and to whom, together with Peter, the announcement of the resurrection is first made (John 20:2)—is in fact John. There is only one early Christian tradition, dating from the end of the second century, that identifies the unnamed favorite disciple as John, son of Zebedee. Though we have no reason to doubt this tradition, it is more than curious that the name of this beloved disciple is not otherwise mentioned.

In his intuitive book on Jesus, Hans Blüher provides an apt characterization of John: "The closest one to [Jesus] is John, the disciple, who leans on his breast; but even this disciple has no striking features. He is a young, impulsive upstart, who is always asking *totally inappropriate questions*" (*Aristie*, 121). Blüher intuits that the disciple John is the one "who does not know how to ask."

And yet here at this Seder celebration he asks precisely the right question. It is obviously question number three of the four questions of the *Ma nishtanna* text, which the youngest person still today recites as a catechistic leading question at every Seder celebration. That is clear from the answer that Jesus gives.

This third question is framed as follows in the text of the Haggada: "On all other nights, we are not required to dip even once; tonight we are required to dip twice."[78] Jesus answers the disciple's question about who will betray him by saying, "It is the one to whom I give this piece of bread," whereupon he dips the bread and gives it to Judas, Simon's son, called Iscariot (John 13:26).

We recognize the ceremony of the Seder night in all details, but modified into the institutional celebration of the new covenant.

Here again the number four is clearly the leading motif of the Passover Seder ritual. We can observe a conscious deviation or reinterpretation of this ritual at four central points of the Last Supper.

We have already mentioned three such reinterpretations: first, the matsa, the unleavened bread, which Jesus distributes as 'afikoman to the disciples around the table, symbolizes his body, which is now broken; second, the cup of anger, which is reinterpreted as the cup of blood shed for the remission of the sins of many (all Israel); third, the dipping of the symbolic course (probably the bitter herb, since the concern here is with the bitterness of death), which becomes the sign that identifies the betrayer.

The fourth conscious modification of the Seder ritual has to do with the washing of feet (John 13:3–20). As John presents it, Jesus first takes off his outer robe before the Seder celebration begins, ties a towel around himself, and proceeds to wash the disciples' feet and dry them with the towel. Peter objects to this humbling gesture, but Jesus insists that he obey. In the end, Peter begs that not only his feet be washed but his hands and head as well (v. 9).

What is going on here? At the beginning of the Seder celebration the host washes his hands, although the guests are not required to do so. It is common at this point to wash the hands of the participating eldest member of the house, for on this evening he is a "king" among his friends and loved ones, a free man, redeemed from Egyptian bondage. And now, according to the report in John's Gospel, Jesus consciously transforms this ritual into its opposite. He does not have his hands washed; instead he himself washes the feet of his disciples. He explains this curious action by saying,

"Do you know what I have done to you? You call me Teacher and Lord— and you are right, for that is what I am. So if I, your Lord and Teacher, have washed your feet, you also ought to wash one another's feet. For I have set you an example, that you also should do as I have done to you.

Very truly, I tell you, servants are not greater than their master, nor are messengers greater than the one who sent them. If you know these things, you are blessed if you do them." (vv. 12–17)

This footwashing becomes understandable against the background of the Seder ritual. In the very night of his glorification the master, in whom the disciples see not only the king of this night but the king of the Jews, humbles himself. In this night in which all of Israel avows its redemption from servitude, Jesus insists that the servants (of God) must not become proud. He concludes his explanation of the newly instituted ritual, which is a transformation of the old one, with the remark "If you know these things, you are blessed if you do them."

We hear in this statement once again one of Jesus' basic principles, transmitted to us in the reading following Luke 6:4 found in the Codex Bezae: "If you know what you are doing, you are blessed; if you do not know what you are doing, you are accursed and a violator of the law."

This means that if, in full knowledge of the new covenantal relationship, the Seder celebration is transformed into a commemorative meal for Jesus, the innovators are to be praised as blessed. If the innovators are ignorant of the deep relationship, however, and transgress the laws of the Seder ritual, then they are nothing but accursed sinners.

The four deviations, or transformations, share the key statement "Do this in remembrance of me" (Luke 22:19). Jesus certainly did not, however, mean to do away with the Passover celebration, the Seder meal. Nothing of the kind. It was far from his intention to replace the Seder celebration with the Last Supper, the Eucharist, an event that developed completely independently of the fourteenth day of Nisan. His purpose was rather to take this meal that commemorates the Exodus from Egypt and append to it the memory of his own sacrificial deed, thereby creating a synthesis through the act of *zikkaron,* 'holy memory.'

Over this Seder celebration lies the shadow of the betrayal. The betrayer is Judas Iscariot, the most enigmatic figure of the gospel story. This figure continues to be oddly shadowy; only in Matthew and John does Judas acquire recognizable traits, and the Acts of the Apostles (1:18–20) provides a variant on his death. We know nothing else about this dark disciple Yehuda Bar-Shim'on. Some assume that he was the only Judean in the circle of Galileans around the Nazarene, but that too remains only a supposition based on his being called the "man from Cariot." Attempts to specify the location of Cariot in Judea have been unsuccessful. As mentioned earlier, it may have been one of the suburbs or towns (*krayoth*), but that still does not narrow the search. Perhaps, however—and this seems more likely to me— "Iscariot" may relate to Judas's membership in the Sicarians, the anti-Roman activists.

The motives for the betrayal are not at all clear. There is reason to suppose that his political or eschatological activism forced Judas into his apparent betrayal. Judas belongs to those who "hasten the end time" (cf. Isa. 60:22). He hopes to maneuver his master into a situation in which he cannot avoid revealing himself to be king of the Jews. Judas's deed, which the Evangelists understand as a necessary *skandalon*, or stumbling block, in the great process of salvation, was probably intended as a way of forcing the hand of his master to display his messianic powers. The anthroposoph Rudolf Steiner once asserted, with the combinatory logic for which he was renowned, that Judas Iscariot was a reincarnation of Judas Maccabaeus; this connection obviously owed in part to the similarity in names. Although I would not attribute any scientific or historical validity to Steiner's remark, it is useful as an intuitive characterization of Judas.

There is no reason to doubt the historicity of Judas; we cannot imagine anyone having wished to invent a character so embarrassing to the original community. Nevertheless, the figure of Judas did undergo mythologization.

Three traditions are recognizable in the composition of the figure of Judas: the midrash of the four sons in the Haggada; the midrash on the prophetic book of Zechariah; and the Qumran tradition of the sons of darkness, who are locked in battle with the sons of light.

The *rasha*, 'evil one,' is introduced as the second son of the Haggada among the four types of questioners. The Haggada says of him, "And since he excludes himself from the community, he denies what is most important . . . and even if he had been present, he would not have been redeemed." That is directly relevant to Judas, the "son of destruction" (John 17:12, variant reading). He excludes himself from the community of disciples, abandons the round table in order to go out and betray the master. He is present at the institution of the Last Supper, but he excludes himself from redemption by his deed. He therefore bears the traits of the "evil one" in the Haggada, and he himself is a son of the evil one, Satan, who enters and demonizes him. Satan is presented in the New Testament in totally personal terms, and here again we hear an echo of the book of Zechariah (3:1–2), for only in Zechariah and in the prologue to the book of Job does Satan appear personified in an Old Testament narrative (cf. also 1 Chron. 21:1 and Ps. 109:6).

And thus we again have an echo of the Zechariah midrash. Let us look at the passage in chapter 11, verses 12 and 13, as it can be applied to Judas. I quote from the translation by Martin Buber:

"If it seems right to you,
give me my wages;
but if not, keep them."
So they weighed out as my wages
thirty shekels of silver.
And *he* said to me,
"Throw it into the treasury,
the price that I am worth to you."
I took the thirty shekels of silver
and threw them into *his* house, the treasury.[79]

These shekels are the thirty pieces of silver that Judas receives from the Sanhedrin for the betrayal of Jesus' whereabouts and later, seized by regret, throws back into the temple treasury (Matt. 27:3–5). The typological aspect of this narrative is transparent. In his book on the twelve minor prophets, Karl Elliger correctly points out that "the relationship between the thirty shekels of silver in Zechariah and those of the Passion story is quite superficial, and the typological interpretation given by Matthew makes as little sense as the allegorical interpretation of the rabbis who discover here thirty commandments or thirty just men" (*Das Buch*, 165). It cannot be otherwise; in the story of Judas a historical event undergoes mythologization and typologization and is integrated into the Zechariah midrash.

Matthew clearly misunderstands this context and alludes to a statement of Jeremiah: "And they took the thirty pieces of silver, the price of the one on whom a price had been set, on whom some of the people of Israel had set a price, and they gave them for the potter's field, as the Lord commanded me" (Matt. 27:9–10). According to Matthew's version, with the betrayal money that is returned, the thirty pieces of silver, a field of clay soil in Jerusalem—*Chakal Dama*, 'the Field of Blood,'—is purchased by the chief priests as a burial site for foreigners. This purchase is associated in Matthew with the purchase of the field at 'Anathoth mentioned by the prophet Jeremiah (32:9). The purchase price there is not thirty but only seventeen shekels of silver, whereas Zechariah explicitly indicates the sum of thirty silver shekels. But neither should the field at 'Anathoth (a country town named for the Canaanite goddess 'Anath) be associated in any way with the Field of Blood. The field at 'Anathoth is in fact a sign of promise: "Houses and fields and vineyards shall again be bought in this land" (Jer. 32:15). Although a gloomy fate is already drawing over Jerusalem, the prophet must try to demonstrate, through the symbolic purchase of this field belonging to his cousin, that there is still reason for hope. How does this relate to Judas's Field of Blood?

The Zechariah midrash itself underwent a reinterpretation as well. The text, however, has nothing to do with this field, which according to the Acts of the Apostles (1:18) was purchased by Judas, but only with the reward of the thirty pieces of silver. In Zechariah it is a shepherd who receives the reward that he does not wish to keep. In the story of the Passion, the shepherd figure is messianically reinterpreted as the suffering servant of God who is sold for this price, just as Joseph was sold.

The third motif at work in the figure of Judas is that of the sons of darkness. It comes from the war scroll of Qumran, which describes the battle of the sons of light against the sons of darkness. The Gospel of John portrays Judas as a son of darkness, remarking with startling brevity, "So, after receiving the piece of bread, he immediately went out. *And it was night*" (13:30). It is the night "when no one can work"

(9:4)—no son of light, that is, whereas the son of darkness is in his element at night. Now this night is, of course, *Leil-Shimmurim,* the Night of Protection, in which the demons are thought to be impotent; but this too rests upon a reinterpretation. Precisely because Satan, through the betrayal of Judas, is given power over the son of man in this Night of Protection, his power is broken, for it is out of this betrayal—predestined, according to the faith of the community, in God's plan of salvation—that redemption emerges. The dialectic of this process is obviously kerygmatic. The disciples must have been stunned and confused by the betrayal, and its theological rationalization evolved only gradually.

Jesus, of course, must not appear to be surprised, since he knows about the betrayal in advance; indeed he more or less commands Judas to do his deed, or misdeed. Hans Blüher's speculation that Jesus used telehypnotic power to command Judas (*Die Aristie,* 126) seems to me completely off the mark, however, since the text is not concerned with a factual registration of processes but rather with their midrashic interpretation.

Matthew says that Judas hangs himself out of remorse for his betrayal (27:3–5). According to the Acts of the Apostles, "falling headlong [in his field], he burst open in the middle and all his bowels gushed out" (1:18).

There is a curious representation on one of the bronze portals of the cathedral at Benevento from the year 1279 (La Farge, *Europe,* pl. 118). The relief shows Judas hanging from a palm tree, his body burst apart and his entrails pouring out (the two versions, Matthew and Acts, are combined here). But the figure of the hanged Judas is embraced by an angel, who kisses the betrayer. What an insight on the part of this anonymous artist! Judas is depicted as the disciple who sacrifices himself, who sacrifices his own salvation, in order to instantiate the redemptive act of his master. Even as the curse lies upon him—"Occasions for stumbling are bound to come, but woe to the one by whom the stumbling block comes!" (Matt. 18:7)—grace, the angel, lifts him from above, for the sacrifice of Judas is no less necessary to the plan of salvation than Jesus' own path of martyrdom. Something of this insight has been retained in the theology of the Eastern church, whereas for the rest of Christendom, Judas remains a purely negative figure. The name "Judas," which became identified with the Jews, has an ominous quality about it, although in the New Testament there are altogether positive Judas figures; they include the brother of Jesus (Mark 6:3; Matt. 13:55), who is presumed to be the writer of the epistle of Jude. But only the figure of Judas Iscariot was projected onto the Jewish people, thus making them a Judas people, and leading to fatal consequences in the Jews' history of suffering. To the Christian mind, Judas remained the son of darkness in opposition to the children of light (John 12:36), entirely in the style of the Qumran tradition. But the Jews as a whole were viewed as the sons of darkness, which of course is an entirely different problem from that of Qumran.

Judas therefore stands before us overshadowed by three mythological motifs, yet recognizable as the figure of one who hastened the end time. Judas is the most tragic figure of the New Testament. He must bear the *skandalon*. He is testimony to the fact that the *sitra 'achara*, 'the demonic side' (as it is known in Jewish mysticism), is integrated into God's plan of salvation. He becomes the "night side of 'Elohim," an expression used by the Hebraic mythologist Oskar Goldberg. Once again the slayer is afoot on the Passover night, now in the form of the fallen disciple.

We determined earlier that the sacred number four distinguishes the ritual of the Pesach night. In apparent opposition, we have the statement of Rabbi Gamaliel, the teacher of Paul: "Whoever has not mentioned these three things at Pesach has not satisfied his obligation: the Pesach sacrifice, the matsa, and the bitter herb" (Mishna, Pesachim 10.5).

Rabbi Gamaliel mentions only three elements here. In an obvious effort to complete the number four, however, wine was added as an indispensable fourth element very early on. Thus we have the four ingredients of the feast: the paschal lamb, the unleavened bread of the matsa, the bitter herb, and the four prescribed cups of wine. All four of these elements are transformed in the Seder of Jesus of Nazareth. This is probably the root of the concept of the transubstantiation of the elements in the later Eucharist.

The paschal lamb becomes the Agnus Dei referred to by John the Baptist (John 1:29 and 36) and by John of Patmos (Rev. 5:12 and elsewhere). The matsa becomes the broken body of Jesus. The bitter herb becomes the symbol of the bitterness of his death, offered to him yet again on the hyssop stick; this hyssop points further to the smearing of the posts on the Hebrew houses in the land of Goshen in Egypt on the first Passover night.

Finally, the wine becomes the blood of Jesus that is poured out for the redemption of many.

11   *The Fifth Cup*

Immediately after the conclusion of the Seder meal, Jesus and his disciples retire to a somewhat isolated and peaceful grove of olive trees, a garden known as *Gath Shemani*, which means 'oil press' (Mark 14:32). Apparently, Gethsemane had served previously as the location for quiet gatherings of the master and his pupils. Here in the vicinity of the temple, but protected by the Kidron Valley from the noise coming frequently from this worship center, he would often meet with his closest friends to talk things over. His final journey as a free man leads him to this spot—and here, all too easily, he can be found by the betrayer, the dark disciple Judas, the man from the *krayoth*.

After the last, fateful meal, which turned into a moving farewell to his friends, Jesus feels compelled to go out into the full-moon night. Having celebrated the liturgy of the holy night with his disciples, he desires solitude in order to perform the *tefillath-yachid*, 'the individual's prayer,' which he has recommended to his pupils, telling them to "go into your room and shut the door and pray to your Father who is in secret" (Matt. 6:6).

It was common after the often sumptuous Seder meal to go out into the open air in order to experience the *Chag Ha'aviv*, the Feast of Spring. Pesach, after all, is not only a celebration of freedom, of salvation from the Egyptian house of bondage, a commemoration of the Exodus from *Mitsrayim* (Egypt); it is simultaneously, like all pilgrim festivals in Israel, a celebration of nature. The company at table, who would gather around the sacrificial lamb and celebrate the *Leil-Shimmurim*, the Night of Protection, enjoyed going out into the night after the meal. The rabbis took a dim view of these late-night walks after the Seder meal, since it often happened that they turned into Greek-style orgies. The rabbis prescribed, therefore, *'Ein maftirin 'achar hapesach 'afikoman*—that the Pesach meal should not end with going around from one party to another (BT, Pesachim 119b; JT, Pesachim 10.8). That is probably the original sense of the proscription still found in the Haggada of the Pesach night but now naively translated "One is not to enjoy any dessert after the Passover meal." The Greek loan word *'afikoman* (more correctly *epikomion*)[80] is ambiguous and can be interpreted in three ways: as dessert, as table music, or as a festive procession from one party to another.

As we have seen, from the meal commemorating the Exodus from Egypt, which was originally taken in great haste, a kind of Greek *symposion* developed which entailed lavish consumption of wine, lengthy table discussions, and reclining at table on pillows. To this *symposion* event were added flute playing and uninhibited merriment, with the result that the holy celebration sometimes degenerated into a bacchanal.

The little troop consisting of the rabbi from Nazareth and his remaining eleven followers, however, does not engage in the kind of revelry that one might associate with, say, the satyr play after a tragedy or the burlesque after a drama. Profound earnestness marks this band as it makes its familiar way to the olive grove at Gethsemane. All have been seized by a premonition of what is to come, and all are exhausted from the extreme emotional intensity they have been under. These men do not know what this night of decision will yet bring, and they are troubled by the unfathomable words of their master, who has been growing increasingly enigmatic.

And now he bids them to watch and wait—and to leave him alone. Their rabbi goes a stone's throw away in order to pray in solitude.

They know these prayerful exercises of their master and stand back timidly whenever he speaks with his Father in heaven, face to face with an immediacy of communication that leaves them awestruck.

It is oppressively hot. A *chamsin* or *sharav,* a dry desert wind, sweeps across Jerusalem, causing the man in prayer to break into a sweat. The night is so sultry that no one takes much notice of a young man who has slipped into their ranks somewhere along the way. Clad only in a shirt or tunic, he later, in the moment of danger, leaves his garment behind in the hands of the arresting officers to avoid being identified with the *chasidim,* the disciples of the foreign rabbi from Nazareth (Mark 14:51–52).

Jesus steps away from the company and prays. He falls upon his face, as one would pray in the temple, and cries out fearfully to his God (Mark 14:35; cf. Luke 22:44). Now, now he knows, with an absolutely certain feeling, that he is lost. Suddenly, it is clear to him that his path to Jerusalem was a path of martyrdom and that, standing in the shadow of the *'eved-hashem,* 'the servant of God,' he must take that suffering unto death upon himself in servile obedience.

And yet—is it not *Leil-Shimmurim,* the night in which the Lord by his strong arm so wondrously proved his faithfulness to his people Israel? The night in which he led Israel out of slavery into freedom? The night in which he spared his firstborn Israel even as he slew the firstborn of Egypt? But *Leil-Shimmurim* also—and especially—means the Night of Watching. In this night Israel is likened to its God, of whom it is written, "He who keeps Israel will neither slumber nor sleep" (Ps. 121:4). Neither shall Israel slumber nor sleep on such a night of miracles and grace. So it was that the story (from the Passover Haggada) was later told of the wise men at the time of the Bar-Kokheva rebellion. Led by Rabbi 'Akiva, they stayed awake the entire Pesach night in the little town of Benei Berak in order to tell over and over the story of God's act of salvation in Egypt. At last their students came to them and said, "Masters, it is time to say the morning prayer."

Now the master asks his disciples on this *Leil-Shimmurim* to watch and to pray. To watch for *him,* in order that this be the Night of Protection for him as well. But they are weak and drift off to sleep.

He, however, watches, shaken by the creaturely fear of death. One cannot read this report in the Gospels without being moved to tears. This is no hero standing here, no demigod, no myth! This is a man trembling in mortal fear for his very life. And in this hour of fear Jesus is especially close to us. It is inconceivable to me how anyone could interpret this human tragedy in the dogmatic terms of the twofold nature of Christ: true man and true God.

The one who stands before us now, seized by the fear of death, is the true man—man who is born with the fear of death—whose life is ever a living toward death, and whose thoughts and actions all represent a flight from death. Jesus prays, "My Father, if it is possible, let this cup pass from me; yet not what I want but what you want" (Matt. 26:39).

The man in prayer is still operating entirely within the Seder ritual that has just ended. He and his disciples have emptied four cups together. As we have seen, the fourfold act of God's salvation is celebrated with four cups at the Pesach meal in this holy night.

Vehotseithi, 'I have led you out.' The first cup is raised. *Vehitsalti,* 'I have rescued you.' The second cup is raised. *Vega'alti 'ethekhem,* 'And I have redeemed you.' Another cup, the third, is emptied, the cup of fulfilled salvation. *Velakachti 'ethekhem,* 'And I receive you, you sons of Israel.' This is the fourth and last cup, also a cup of salvation, the *kos yeshu'oth,* given to the people of the covenant, chosen through grace—the cup to which Jesus has given his own interpretation.

But is it really the last cup? That is the question asked by the lonely man in prayer in Gethsemane. Is there not yet a fifth cup foreseen in God's plan for him in this night? An awful cup, like the cup of delirium [81] that God offers those whom he has elected for destruction.

A fifth cup—the one that Jesus prays might pass from him—is possible, if controversial, in the ritual of the Seder night. The question of a fifth cup could never be decided; it was therefore postponed "until Elijah comes" (the usual talmudic expression in the case of undecided questions of doctrine [cf. note 73]). Popular belief seized on this development and called the fifth cup the "cup of Elijah," which is set out on the festive table in expectation of the return of the prophet. The prophet Elijah is expected to return as the herald of the Messiah, who will reconcile the hearts of parents and children (Mal. 4:6) before the awesome Day of Yahweh. Jesus now recognizes, however, that the Father is offering this cup of suffering to *him.*

Oh, if only this last cup, the cup of bitterness, could pass from him! Jesus longs to be like everyone else now, like one of the elected people of the covenant, to whom only four cups are offered: the cups of freedom, rescue, salvation, and election. If it is possible—if it is *still* possible—then let this last cup, this very last cup, pass from him. Earlier among his friends he had become so deeply resigned to his inevitable fate that he was able to avow, "I tell you, I will never again drink of this fruit of the vine (*peri-hagefen*) until that day when I drink it new with you in my Father's kingdom" (Matt. 26:29). He was referring to the *yayin hameshummar,* the drink prepared for the citizens of the kingdom of God.

Now, in this night when no one can work, when the slayer once again goes about as in the night of the Passover in Egypt, Jesus sees the image of the cup of the holy night with entirely different eyes. In this night of the four cups of salvation, the cup of destruction is meant for him.

He begs God to let *this* cup pass from him. And yet that is not his final word: *Not my will, Father, but yours be done.*

The author of the epistle to the Hebrews understood the problematic nature of this hour in a profound way. For the kerygma of the brotherhood of Jesus, the master was God's son. How, then, are we able to harmonize the contradiction between his human and divine will, his dejection and the sacrifice required of him by the Unfathomable One? The author of the epistle answers, "Although he was a Son, he learned obedience through what he suffered" (Heb. 5:8).

Obedience—the central, sorrowful motif of the Passion that begins in this hour, that reaches its culmination in this hour. In this prescient prayer of Jesus the bitter suffering unto death is already present as an emotional certainty. There is no more hope of rescue. He now humbles himself completely in the hands of the living God—a dreadful thing, according to Hebrews 10:31.

The Night God—the night side of God, the demonic, night side of 'Elohim—is now revealed to Jesus. This is the God who wrestled with

Jacob at night (Gen. 32:22–32). This is the God who visited his servant Moses in the night lodging on the road to Egypt, intending to kill him; only the blood of circumcision could appease the nocturnal-demonic Yahweh (Exod. 4:24–26). This is the God who made his terrifying rounds on this night in Egypt, slaying all the firstborn. Only the blood of the lamb, smeared with hyssop branches on the doorposts of the Hebrew homes in Goshen, could appease him.

This Unfathomable One thirsts for blood at night. Jesus sweats blood: "his sweat became like great drops of blood falling down on the ground," as Luke reports (22:44). This blood-sweat is not accepted, however. The blood of this man, who has been so horrifyingly elected, must be shed as redemption money for many. Now Jesus realizes that the kingdom of God can be purchased only with blood—his own blood, his own life, which God requires of him.

Of course, we have no details about Jesus' prayer. Because the disciples had gone to sleep, it was a prayer without witnesses. What has come down to us, therefore, is a piece of kerygmatic tradition of the early community. And yet we do sense that this could be a genuine prayer of Jesus—of the Jew who leaves the Seder meal to go out into the night of death, who must recognize that he, the elect of the elected, has been chosen for bloody martyrdom. In this hour he is Israel, which again and again is led into the Passion by the choosing and saving God, and which must suffer in order to save this fallen world. "Do you have eyes, and fail to see? Do you have ears, and fail to hear?" (Mark 8:18).

"Yet not what I want but what you want." Thus Jesus prays in death's dread, repeating the formula from the prayer that he had taught his disciples ("your will be done") but now varying and individualizing it: "Yet not what I want but what *you* want."

How peculiar this statement seems in contrast to the powerful *I* words of the Johannine Christ: "As you, Father, are in me and I am in you, may they also be in us" (John 17:21). Indeed, if they are one, how can there be any division between the will of Jesus and the will of God?

Only a later dogma could have turned this into an insoluble problem. If we look at it undogmatically, the holy unity is completed in this moment. In humbling his will to that of the Father, Jesus becomes one with him: he accepts the last cup of suffering from the hand of the Father. He does not want this cup. He does not want to suffer — any more than did the rabbi who, as he lay on his death bed surrounded by friends seeking to console him with thoughts of the reward to come in the afterworld for his suffering, dismissed them, saying, "Neither the suffering nor the reward!"

Still a young man, he loves the world and wants to live. He has no lust for suffering, unlike those later saints who mistakenly presumed to imitate him with their masochistic self-flagellation. He wants to rejoice together with all of Israel in this night of joy: *Father, let this cup of the last bitterness, which has been added to my Seder meal, pass from me.*

In the end, after all, Jacob was spared by the avenging Night God, though wrestling with this God in human form did leave him with a limp. Moses too was spared after his wife, Zipporah, offered the bloody foreskin of their son to God. The avenging God, satisfied by the blood of the lamb, also spared Israel on this Passover night, just as he spared Isaac, the son of the promise, who, lying bound upon the altar at Moriah, was redeemed by the blood of a ram. Might not some vicarious blood be found now as well for him, the son of man?

But greater even than his fear, which is so palpable, is Jesus' obedience. "The soul is yours, and the body is yours." Thus worshipers pray in the synagogue on the Day of Awe, Yom Kippur, in the same sense as Jesus did on that night: "and we are slaughtered daily for your sake, like sheep led to the slaughtering-house."

The consoler of the Babylonian Exile sang of the same thing in his *kina*, his threnody on the unknown blood witness, the servant of God:

He was oppressed, and he was afflicted,
yet he did not open his mouth;
like a lamb that is led to the slaughter,
and like a sheep that before its shearers is silent,
so he did not open his mouth. (Isa. 53:7)

That was the great and as yet unachieved ideal. "He," Jesus, again opens his mouth, prays that the fifth cup might pass from him. He has not yet fallen silent; it is still written of him, "In the days of his flesh, Jesus offered up prayers and supplications, with loud cries and tears, to the one who was able to save him from death, and he was heard because of his reverent submission" (Heb. 5:7).

The epistle to the Hebrews says candidly, "with loud cries and tears." Jesus' Oriental-Jewish nature, wild and unchained, is depicted realistically here. He does not yet behave as a servant, with silent submission. He will accept this silent submission and reject active resistance only at the moment of his arrest, shortly after having wrestled in prayer. Again he seizes on the image of the undesired, final, supernumerary cup of his last Seder meal, saying to Peter, "Am I not to drink the cup that the Father has given me?" (John 18:11). Now at last he will say yes to his fate. It is not easier, but it *makes more sense* when accepted as part of God's plan. He drinks the fifth cup. And *that* is what is meant by the final words "It is finished," which he utters in dying on the cross (John 19:30), having swallowed the bitter vinegar handed to him on a sponge attached to the hyssop stick (symbol of the first Passover night in Egypt). A terrible caricature of the festive cup. The conclusion to the tragedy.

Stronger, or at least certain now, as a result of his solitary struggle in prayer, Jesus returns to the slumbering disciples—even as fate approaches in the figure of the last disciple, *Judas.* It is Judas who leads a detachment of soldiers to the spot where Jesus' disciples are gathered in the Garden of Gethsemane. The detachment obviously comprises a mixed cohort from the temple police, the palace guard of the officiating chief priest, and several Roman legionnaires under a Roman tribune (John 18:12), whose presence gives legality to the arrest.

It is an armed detachment: the Romans carry swords; the Jews, clubs. It was apparently assumed that Jesus and his disciples would offer physical resistance. That is hardly surprising, since the accuser himself, Judas, belonged to the activists and could not imagine any other response. But in fact he now sees his master submit to the cohort without violence.

Judas approaches him and greets him in the traditional way: *Shalom 'aleykha Rabbi u-Mori,* 'Peace be with you, my Rabbi and Teacher,' and gives him a kiss.

Much ink has been spilled in the attempt to understand this kiss of Judas. In the Gospels it is presented as a sign of recognition. But surely it would have sufficed simply to point at Jesus and say, "There is the man you seek!"

But Judas kisses his master, and with this kiss the death of the Just One is sealed. That is what the kiss signifies.

The motif of *mitha bineshika,* 'death by a kiss,' is disguised, distorted, even gruesomely caricatured. In the haggadic view, a Just One is to die with a kiss that is the kiss of God. This conception derives from the story of the death of Moses, alone on the mountain where, according to Jewish legend, God kisses Moses' soul away. It is not the horrible angel of death that approaches the Just One here; God the Father bends down, kisses his son, and takes back the soul he had given him.

Something of this conception of the kiss of death reserved for the Just One is implied in Judas's kiss. With this kiss Jesus' fate is sealed. God, who makes use of both Satan and the dark disciple in his plan of salvation, sends the kiss to the one selected for death as a *sign of recognition.* Judas's kiss is a signal, not only for the arresting officers but for Jesus as well.

Jesus turns to the fallen disciple and says, "*Friend,* do what you are here to do" (Matt. 26:50). Jesus himself fulfills the commandment from the Sermon on the Mount literally: "But I say to you, Love your enemies" (Matt. 5:43). He now calls the enemy a friend, no longer simply a disciple. The distant relationship between master and pupil is dropped: "Friend"! Precisely in this hour. As the Gospel of John presents it, at the moment when Jesus reveals his identity, everyone falls to the ground (18:6). That is attested by no other Gospel, but Judas may well have fallen to his knees—Judas, even *before* the Apostle Thomas fell in adoration at Jesus' feet—overcome by the serenity, calm, and forgiving love of the teacher who greets him, at this moment, as "Friend."

Peter, no doubt along with some of the other disciples, thinks that they should put up a fight. He draws his sword and, according to John's account (18:10), cuts off an ear of one Malchus, servant of the high priest. Jesus immediately heals the wound. The story is obviously a legend that was not thought through to its proper conclusion, for the attacker, Peter, who leads the active resistance, would have been arrested at once. That does not happen; in fact, he is allowed to accompany Jesus, who is taken into custody. He is repeatedly asked whether he does not belong to the band of Galilean followers of Jesus; he strongly denies that he does. No, Peter offers no resistance; like all the other disciples, he takes to his heels. Because they are certain that the anointed king, this man Jesus whom they regard as the Messiah, the savior, is about to reveal himself in his God-given might, the disciples do not interfere; Jesus is simply allowed to be arrested and led away.

"Truly I tell you, this very night, before the cock crows, you will deny me three times" (Matt. 26:34). Thus Jesus speaks to Peter, who had boasted so loudly of his undying loyalty to his master. The cock must be taken as symbolic here. Why? Could Jesus not simply have said, "Before morning comes you will betray me three times"? Instead, he chooses the imagery of the cock, alluding to the liturgical formula in the first benediction of the morning prayer: "Blessed art thou, Lord our God, king of the universe, who has given the cock (sechvi) the intelligence to distinguish between day and night."

The cock has the ability to distinguish between day and night, and thus presumably between light and darkness as well, as understood by the Qumran community. *But not you, Peter, Shim'on Bar-Yona, whom I took to be the pillar and foundation of my community.* What an irony in the image of the cock!

Jesus does not resist arrest. He may have anticipated being arrested in the forecourt of the temple, where he taught publicly. But the authorities were careful to avoid that scenario—to avoid any commotion at all. Jesus was to be arrested at night and in secret, for his following among the population of Jerusalem and the pilgrims attending the festival was too large.

He is first led away to the palace of Caiaphas, the officiating high priest, where the night hearing proceeds. This is the hearing preliminary to the trial before the procurator, Pontius Pilate.

12 *The Longest Short Trial*

It took only a short trial to dispose of Jesus of Nazareth. That short trial has gone on, however, longer than any other in the history of the world. The trial of Jesus is surely the greatest and most consequential of all trials, despite its having been concluded in exceptionally short order.

When the nation of Israel was founded in 1948, Christian theologians from around the world filed a number of petitions with the Jerusalem chancellery, seeking a revision of the trial of Jesus after nearly two thousand years. One of the first to file such a petition was a Dutch engineer by the name of Robbé Groskamp.

Groskamp reasoned as follows: now that the Jewish people at last had their own sovereign system of justice, the time had come for a legal revision of the trial of Jesus of Nazareth. Dr. Moshe Smoira, a legal scholar and chief justice of Israel from 1948 to 1954, proceeded to examine the validity of these petitions in detail. In the end, however, he had to deny them, given that all court records necessary for such a revision were missing and that the only extant records were the tendentious reports in the Gospels of Mark (14:53–15:20), Matthew (26:57–27:31), Luke (22:66–23:25), and John (18:12–19:16).[82] The reports in the Gospels were too contradictory to justify revisiting the trial, and no reports of the trial were to be found in talmudic sources.[83]

Legal minds may have difficulty in reconstructing a basis for revisiting the most significant trial in the history of the world. Historians, on the other hand, have means of eliciting a good deal of evidence that exists, as it were, between the lines of the Gospels. After centuries in which only theologians had concerned themselves with the trial of Jesus, toward the end of the eighteenth century, historians finally began to have an equal say; jurists did not join this investigation, however, until the mid–twentieth century. Among them was Haim Cohn, a judge in the Jerusalem Court of Appeals. In October 1966, on the fifth anniversary of Dr. Smoira's death, Justice Cohn delivered a speech before a gathering of lawyers at the Hebrew University in Jerusalem, in which he examined the legal issues involved in the trial of Jesus. We will have more to say about this below.

But first, two lengthy works on the trial of Jesus should be mentioned: *Der Prozeß Jesu* (The trial of Jesus) by the Jesuit Josef Blinzler, and *On the Trial of Jesus* by the Jewish legal historian Paul Winter.

Blinzler's premise is that Jews unquestionably must bear the primary guilt for the condemnation of Jesus: "The primary responsibility is on the side of the Jews," Blinzler affirms (334). By contrast, Paul Winter's conclusion, based upon the report of the trial used by Mark, is that no criminal proceeding against Jesus took place within the judicial system of the Jews.

In his memorial lecture, published in 1967 as "Reflections on the Trial and Death of Jesus," Justice Cohn took a position similar to Winter's. Cohn argues that even prior to the proceedings against Jesus of Nazareth before the procurator Pontius Pilate, the high priest Caiaphas had made a final attempt to persuade Jesus to withdraw his self-proclamation as "King of the Jews." After this failed, and the defendant refused to cooperate with the Jewish authorities, Caiaphas had no alternative but to hand Jesus over to the Romans.

Cohn thus restores the honor of Caiaphas and the Sanhedrin (this is developed further in his 1971 book *Trial and Death of Jesus,* chap. 5).

In his tendentious book on Jesus, the New Testament scholar Ethelbert Stauffer also undertakes to restore the honor of Caiaphas, but in a much different way:

> The sentence of capital punishment handed down by the Great Sanhedrin did not amount to official murder by the court but was completely justifiable under the law. Jesus' violations of the sabbath were massive and overt, his assaults on the Torah provocative in the extreme. Under these circumstances his "powerful deeds, omens, and portents" had to be branded, in keeping with Deuteronomy 13:1–5, as arts of enticement of false prophets (cf. Mark 3:22).

Stauffer once remarked to me in private, "I am probably the only person today who supports the restoration of Caiaphas's honor." This restoration of honor strikes me, however, as dubious, since Stauffer otherwise pictures Caiaphas as a ruthless Grand Inquisitor, though one who upholds the formal letter of the law (*Jesus and His Story*, 121–28). The Torah infractions alleged by Stauffer are nowhere mentioned in the trial reports of the Gospels as evidence against Jesus of Nazareth.

This brief overview has taken into consideration only a handful of the many interpretations of the trial of Jesus. Blinzler's wide-ranging and highly learned study defends the dogmatic thesis that the Jews bear the major responsibility for the cross. Winter takes the path, either consciously or unconsciously, of the Jewish apologists who seek to deflect, if not remove, the guilt from the Jews for the condemnation of Jesus. Haim Cohn, in arguing that Caiaphas attempted to convince Jesus to recant, operates on this same track. Stauffer wishes to demonstrate a fundamental faith conflict between the Torah and the New Testament.

In my estimation, all these interpretations do violence to the sources. The trial against Jesus of Nazareth was a political trial. At its root lay the question of the right of the threatened Jewish people to survive in a land occupied and oppressed by the Romans.

There is a kind of scientific dogmatism that is blind to this insight, because it ignores the relevance of the fourth Gospel. Although the so-called Ur-Mark, from which Matthew is presumed to have borrowed, never fails to fascinate, and although Luke's expansions are accepted as valid at least in part, John is typically dismissed out of hand. But it is precisely in John's Gospel that some real light is shed on the trial of Jesus. Here we find the event's true motivation in the words of Caiaphas to the Sanhedrin that "it is better for you to have one man die for the people than to have the whole nation destroyed" (11:50). John reminds the reader of Caiaphas's statement later on when Jesus is brought before the high priest (18:14).

We have only to visualize the situation in which the oppressed Jews were languishing in their occupied homeland. It is altogether reasonable that the authorities should have done everything in their power to neutralize a troublemaker like Jesus of Nazareth, to whom so many of the common people were flocking, including political activists of the likes of Judas Iscariot.

Caiaphas and his friends realized with whom they were dealing in Pontius Pilate. Philo of Alexandria claims that King Agrippa I called Pilate an "unbending, cruel, and evil man" (*De legatione,* 301). Josephus reports that Pilate ordered the slaughter of unarmed Jewish pilgrims as well as Samaritans (*Jewish Antiquities,* 18.3.2, 18.4.1).

The New Testament, particularly the Gospel of John, takes pains to relieve Pilate of his guilt, since the first Christians, after having separated from the Jews, hoped to work out an acceptable relationship with the Roman imperial authorities. But no amount of softening can avoid confirming the gruesome character of the procurator. Luke 13:1 reports, "At that very time there were some present who told [Jesus] about the Galileans whose blood Pilate had mingled with their sacrifices." This sentence apparently slipped unintentionally into the text; Fritz Rienecker observes that it concerns an event "not known to secular history" (*Evangelium des Lukas,* 328). The story seems to be that a band of Galilean travelers, on their way to Jerusalem for a pilgrim festival, was wiped out by the legionnaires of Pilate, presumably for protesting either the images of Caesar or certain signs of Roman authority in the temple. Caiaphas and his company perhaps saw the massacre as a warning of an imminent pogrom against Galileans and therefore decided to neutralize this latest rebel from Galilee by taking him into custody.

Caiaphas, the officiating high priest, and the members of the Sanhedrin would hardly have been decent Jews and lawyers—"Torah lawyers," as Stauffer is wont to call them (*Jerusalem und Rom*, chaps. 5 and 6)—if they had simply handed over the Galilean to the Romans without a hearing. Their interest was to find formal grounds on which to justify, both politically and on the basis of Halakha (religious law), handing Jesus over to the Romans.

By drawing evidence from all four Gospels, without preference for one over the others, we may distinguish several phases in the trial of Jesus. Immediately after his arrest in Gethsemane Jesus is brought before Annas, the father-in-law of Caiaphas, for a preliminary hearing (John 18:13–15). Annas's son-in-law has already made him aware that Jesus represents a public danger. As the only judge present, Annas proceeds with the preliminary hearing in a general way, questioning Jesus about his doctrine and his disciples. It would appear that Annas was able to draw on some previous testimony (possibly that of John the Baptist). I am inclined to accept that this preliminary hearing did indeed take place before Annas, who then transferred the defendant to the court. The court, under the jurisdiction of the officiating high priest, then formulated three complaints:

(1) Profanation of the temple (Mark 14:57–58). The harsh words of Jesus regarding the temple, which he believed was worthy of being torn down and replaced in three days at the same location by a true temple, were felt by the prosecution to be especially troubling. It is important to understand that the Sadducees, the party of the high priests constituting the majority in the Sanhedrin, had become extremely sensitive to profanation of the temple.[84] They had two reasons for their sensitivity. One was that the number of synagogues was increasing at this time, a tendency that threatened to eclipse the status of the temple as the cultic center. The priesthood looked unfavorably on this tendency, since in the synagogue the prayer service was, as it still is, conducted by the laity. The concept of the synagogue as a place of prayer to God in spirit and in truth—that is, as a place of verbal worship rather than of sacramental, sacrificial worship in the Holy of Holies—had by this time penetrated the temple itself; a synagogue had already been located there. The second reason was that the sect of Qumran, with which Jesus was obviously connected and which originally had been a saducean sect before breaking with the rul-

ing priestly dynasty, had completely severed ties with the temple in Jerusalem.

(2) Tax evasion with respect to the imperial government (Luke 23: 2). In our discussion of the coin of tribute, we emphasized that tax evasion was one of the accusations leveled against Jesus in his trial. Although Jesus avoided the trap, witnesses obviously were found who interpreted his ambiguous answer as favoring tax evasion. This would have provided the political motive, an important condition for arguing the necessity of remanding Jesus to Pontius Pilate.

(3) Presumptive messiahship. This is the third, and central, motive for the internal Jewish involvement with the case. Caiaphas himself asks the pointed question, "Are you the Messiah, the Son of the Blessed One?" (Mark 14:61; cf. Luke 22:66–68). In Matthew 26:63–64 he is even more specific. He does not simply ask; he *adjures* the plaintiff under oath to "tell us if you are the Messiah, the Son of God."

In this interrogation it is striking that the Messiah is designated "the Son of the Blessed One" and "the Son of God." This should not be understood in the sense of the later Christian dogma of the only begotten son of God. According to Psalm 2:7, God says to the king at the moment of coronation, "You are my son; today I have begotten you." When a king of the Jews mounts the throne, he is considered to be, as it were, the newly begotten son of God (a conception also attested in Psalm 89:27–29). In not explicitly denying that he is "the Messiah, the Son of the Blessed One" (Mark 14:61–62), Jesus may also be making a veiled reference to himself as the King of the Jews in the sense of Psalm 2:7 (i.e., as son of God). However that may be, he is purposefully evasive (Matt. 26:64), implying only that he is the "Son of Man."

To Caiaphas's order to "tell us if you are the Messiah, the Son of God," Jesus replies ambiguously with the famous words 'Atta 'amarta, 'You have said so' (Matt. 26:64). This answer can be interpreted variously, depending on the element that is stressed: *You* have said so, or you have *said* so. Employing the same tactic, Jesus later responds in a similar fashion to Pilate's question, "Are you the King of the Jews?" (Mark 15:2).[85]

After the preliminary hearing before Annas, Jesus is led to the Sanhedrin for a pretrial in a night session; here the witnesses provide unsatisfactory statements. A sufficient justification is being sought for turning this dangerous insurrectionist over to the Romans, but the strict rules of protocol, which we know from the tractate Sanhedrin in the Talmud, disqualify the conflicting statements in Mark 14:53–65 as unreliable. A great deal has been written, predominantly from the Jewish side, against the credibility of the trial reports in the Gospels, quite simply because they contradict Jewish trial procedure. I do not agree with this particular objection, however. People in our own time have been eyewitnesses to far too many political trials, both in Western and Eastern Europe, as well as in Africa and Asia and in America, to be persuaded by this type of evidential reasoning. Political trials, which are predicated on reasons of state, are not always conducted in harmony with every paragraph of legal protocol. Besides, trial procedures were not even codified until much later, after the judicial system had become an autonomous branch of government. In the tractate Sanhedrin we have an example of ideal trial procedure, though it was by no means always followed. The Talmud in fact singles out the clique around Annas and Caiaphas for sharp criticism: "'Abba Sha'ul Ben-Botnith spoke for 'Abba Yosef Ben-Chanin about people of that kind: 'Woe is me because of the family of Boethos; woe is me because of their cudgels [these are the clubs mentioned at the arrest of Jesus]; . . . woe is me because of the family of Annas; woe is me because of their whisperings. . . . They themselves were once high priests and their sons-in-law were trustees of the temple, and their servants beat the people with sticks" (BT, Pesachim 57a).

Where such a clique intends to remain in power at any cost, it is hardly surprising, when push comes to shove, that finer points of legal protocol are ignored.

It has been objected that the Jewish authorities ignored two external circumstances in the trial against Jesus of Nazareth: for one thing, the proceedings took place at night; for another, they took place in the official quarters of Caiaphas, which probably adjoined the apartment of his father-in-law. According to the rules of trial law, a legitimate hearing—and this applied a fortiori to capital punishment trials—could take place only in the daytime and in the temple's Hall of Hewn

Stones, the official seat of the court. Moreover, a death sentence that was handed down unanimously was considered legally invalid, since it was thought to reflect bias on the part of the court.

With regard to the nighttime hearing, the Evangelists themselves are conscious of the problem. According to Mark 15:1, the Sadducees, the party of the high priests, summon the Pharisees, the party of the legal experts, for a consultation only the following *morning*: that is, only after the hearing of the previous night (cf. Matt. 27:1-2). What this seems to indicate is that after the preliminary hearing before Annas, the pretrial takes place among the men belonging to the sadducean clique. In the morning, as soon as the trial rules allow, the Pharisee members of the Sanhedrin are co-opted in order to ensure a full assembly of seventy-one judges, and it is agreed to hand Jesus over to Pilate. In this way they are able to skirt the obstacle of a nighttime judgment.

Regarding the location of the Sanhedrin in the *Lishkath Hagazith*, 'the Hall of Hewn Stones,' Haim Cohn notes that the Sanhedrin is thought to have abandoned this chamber and withdrawn to a provisional location known as the *chanuth*, 'tent of commerce,' forty years before the destruction of the temple in 70 C.E., but Cohn himself doubts that this is historically valid (*Trial and Death*, 346-49). I think, however, that it does imply at least that sessions were sometimes held *also* outside of the Hall of Hewn Stones around this time, particularly when there was no plan to carry out an execution but only to remand a prisoner to the Roman occupational authority. Whether the Jews possessed the right of capital punishment at that time is debatable. The Gospels indicate that they did not, although we know that the stoning of Stephen took place (Acts 6:8-7:60) *after* the execution of Jesus. That this may have amounted to some kind of vigilante justice seems more than doubtful to me. Even if no formal right of capital punishment existed any longer, such acts could be carried out occasionally without stirring up the Romans over Jews dealing with Jews according to their own law.

In the case of Jesus of Nazareth, however, publicly remanding him to Rome was meant to remove any suspicion that the dangerous and cruel Pontius Pilate had acted counter to the temple and the population of Jerusalem, or to the multitude of pilgrims at Passover.

The unanimous decision was therefore acceptable to the Sanhedrin, since it involved only the *remanding* of a rebel considered dangerous to the state.

Jesus of Nazareth does not defend himself before the Sanhedrin. He knows he will not be believed and therefore prefers to focus exclusively on the fact that he has taught publicly rather than in secret, implying that further questioning would be superfluous. During his period of public ministry, Jesus in fact never did proclaim himself to be the Messiah, as we have noted repeatedly. In the present situation, however, he considers it beneath his dignity to defend himself in front of his sworn enemies. He will adopt the same behavior a few hours later before Pontius Pilate.

The high priest Caiaphas tears his undergarment at the moment when Jesus alludes to his kingly nature (Mark 14:61–62). Haim Cohn explains this action according to the Jewish custom of mourning: the mourner is to rip apart, or rend, his garment (*Trial and Death,* 129–34). This may be the correct interpretation of the gesture, whereas the Gospels take it as a gesture of outrage at the blasphemy of the accused. However that may be, there is still another symbolic meaning in the act of rending the garment of the high priest: as a narrative technique, it precedes the rending of the curtain in the Holy of Holies at the hour of Jesus' death on the cross (Matt. 27:50–51).

In the tearing of the garment the bond between Jesus and his people is also torn and his deliverance to Pontius Pilate decided.

This act initiates the second or, more precisely, the fourth phase of the judicial process. It is the second insofar as the trial now is transferred from an internal Jewish sphere to the Jewish-Roman sphere; it is the fourth if we divide the internal Jewish process into three segments:

(1) the preliminary hearing before Annas;

(2) the nighttime preliminary trial before Caiaphas;

(3) the full session of the Sanhedrin, including the Pharisees, in the early morning hours.

The night of decision is past. For Jesus of Nazareth and his disciples it was the night of the Pesach. For Caiaphas and his company it was the night before the Passover meal, the period of *bedikath-*

chamets, the removal of the leaven prior to the feast. The New Testament itself explains this removal in a figurative, theological sense as the removal of the leaven of the heart: that is, of sinful thoughts and biases (1 Cor. 5:7–8). For the Sanhedrin, however, this process meant both seeking out and removing a dangerous kind of leaven: *bedikath-chamets* is the search for leaven; *bittul chamets* is the destruction, or burning, of the leaven. This Passover motif is implicit here.

The decisive phase in the procedure against Jesus of Nazareth begins when he is brought before Pontius Pilate. Here the charge of Jesus' presumptuous claim to royalty is of central importance; remarkably, the problem of tax evasion is not explicitly mentioned. The presumption of the royal title is tantamount to lèse majesté, according to the *Lex Iulia,* the prevailing form of law, and punishable by the most horrifying of all death sentences: crucifixion.

The hearing before Pilate is limited to the question of kingship. Again, Jesus prefers for the most part to remain silent and, when he does speak, to utter only the ambiguous phrase "You say so." The pains taken by the Gospels to protect Pilate are striking. Among the motifs employed are the legendary dream of the wife of Pilate (Matt. 27:19) and, most famously, the scene in which Pilate washes his hands of the whole affair (Matt. 27:24). The latter event is patently false, for the same Pilate who says to Jesus "I am not a Jew, am I?" (John 18:35) can hardly have known or been alluding to the statement in Psalms that is alluded to in Matthew: "I wash my hands in innocence" (Ps. 26:6; cf. 73:13).

The Evangelist who sees most deeply into the antagonism between Jesus and Pilate is John, though John too does his utmost to rationalize Pilate's actions and to depict him as nothing more than a facilitator of the wishes of the mass of Jews crying out for Jesus' crucifixion. To the summarizing remark of Pilate "So you are a king," Jesus replies, "You say that I am a king," and he adds, "For this I was born, and for this I came into the world, to testify to the truth." Pilate responds, "What is truth?" (18:37–38).

Pilate's question "What is truth?" reveals the chasm that exists between Jesus and his judge. In the exchange between Jesus and Caiaphas, belief contended against belief; what was at stake, beyond all political implications, was a decision of faith. In the dialogue with

Pilate, on the other hand, there is no common language. Pilate does not ask about the truth but puts truth in question. For him there is no truth, only power. Whoever has power is in the right and possesses authoritative truth; truth is, in the final analysis, what is useful to Rome.

During the course of the hearing, Pilate discovers that Jesus is a Galilean, and since his own territorial prince, Herod Antipas, is then residing in Jerusalem on the occasion of the Passover celebration, Pilate remands the accused Galilean to his prince (Luke 23:6–7). With that, the trial enters a new phase, if only an entr'acte. Herod has heard a great deal by this time about his famous, or infamous, subject Jesus of Nazareth and is eager to know personally this dangerous man (Luke 23:8), who, as he is aware, has called him a fox (Luke 13:32). But these encounters never turn into conversations. Before his Jewish judges Jesus remains taciturn; before Pilate he is almost completely mute; and before the collaborator Herod he says nothing at all.

Too little note has been taken of the fact that after this disappointing encounter, Herod sends Jesus back to Pilate in a white[86] garment (Luke 23:11). This gesture must be looked at together with the scene in which Pilate's soldiers put a purple coat on Jesus as he is being mocked and scourged (Mark 15:17). The texts then mention that Jesus is allowed to put on his own clothing again before the crucifixion. This twofold changing of garments (whether it actually took place or not) with its three-stage sequence (original-new-original) serves a narrative purpose, in that it has implications for Jesus' *death of atonement,* which is meant to serve as a substitution for the great Day of Atonement, Yom Kippur. In the ritual of the Day of Atonement (Lev. 16:4, 24) the high priest, who carries out the act of atonement, exchanges his white vestments for a golden garment, only to have his original vestments brought to him again following his completion of the atonement ritual. This sequence is explicitly described in the Mishna (Yoma, 7.3–4):

> If he (the high priest) read[87] in linen garments, he sanctified his hands
> and feet, stripped, went down and immersed himself.... They brought
> him golden raiments and he put them on and sanctified his hands and
> feet; and he went out and prepared his ram.... He (then) sanctified his

hands and feet, stripped, and went down and immersed himself. . . . They brought him white garments and he put them on.

For the Gospel writers, the great Day of Atonement is annulled by the sacrifice of Golgotha. Jesus is viewed as the high priest, as this changing of garments clearly symbolizes. In the eyes of his disciples the white garment worn before Herod symbolizes Jesus as the true high priest; the purple garment of mockery symbolizes him as the true king. There is also a response to Qumran implied here. At Qumran the distinction was made between a priestly and a kingly Messiah, a distinction to which the epistle to the Hebrews alludes. The white garment before Herod and purple garment before the legionnaires symbolize Jesus as both the high priestly and the kingly Messiah; his own simple garment, by contrast, represents the suffering Messiah.

After Herod Antipas sends Jesus back to Pilate, Luke remarks, "That same day Herod and Pilate became friends with each other; before this they had been enemies" (23:12). Here one can speak of unification through the enemy. The opponents Pilate and Herod, rivals for the favor of Caesar, become friends through their common enemy, Jesus of Nazareth. Thus the historians understand it, but the Gospel texts anticipate the epistle to the Ephesians: "For he is our peace; in his flesh he has made both groups into one and has broken down the dividing wall, that is, the hostility between us" (2:14).

Ephesians, of course, is speaking of the legal wall between Jews and gentiles, but the wall of enmity between the Roman Pilate and the half-Jew Herod Antipas is removed by Jesus as well: thus Luke's remark. The sworn enemies of Jesus are the first to be reconciled through him.

The Barabbas episode, which follows (Mark 15:6–15; Matt. 27:15–26; Luke 23:18–25; John 18:39–19:16), must also be understood in this sense. In keeping with the Passover festival amnesty, Pilate declares his willingness to free one of the accused men, either Barabbas—a political prisoner charged with insurrection and murder—or Jesus. While the crowd voices its desire that Barabbas be pardoned, Pilate repeatedly attempts, with unmistakable irony, to send their "king" back to the Jews. But they do not wish to see this "king" again and demand that he be done away with.

A great exegetical riddle surrounds this Barabbas pericope. Whether the events as portrayed here are historically accurate is not certain. In the first place, there is the problem of the so-called Paschal privilege, the release of a condemned prisoner on the occasion of the Passover feast; this privilege is not documented in any historical source.[88] The Gospel texts speak of it as though it were common knowledge, but that cannot have been so. Furthermore, a difficulty exists within the narrative itself. If, in fact, Jesus was removed primarily because the leading Jewish estate feared that a rebel might endanger the community, then it is difficult to understand why this same group of leaders should have contemplated releasing another insurrectionist.

Several manuscripts of the Gospel of Matthew (27:16–17) provide the full name of Barabbas: *Jesus* Barabbas. The name suggests a possible interpretation of this episode as a soteriological transformation of the *lex talionis* (an eye for an eye, a tooth for a tooth): *Jesus for Jesus,* in other words. The innocent Jesus is sacrificed in lieu of the guilty Jesus. A similar conception is contained in a later Jewish ritual, the so-called *kappara* rite, where, on the eve of the Day of Atonement, the person who prays brandishes a cock about his head and sacrifices it for his sins. An analogous wordplay may underlie this practice as well: *gever tachath gever,* 'a man for a man,' for in Hebrew the word *gever* can be used for both a cock and a man.

Viewed in this way, Jesus for Jesus is the deeper meaning of the Barabbas episode, and Barabbas is the first fruit of the redemption through the sacrificial death of Jesus.[89]

To later editors, however, it seemed unfitting that a "bandit," as Barabbas is derogatorily and inappropriately described (John 18:40), should bear the name of Jesus. Furthermore, a certain religious fear developed, given the reverence for a name now considered holy (Phil. 2:9–10), of calling anyone else by the name of Jesus, particularly someone of dubious reputation. But at the time, the name Jesus (Yeshuʻ or Yeshuaʻ) was widely in use. We think, for example, of Jesus Sirach, the author of the apocryphal Book of Wisdom. Even in the New Testament another Jesus is attested, the servant to Paul who sends his greetings in the letter to the Colossians (4:11). There the name of Jesus is altered to Justus: "And Jesus who is called Justus greets you." In the Christian community, apparently, whether out of respect or fear, the holy name of Jesus was not given to others, and persons already having the name were renamed, as in "Jesus who is called Justus." In the case of Barabbas, the first name was simply struck—and with it, the very point of the original narrative.

Still, I cannot go as far as Herbert Landau, who understands "Barabbas" as Jesus' honorific title Bar-Rabban, 'Son of a Rabbi,' and assumes that the narration was transfigured for apologetic reasons (311–12). In other words, the people were actually demanding the release of Jesus. But this simply cannot have been so, when we take into account the general spirit of all four versions of the narrative.

In fact, an entirely different issue is probably being raised here. In the Gospel reports the people demand the release of Barabbas and the condemnation of Jesus. Pilate is portrayed as hesitant and weak. He finds no guilt in Jesus, but because he wants to avoid a falling-out with the people over his leadership, he ultimately gives in. It has been pointed out again and again that this presentation of the facts is unconvincing and that, as we noted above, what is in fact mirrored in this report is the effort of the young Christian community to achieve a tolerable relationship with the Roman national authority.

There are two parties, then: Rome and Jerusalem. But a third is missing in this version: the group of Jesus' disciples, which in fact constituted a *chavura,* a more or less self-contained community. The concept of the *chavura* is exemplified here. Two parties must have formed out of the larger mass of people: the *chavura* of Jesus of Nazareth and the *chavura* of Barabbas. It appears, however, that Barabbas alone had highly vocal adherents, determined people who dared to demand of the Roman procurator the release of their partisan, whereas the disciples of Jesus had long since taken flight. Peter's betrayal, which is described at such length, is merely one indication of that. Just as Peter betrays Jesus, so all the other disciples betray him as well, probably even his beloved disciple John, who, though present for a time at the preliminary hearing (John 18:15), offers not a single word in defense of Jesus. The only betrayer to behave in an accountable fashion is Judas. Seized with remorse, he commits suicide.

After having betrayed his Lord three times, Peter weeps bitterly, but later on he allows himself to be venerated as the head of the community of Jesus.

The adherents of Barabbas stand beside their comrade in the hour of danger. The adherents of Jesus, though obviously quite numerous, do not dare to do so. That must have been an embarrassing fact for later Christian historiographers (though this term may not be altogether fitting for the Gospel writers). This difficulty may explain why the version of the story that has come down to us could not be dismissed by the later kerygmatic tradition.

Although no outcry on behalf of Jesus rises from the horde of people gathered before the residence of Pontius Pilate—only for reasons of ritualistic purity on the eve of the Passover does the group not enter the administration building of the heathen Pilate—one hideous cry does ascend toward heaven in Matthew 27:25: "His blood be on us and on our children!" The text continues (v. 26), "So he released Barabbas for them; and after flogging Jesus, he handed him over to be crucified." This self-cursing of a stirred-up mob in a moment of political mass hysteria would become a historical curse on the Jewish people. The utterance, which is documented only once in the Gospels, has all too readily found terrible resonance down through the centuries. On the basis of this alleged self-cursing, innumerable acts of violence have been perpetrated on Jews by so-called Christians. There is no way to know whether this cry was ever in fact uttered. I consider it at least possible; although the formulation is unusual, a similar formulation does exist in the oath of David (2 Sam. 1:16), but in the second person: "Your blood be on your head; for your own mouth has testified against you, saying, 'I have killed the Lord's anointed.'" What was intended in the so-called self-cursing of the Jews was probably an allusion to this Old Testament passage.

In the theological view, the self-cursing of the people—assuming it happened at all—is lifted and removed by the prayer of Jesus on the cross: "Father, forgive them; for they do not know what they are doing" (Luke 23:34). It is, in fact, lifted in a double sense: first, lifting the curse annuls its legal validity; second, it elevates the curse to the status of a prayer. What is more, to the Christian mind this alleged self-cursing would have contained an element of salvation. Whereas the blood of Abel cries from the earth for vengeance (Gen. 4:10), the blood of Jesus purifies, according to the faith of his community, from all sins. Only in very recent history has this sentence found new meaning for the richly developed theology of the blood of Jesus and been reinterpreted in positive terms. Although it may have happened that a handful of fanatics or hirelings from the clique of the high priest shouted out some such utterance, an outburst of organized popular hysteria can hardly be blamed on the Jews of Jerusalem as a whole; or on the festival pilgrims from abroad; or on the Jews of the diaspora; much less on the mass of Jews from other countries, who had not the slightest inkling of what was going on in Jerusalem; certainly not on the communities from Alexandria to Rome; and least of all on the Jews of later generations. And yet the church construed a theory of collective guilt from which legal license has been derived down through the centuries to discriminate against the Jews, even to expel them, and to justify their extermination. Whether this fateful self-cursing ever occurred, we will never know. But that it was effective, we have no lack of evidence. What is most obvious in all of this is that Christ's church has never really taken to heart the commandment to love one's enemies.

The proceedings before Pilate as reported in the Gospels give the impression that an antagonism existed between Jesus and "the Jews." This impression is of course the result of a later pagan-Christian representation, for Jesus of Nazareth is in fact accused of being a Jewish patriot who is purported to have called himself the "King of the Jews." Such is the crime that leads to death, as indicated by the inscription put on the cross, which states the reason for the crucifixion. According to the Law of Augustus proclaimed in the year 8 B.C.E., the sentence of death was applied to any similar act of lèse majesté. This was probably the real reason that "the Jews" hesitated to carry out the sentence of death on Jesus, one of their own, despite having been charged to do so by Pilate (John 19:6).

"The Jews" cannot be viewed monolithically in this whole affair. There were, of course, sworn enemies of Jesus, especially in the clique around the officiating high priest; there were also the worried but less involved pharisaic legal experts; and finally, there were the adherents of Jesus, who seemed to demonstrate very little civil courage and, in the hour of danger, fell away. Most important, however, there was also the overwhelming mass of Jews who had nothing whatsoever, in any practical sense, to do with this quick process. Nevertheless, the tendentious report in the Gospels gives the impression that "the Jews" as a whole were sworn enemies of Jesus. Even at that, the writers are compelled to report that certain leading Jews did at least concern themselves with arranging a worthy burial for the crucified man.

The entire procedure thus happened in great haste, under pressure of the coming festival and Sabbath.[90] Given the tempo of this proceeding, it was impossible for the scattered Jewish followers of Jesus to be informed. Indeed, the puppet master of the clique intentionally arranged it so. It would have been natural, in fact, for Caiaphas and his company to delay handing over Jesus to Pilate until after the Passover feast and to hold the prisoner in custody through the week of the festival. That would likely have been the case if Jesus had not had so many adherents among the Jewish people. The clique doubtless feared that the news of his incarceration would spread rapidly among the people and festival pilgrims, possibly giving rise to resistance groups and counteractions. Such activity was to be prevented by creating a fait accompli. Their haste is therefore understandable, in that "the Jews" involved disagreed on how to handle the situation; in fact, the mass of simple folk, the 'am-ha'arets class, stood on the side of Jesus, thus prompting the Jewish collaborators to encourage the Roman Pilate to expedite the case.

Pilate hands over Jesus to the Roman soldiers for scourging—perhaps twice, it would appear. At this point, all the pro-Roman retouches in the gospel texts fail. We see the Roman legionnaires, driven by hatred and scorn, as they mock the "King of the Jews" and, in mocking him, his entire Jewish people, already disenfranchised and beaten down. The soldiers throw a purple officer's coat around him, exactly as the legions would throw a purple coat around the shoulders of their field general as a sign of having chosen him to be their Caesar.

A talmudic parable, reported in the name of the 'Amora Levi[91] (from the third century C.E.), sheds important light on this event:

> It is like the case of a general to whom his legions have thrown the purple cloak. So what does he do? He remits the arrears of taxes, burns the roll [i.e., the documents of delinquency], and leads the legions out [on parade], and this is counted as the beginning of his reign. So also . . . the Holy One, blessed be He, ruled in Egypt. He remitted their taxes [those

of the children of Israel]; . . . He burnt the roll. . . . He brought out His
legions, and this dated the beginning of His reign. (*Exodus Rabbah* 15.13)

Even though it is not reported until relatively late, this midrash
or a similar idea may well stand behind the report of the mocking
of Jesus by the soldiers. They throw the purple coat around his shoulders, thereby making him their "Caesar," and glorify him. But what
is really meant by this action? In the terms of the midrash just quoted,
it signifies the remission of outstanding debts, the burning of the
documents concerning the debts, and guided passage to freedom. In
theological terms, the coronation of Jesus with the crown of thorns
and the purple coat signifies the beginning of the new age, in which
all debts are forgiven as a result of the sacrifice of this powerless
"Caesar."

I consider the appeal to a midrash justified here, since no one from
Jesus' original community was present specifically at his scourging,
mocking, crowning with thorns, and arraying in the purple coat. It is
possible that certain of the acts committed in the torture chamber
found their way into public knowledge. According to reports, Jesus
was presented a second time in this officer's coat to the public. The
reports, however, are so much later that a midrashic interpretation of
them is completely justifiable, especially since the *moment of fulfillment*—as son of man, servant of God—dominates the Passion story.

It is the "King of the Jews" whom Pilate now hands over for crucifixion. Pilate repeatedly presents their "king" to the people with unmistakable anti-Semitic overtones, and it is not difficult for us to picture the easily disgusted Roman procurator. The caricature of a king
that he offers is the new Jewish king. The Jewish clique gains nothing
by distancing itself as far as possible from Jesus. To the imperialist
Pilate, they all belonged together, accusers and accused alike, these
"Jews among themselves" whose internal squabbles were of no consequence to Rome's mouthpiece. Rome had already hung so many
Jews on crosses that the wood supply in Israel could no longer meet
the demand. It is said that during the Jewish wars some five hundred
Jews a day were crucified. To the Roman Pilate it was totally irrelevant
whether one Jew more or one Jew less hung on a cross.

Anatole France perceptively intuited the situation in his novella about Pontius Pilate, "The Procurator of Judaea." At the end of the work (25) he presents a dialogue between the elderly Pilate, now retired in Rome, and his friend Lamia. Lamia is telling about a lover who has left him:

> "Some months after I lost sight of her, I learned by chance that she had attached herself to a small company of men and women who were followers of a young Galilean thaumaturgist. His name was Jesus; he came from Nazareth, and he was crucified for some crime, I don't quite know what. Pontius, do you remember anything about the man?"
>
> Pontius Pilate contracted his brows, and his hand rose to his forehead in the attitude of one who probes the deeps of memory. Then after a silence of some seconds—
>
> "Jesus?" he murmured, "Jesus—of Nazareth? I cannot call him to mind."

The poet here says more than the historian is able to say or the theologian cares to say. He speaks the truth about the man who once asked, "What is truth?"

13 INRI, or The Curse of the Crucified

The tragedy of the life of Jesus now approaches its high point. The Apostles' Creed summarizes it succinctly in the words "suffered under Pontius Pilate, was crucified, died, and was buried." The formulation reflects the belief that it was Pontius Pilate who bore—and still bears—the chief responsibility for the crucifixion of Jesus, despite the Gospels' later efforts to exonerate the procurator by depicting him as nothing but a tool in the hands of the Jewish authorities.

Crucifixion as capital punishment was not a Jewish but a Roman form of execution, the most gruesome and horrifying form known to antiquity. Jewish law recognized four kinds of capital punishment: stoning, burning, decapitation, and strangulation.

The Mishna, in the tractate Sanhedrin 7, is specifically concerned with these forms of execution and details the crimes punishable by each.

After the sentence of death was carried out, the executed individual was then hung on a pole as a means of holding him up to public display. According to religio-legal prescriptions, this applied only to male blasphemers and idolators. The corpse had to be taken down by evening and buried. This prescription was strictly observed in the crucifixion of Jesus.

The idea that a man had to be taken down before sunset is ancient. It is documented as early as Joshua 8:29 and 10:27, which state that even enemy kings who had been hanged were taken down from the tree or gallows prior to sunset. The shocking story of the impalement of the sons of Saul's concubine, Rizpah Bath-Aiah (2 Sam. 21:8–14), provides further documentation that anyone not taken down from the pole, and left unburied, was considered especially cursed. The relevant prescription is found in Deuteronomy 21:22–23:

> When someone is convicted of a crime punishable by death and is exe-
> cuted, and you hang him on a tree, his corpse must not remain all night
> upon the tree; you shall bury him that same day, for anyone hung on a
> tree is under God's curse. You must not defile the land that the Lord your
> God is giving you for possession.

In his commentary on the book of Deuteronomy, Gerhard von Rad remarks on this prescription:

> The regulation about the body of a man who has been hanged . . . starts
> from the very ancient conception that the land must be protected against
> ritual pollution. From this point of view the customary degrading exhibi-
> tion of the corpse should be limited in time. The maxim in v. 23 explain-
> ing the reason for the ordinance uses as an argument a conception which
> must have been generally widespread, namely, that the corpse of a hanged
> man is a threat to the cultic purity of the land, and thus might interfere
> with its yield. (138)

One who has been hanged is under God's curse. And it is precisely this fate that is hastening even now toward the man who has been honored by his community as the bringer of salvation. The paradox of Christianity culminates in this event. Its reinterpretation demonstrates the power of the Good News to transform what is horrible into a proclamation of salvation: "Christ redeemed us from the curse of the law by becoming a curse for us—for it is written, 'Cursed is every-one who hangs on a tree'" (Gal. 3:13).

Between the archaic understanding of Deuteronomy and the Pauline soteriological interpretation we have that of later Judaism, as expressed in Rashi's commentary on the passage in Deuteronomy:

> For he that is hanged is a degradation of the Divine King, for a man is created in *His* image, and the sons of Israel are *His* children. Here is a parable! It is like twin brothers who resembled one another. One became king, and the other was apprehended as a robber and hanged. Whoever looks upon him says, "The king has been hanged."

This parable is also referred to in the Babylonian Talmud (Sanhedrin 46b), which concludes by saying that the king ordered that the man be taken down.

Thus we see how the curse of one who has been hanged was subjected to manifold transformations of meaning.

Although the sentence of crucifixion is not provided for in Hebrew law, it was nevertheless known only too well in Palestine long before the crucifixion of Jesus. Here we think of the passage in Ezra 6:11, which deals with an edict of the Persian supreme king, Darius the Great, around 510 B.C.E. concerning the reconstruction of the temple in Jerusalem. Whoever did not wish to take part in the work was threatened with a terrible punishment: "Furthermore I decree that if anyone alters this edict, a beam shall be pulled out of the house of the perpetrator, who then shall be impaled on [fastened to] it." Hence, the threat of crucifixion was known in Palestine by way of Persian culture some five hundred years before Jesus. To be sure, it was only a threat; we have no proof that this gruesome form of execution was actually practiced at that time in the biblical land.

There is also a report concerning the Hasmonean king Alexander Jannaeus (reigned 103–76 B.C.E.), which claims that he had eighty Jewish citizens crucified. The Dead Sea scrolls offer indirect proof and at the same time stress that crucifixion was scandalous and not widely practiced: the so-called Nachum Commentary from the scrolls of Qumran speaks of a "lion" that crucified his victims; this was something, according to the commentary, "which never happened in Israel."

Justice Haim Cohn notes that the verb *tsalav* (crucify) is employed imprecisely in the Aramaic texts of the rabbinic literature and occasionally applies to hanging (*Trial and Death,* 209–10). Some passages describe crucifixion as *kederekh hamalkhuth,* 'in the manner of the empire.' The old legal literature of the rabbis also equates strangulation with hanging.

It is remarkable that the phrase expressing the curse of hanging (Deut. 21:23) is translated in the Aramaic Targum (the translation of Yonathan Ben-'Uzzi'el) as "for the crucified is a curse." Here again, hanging and crucifixion are equated.

Of the four kinds of capital punishment in Hebrew law, the fourth, strangulation, is described in the Aramaic Targum to Ruth 1:17 as crucifixion—though it should be noted in this instance that strangulation and hanging are synonymous. As Haim Cohn demonstrates (*Trial and Death,* chap. 8), these strikingly inexact usages are not difficult to explain. Cohn observes that capital punishment had gone out of practice long before the rabbinic authors in question were writing. Nor should we always equate the presence of a codified law with the actual carrying-out of the punishment.

After being scourged, Jesus of Nazareth is led by the Roman soldiers to the place of execution. He is made to bear his own cross. The sight of a condemned man bearing a cross is deeply etched in Jewish consciousness. An example is provided in the Midrash Rabba to Genesis 22:6: "Abraham took the wood of the burnt offering and laid it on his son Isaac." The midrash comments, "Like one who carries his stake on his shoulders." Isaac, who bears the wood to the sacrificial altar on Mount Moriah, is portrayed as one bearing a cross. It is not necessary to see in this an allusion to the Passion of Jesus, for the cross-bearing Jew had long since become a widely known phenomenon.[92]

According to the synoptic Gospels (Matt. 27:32; Mark 15:21; Luke 23:26), the Roman soldiers of the execution cohort force a peasant by the name of Simon of Cyrene, who is returning home from the fields, to take the cross from Jesus and bear it for him. We do not read that Jesus collapsed under the weight of the cross, although that may be assumed, since otherwise there would have been no reason to require that Simon take the cross. But as a narrative device it alludes to

Jesus' statement in the Matthew text that "whoever does not take up the cross and follow me is not worthy of me" (10:38). Cause and effect are unclear in this instance. Did this saying regarding imitation in the sign of the cross arise from the episode with Simon of Cyrene, or was the Simon episode interpolated to illustrate an earlier saying? I am inclined to think that it served the purpose of illustration, since it is only weakly documented and not explicitly motivated. It is typical of the style of the Passion story that specific models are provided for all later theological matters: Pilate and Herod as the first to be reconciled through Christ; Barabbas as the first to be redeemed through the vicarious suffering of Christ; Simon of Cyrene as the first to follow in the imitation of Christ.

In any case, the reference to Simon of Cyrene provides us with a factual clue that the walk to the place of execution occurred in the middle of a workday. Simon is returning from the fields during the morning hours because it is 'Erev Pesach, the day of preparation for the Passover celebration, which is to begin that evening. Since the first day of the festival was also the Sabbath, the day was doubly consecrated.

From the terseness of the Gospels' reports we may infer that the execution was carried out in haste, perhaps because it happened on the day of preparation for the Sabbath, and the theme of the Passover celebration is accordingly relegated to the background. There are, in fact, important halakhic reasons for this, since the religio-legal prescriptions for the Sabbath are even stricter than those for the Passover holiday.

The place of execution is called Golgotha, derived from the Hebrew gulgoleth, 'skull.' Hence the name "place of the skull" (Greek kraniou topos). The attempt to derive the word from the presumption that there were skulls lying all about is specious, however, since such a situation would have flagrantly violated the codes of cultic purity in Jewish law. Rather, we must imagine a high rocky place resembling a skull in shape. Although archaeologists have raised many objections to the so-called Gordon Garden Tomb on the Golgotha cliff opposite the Damascus Gate in Jerusalem's Old City, it seems to me that a great deal does speak in favor of its having been the site of Golgotha. I myself have often paused in the shadow of the Damascus Gate at sunset to gaze at this cliff, which could be Golgotha, and which does indeed give the impression of a bald skull with eye sockets. It is still less likely that Golgotha was located in the modern Tomb Church of Jerusalem's Old City. But this is not the place to debate the controversial issue of whether it lay inside or outside the city walls at the time of Jesus. That question should be left to archaeologists. Our own view must remain fixed on the man of sorrows as he stumbles toward the fulfillment of his horrible fate.

The text of Luke, which consistently underscores the role of women, reports the lament of the "Daughters of Jerusalem" for the man being led to the place of execution (23:28). The concern here is not simply with the fate of an individual but rather with a certain custom reported in a *baraitha:* "To the man being led away to be executed a cup of wine with incense is offered for the sake of dulling his senses. The noble daughters of Jerusalem generously donated and served it" (BT, Sanhedrin 43a). The custom is also mentioned in Mark 15:23, with the note that Jesus rejected this narcotic, much as, according to Luke, he turned away the women mourners.

The crucifixion now proceeds in the usual manner. We should stress that it is not essential to hold to the common assumption that Jesus was nailed to the cross. There is good evidence that crucified individuals were bound to the cross with cords, a manner of crucifixion that was, to be sure, gruesome enough.

Jesus is crucified between two other condemned men, who are identified as murderers or robbers—armed robbers, namely, since the death sentence applied only to cases of armed robbery. Presumably, they were insurrectionists in the mold of Barabbas. It is not indicated whether an inscription was attached to their crosses, as it was to Jesus' cross, stating the reason for their punishment. John offers the most explicit version: "Pilate also had an inscription written and put on the cross. It read 'Jesus of Nazareth, the King of the Jews'" (19:19). The Latin form of this inscription is *Iesus Nazarenus Rex Iudaeorum,* the initials of which make up the famous acronym INRI. The inscription was written in the three languages of the land, Hebrew, Greek, and Latin. The Latin INRI has become the standard abbreviation, but the reconstructed Hebrew inscription suggests that it may have meant to invoke the tetragram, the four-letter name for

Jehovah, YHWH: *Yeshuʿ Hanotsri W/u-Melekh Hayehudim.* As so often in the Gospels, the Hebraic intention is concealed by a foreign language.

The clique objects to this title, perhaps not so much because it proclaims the royalty of Jesus—however ironically intended—as out of fear that it would desecrate the tetragram. But Pilate refuses their objection with the statement "What I have written I have written" (John 19:22). This reply recalls the passage in the book of Esther where King Ahasuerus says, "An edict written in the name of the king and sealed with the king's ring cannot be revoked" (8:8). This passage has to do with the decree of the salvation of the Jews, and it was in this way that the inscription on the cross was understood by the original community.

A brief dialogue arises between Jesus and the two men who are crucified with him. According to one version (Matt. 27:44), both criminals deride him, which makes sense psychologically. Reports of political prisoners from concentration camps repeatedly confirm that the intellectual is subjected to particularly brutal scorn and hatred from crude fellow inmates and co-sufferers, who feel—as a final triumph in anonymous degradation—that something higher is being reduced to their own level. In Luke 23:39–43, however, one of the malefactors recognizes the dignity of his suffering comrade, Jesus of Nazareth. Perhaps it was the prayer that Jesus had just offered up, "Father, forgive them; for they do not know what they are doing" (Luke 23:34)—an expression of forgiving love in the moment of the most fearful torment—that so impressed this other man on the cross. He bids Jesus, "Remember me when you come into your kingdom" (v. 42). Jesus answers, "Truly I tell you, today you will be with me in Paradise" (v. 43).

In spite of the objections that have been raised against it by certain scholars, such as Fritz Rienecker in his commentary on Luke (*Evangelium des Lukas,* 350), an alternative reading seems more valid to me: "Amen, I tell you today, you will be with me in Paradise." This reading implies a promise for the long run, which is to say, of life after the resurrection. The idea that Jesus should dwell in Paradise on the very day that he dies—despite the Christian community's own belief that he rose only on the third day and returned to heaven even later—is untenable. My reading has philological difficulties, but these difficulties may have come about as a result of subsequent reworkings of the original text.

In the first part of the Passion story we repeatedly noted the influence of a certain midrash to the book of Zechariah.[93] Now, in the second and final part of the tragedy, there is obviously another midrash at work, this one to the twenty-second Psalm, which begins with the saddest lament imaginable: "My God, my God, why have you forsaken me?" This utterance is transmitted to us by Mark and Matthew as the last words of the despairing man on the cross.

The division of Jesus' clothes under the cross (John 19:23–25) must also be viewed in terms of the midrash to Psalm 22:18: "They divide my clothes among themselves, and for my clothing they cast lots."[94] It was in fact the privilege of the execution soldiers to keep the clothes of the condemned as booty. The seamless tunic of Jesus is easily identifiable as a *tallith*, a prayer shawl. According to the halakhic prescription, the prayer tunic (still worn today in the synagogue) is to have four corners and consist of a *single* piece of material with fringes (Num. 15:37–41; Deut. 22:12).

While these matters are obviously related to Psalm 22:1 and 18, the narrative soon turns back to the Zechariah midrash, to a passage (Zech. 12:10: ". . . when they look on the one whom they have pierced")[95] adapted in John 19:37. John relates it to the piercing of Jesus' side, by which death was to be determined, but this passage in John has also contributed importantly to the Zechariah tradition within Christian exegesis.

Under the cross all kinds of curious onlookers are standing around, as one would expect at a public execution. Followers of Jesus make up part of this anonymous crowd. Luke again mentions the women under the cross. Nothing is said regarding the whereabouts of the remaining eleven disciples from the inner circle; in John's version, the disciple whom Jesus loved (presumably John) is standing beneath the cross (19:26). Also mentioned are the mother of Jesus, an aunt, and Mary Magdalene. Jesus speaks the remarkable words to his mother, "Woman, here is your son," and to the disciple, "Here is your mother" (v. 27).

The distant address to his mother, even now in the final hour of excruciating pain, is reminiscent of his address to her at the wedding in Cana at the beginning of his public activity (John 2:4). It shows once again in realistic terms just how problematic the relationship was between Jesus and his mother. The problem is not diminished by the fact that he shows concern for her continuing welfare in commending her to the protection of the single remaining disciple.

The man on the cross, parched with thirst, again asks for a drink (John 19:28). This time the soldiers place a sponge full of sour wine on a branch of hyssop and hold it to his mouth—an allusion, as we pointed out earlier, to the last cup, the fifth cup, the cup of torment. We also related this moment to the hyssop of the first Passover night in Egypt, significant to John's Gospel in the sense that Jesus is explicitly regarded as the paschal lamb (19:36). Thus, when the soldiers are sent to break the legs of the crucified men, they do not break Jesus' bones, a point related clearly to the commandment in Exodus 12:46 with respect to the pascal lamb: "You shall not break any of its bones."

Three last "words" of Jesus on the cross are transmitted here. According to Matthew 27:46 (cf. Mark 15:34) he dies uttering the cry *Eli, Eli, lema sabachthani?*—"My God, my God, why have you forsaken me?"—the opening words of Psalm 22, which express the dreadful loss of all faith and hope.[96] There can be no doubt that these words are authentic, since they are incongruent with all Christian dogma. We are hearing the cry of a man whose faith has been horribly shattered. Mark expressly mentions that Jesus died with a "loud cry" (15:37). These cries must have been shrill screams, expressions not only of unimaginable physical pain but of the most profound hopelessness at being forsaken by God. That the scoffers standing around thought that he was calling to Elijah may, in fact, have been true. (The wordplay does not work well in Hebrew, however, since *'Eli, 'Eli* and *'Eliya,* or more commonly *'Eliyahu,* are not properly homophonous.) The man who spoke before the Sanhedrin itself of the exaltation of the son of man doubtless expected a miracle until the very end. He must have thought of Daniel in the lions' den; or of Shadrach, Meshach, and Abednego in the fiery furnace; or, above all, of the angel who rescued Isaac on Mount Moriah in his hour of sacrifice. But no angel steps in to halt the inexorable course of this tragedy. The dying man on the cross can only assume that he has been forsaken by God, after his fellowman has long since forsaken him. Whether his cry was uttered in the original formulation of the Psalms or in an Aramaic reformulation is unimportant. This man in pain and despair probably uttered it in his native tongue, Aramaic. There is no question, as far as I am concerned, that Jesus spoke only Aramaic,[97] and his final cry surely resounded in the vernacular as *'Elohi, 'Elohi, lama shevaktani.*

Remarkably absent among the statements from the cross is the Hebrew confession of faith, the *Shema' Yisra'el:* "Hear, O Israel, the Lord our God, the Lord is one" (Deut. 6:4, variant reading), which every Jew speaks in the hour of death and which Jesus himself counted among the highest of all commandments. To me, the absence of the *Shema' Yisra'el* is itself an expression of Jesus' sense of absolute God-forsakenness.

Mark and Matthew record this horrible God-forsakenness with the cry, "My God, my God, why have you forsaken me?" It is important to realize that this utterance does not put the existence of God in question. In times of need the ancient Jew would put this question to God; modern man puts God in question. Luke, however, records the more resigned statement, "Father, into your hands I commend my spirit" (23:46, referring to Ps. 31:5).[98]

Luke, of course, is writing from a greater temporal distance than Mark, whom Matthew used as his source. As the distance increased, the words from the cross were adapted more narrowly into a Christology. The latest Gospel, John, thus says, "It is finished" (19:30). But the reading suggested by Franz Sigge, "It is fulfilled," is probably to be preferred, for the concern now is with the fulfillment of the Old Testament promise. Exegetically, the tragedy is thereby rendered less acute.

Naturally, it is entirely possible that Jesus spoke all these words on the cross as well as a good many others. Unfortunates often remained on the martyr's pole for days at a time (unlike Jesus, who hung on the cross for a matter of hours). We know of instances, in fact, in which entire speeches were delivered from a cross.

The gospel writers consistently retained only as much information as they considered essential to the record, and in general the reports of the New Testament authors display great consolidation of detail. Without attempting to harmonize them, we can summarize the three different last words of Jesus on the cross as follows: first, the wild protest in the moment of God-forsakenness, in which Jesus becomes the new Job; second, the submission to the will of God, now entirely in the "shadow of the servant of God" of Deutero-Isaiah (cf. Isa. 49:2 and 51:16); and third, "It is fulfilled," the statement of the suffering Messiah, who need not be thought of as identical with the servant of God.[99]

After Jesus' sufferings have come to an end in a relatively short time, a darkness (Matt. 27:45; Luke 23:44) and an earthquake (Matt. 27:51–54) are reported; the gospel writers cannot imagine that nature, God's creation, could remain silent at the death of God's own son. At this point the reports lapse into the realm of saga and legend, and it is difficult to reconstruct any historical core from them.

Erich Zehren has examined in detail the question of the darkness after the crucifixion:

> There is an entire series of reports that make reference to the famous solar eclipse in the year 29 C.E., which became visible at the death of Jesus. The reports further conform to the time of day given in the first three Gospels, namely, from about the sixth to the ninth hour, or, by modern reckoning, from about noon until three in the afternoon. If one starts from the fact of a solar eclipse in the year 29 C.E., then another thing is also confirmed: the Gospel of Luke mentions the fifteenth year of the Roman Caesar Tiberius, the very time at which John the Baptist appeared. This fifteenth year of Tiberius corresponds, according to modern time-reckoning, to the year 28/29 C.E. The period of the public activity of Jesus is given by the first three Gospels as occurring approximately one year after Jesus' baptism by John, that is, from one spring to the next. By this reckoning, Jesus could still have died in 29 C.E., the year of the famous solar eclipse. The report of the church father Irenaeus (second century C.E.), that Jesus preached for only one year and was crucified in the twelfth month of that activity, also coincides with these data.
>
> Only one thing among all of these facts remains contradictory: the total eclipse of the sun in the year 29 C.E. did not occur on a day of preparation for the Passover feast . . . but rather on 24 November 29 C.E. (*Der gehenkte Gott*, 69–70)

When we take into account, however, that Matthew wrote around the year 90 C.E. and Luke about five years earlier—which is to say, at an interval of more than fifty years from the event and with a clear missionary goal in mind—then it would seem likely that a solar eclipse occurring sometime around the death of Jesus was later incorporated into the report. The same goes for the notice concerning the earthquake, which is said to have caused graves to open, resurrections to take place (something with which the Gospels are not otherwise concerned), and the curtain in the Holy of Holies of the temple to be torn in two. The symbolic value of these data is clear: an eschatological event is being anticipated.

The simple historical report now proceeds directly to the burial of Jesus. Two respected citizens of Jerusalem, members of the Sanhedrin, take it upon themselves to provide for Jesus' burial: Joseph of Arimathea (in Hebrew, probably Yosef Haramathi) and, according to John 19:39, Nicodemus (Hebrew, Nakdimon), who had once visited Jesus under the cloak of night.

There follows a rather detailed description of the burial custom (John 19:38–42): the wrapping of the body in linen cloths with the application of embalming spices. These details are particularly worthy of attention, since they deviate from the logic of fulfillment that the narrative has been following. The concentration here is *no longer* on the figure of the servant of God, of whom it is said that "he [NRSV "they"] made his grave with the wicked" (Isa. 53:9)—quite the opposite. As Josephus reports in *The Jewish War* (4.5.2), this passage also shows that political criminals executed by the Romans could receive an honorable burial, a privilege not granted normal criminals.

Luke 23:53 notes that the grave, which belonged to the family vault of Joseph of Arimathea, was a new rock-hewn tomb in which no one had yet been buried. Slide-graves of this kind, known as *kukhim,* are common in Israel to this day. Jesus' body was laid in one such rocky niche. The practice was to remove the bones from the tomb after several years and place them in an ossuary, a relatively small stone sarcophagus, thus allowing the same tomb to be used over and over again. (This practice has fallen into complete oblivion among modern Jews.) We should not think of Jesus' tomb, therefore, as one shoveled out of the earth but as a niche in a stone vault. The burial was undertaken in great haste in order that it be completed before the beginning of the Sabbath and Passover festival of the same day. It was for that reason that the women who had been close to Jesus returned to the burial place on Sunday, the first intermediate day of the Passover festival,[100] in order to lend a hand in the worthy burial of their master. But they find the tomb empty. . . .

Here ends the story of Jesus. Here begins the story of Christ. The disciple community construed the disappearance of the body of Jesus as a resurrection. The resurrection, however, remains hidden from our sight. Thus Günther Bornkamm writes,

> The event of Christ's resurrection from the dead, his life, and his eternal reign, are things removed from historical scholarship. History cannot ascertain and establish conclusively the facts about them as it can with other events of the past. The last historical fact available to [it] is the Easter faith of the first disciples. (*Jesus of Nazareth,* 180)

All manner of negative and rationalistic explanations have been put forward to deal with the resurrection of Jesus. The so-called *Toledoth Yeshuʻ,* that dark source to which we referred in chapter 4, fantasized that the disciples stole the body of Jesus. The rationalist Hermann Samuel Reimarus (1694–1768) articulated the same view in *The Goal of Jesus and His Disciples,* one of a series of fragmentary works on religion edited by Gotthold Ephraim Lessing. The fragments relating to the resurrection story were published in 1777 and unleashed a storm of protest in the German theological world.[101]

The presumption of a "rescued Christ" has often been expressed. According to this theory, Jesus was only apparently dead when he was taken down from the cross, and he reawakened soon after being laid in the tomb. In 1965, *The Passover Plot* by Hugh Schonfield created a sensation among the reading public. Earlier, in 1928, Werner Hegemann did much the same with his book *Christ Rescued.* I own a copy of the sixth edition of a much earlier work, published in Leipzig in 1849, that moved in this direction by drawing on purported revelations in ancient manuscripts about the "real" death of Jesus.[102]

I am reluctant to devote any attention to these theories, for speculation contends here against faith. The actual historical resurrection of Christ took place only later in Damascus, with Paul's "Damascus

Road" conversion, an experience rooted deeply in the subjectivity of this contradictory and controversial personality. In 1 Corinthians 15: 14, Paul made faith in the resurrection into a shibboleth: "And if Christ has not been raised, then our proclamation has been in vain and your faith has been in vain." The resurrection of Jesus cannot be apprehended as a historical phenomenon. Even in the Gospels its documentation is insufficient to merit factual status; ultimately, we know nothing about what happened after the burial of Jesus. What we do know is that he has risen time and again in the souls of men and women who have encountered him. And here we begin to touch on the secret of the Christian soul, to which no one can have access who stands outside of this mystery.

Matthew 28:19 says that the resurrected Jesus commissioned his disciples, "Go therefore and make disciples of all nations, baptizing them in the name of the Father and of the Son and of the Holy Spirit" (cf. Mark 16:15–16).

This passage is missing, however, from the oldest manuscripts prior to the Council of Nicea (325 C.E.), as Professor Shlomo Pines proved in 1966 from the evidence of the discovery of a Judeo-Christian manuscript from the early Christian era (*Jewish Christians*).[103]

The words of the resurrected Jesus cannot be traced to any historical collection of sayings, but that does not mean that they were any less meaningful to the Christian community.[104] As Bultmann recognized, they testify not to Jesus of Nazareth but to the exalted *Kyrios,* the Lord, indeed to the *Christos Pantokrator,* 'the ruler of the universe.'

About this personage we have nothing to say. He is hidden from our view. Let us, instead, look once more upon the Jew Yeshua' Ben-Yosef of Nazareth, as he hangs, despised and rejected, there on the cross. His countenance, distorted with pain, is crowned with a diadem of thorns. The martyred body bleeds from countless wounds. Thus we see him once again, the Jew on the cross. His voice carries down through the centuries: *Just as you did to one of the least of these my brothers, so you did to me.*

Notes

([Ed.] = Editors' note)

1. A *baraitha* (Aramaic, 'what is external') is a legalistic saying or collection of sayings not included in the Mishna, the great textual codification of Jewish oral law attributed to Rabbi Yehuda ha-Nasi' and completed around the end of the second century of our era. Baraithoth are scattered throughout the Talmud and are found in certain minor designated collections as well as one major work: the Tosefta (Aramaic, 'supplement'). This work, of uncertain date and authorship, parallels and expatiates upon the Mishna. The relationship between the Mishna and the Tosefta is a matter of intense debate.

The Talmud itself consists of the Mishna, the terse original codification of the law (composed in Hebrew), and the Aramaic interpretive discussions of that law leading to its practical implementation (Gemara), dating from the period 200–500 C.E. The Talmud exists in two recensions: the Babylonian Talmud (Talmud Bavli) (BT) and the Palestinian or Jerusalem Talmud (Talmud Yerushalmi) (JT). The Babylonian Talmud is somewhat later than the Jerusalem Talmud (ca. 500 C.E. versus ca. 400 C.E.), is about three times as extensive, and has exerted an incomparably greater influence on Jewish life. Most of Ben-Chorin's talmudic references in this book are to the Babylonian Talmud.

The interpretive discussions constituting the Gemara are so characteristic of the talmudic style that the term Talmud may be loosely employed to refer specifically to Gemara, and one may speak non-redundantly of Talmud and Mishna. The Mishna has often been printed separately, but the reverse is not the case: the Talmud is never printed without the Mishna. The reason for this is that the Mishna presents the law in a straightforward manner, whereas the Gemara is based on the Mishna text, so its publication in the absence of the Mishna would render it incomprehensible.

The relationship between Gemara and Mishna is such that all Gemaras are based on a mishnaic text, but not all mishnaic tractates have associated Gemaras. Where there exists both Mishna and Gemara, the tractates have identical names, e.g., Mishna, Yoma 7.3, versus BT, Yoma 85b. As may be seen from this referencing system, the Mishna is broken up into chapters (*perakim*) and individual mishnas, whereas the Babylonian Talmud is referenced by page number, the recto being a, the verso b. The Jerusalem Talmud, on the other hand, possess a numeration system like that of the Mishna (e.g., Megilla 4.3). In this book Ben-Chorin often refers specifically to the Mishna. [Ed.]

2. We have been unable to locate this letter. [Ed.]

3. A contemporary scholar who shares this perspective is the Episcopalian Bishop John Spong, who seeks in some of his most recent writings to "liberate" the Christian view of Jesus by reading the gospel story as a narrative that makes use of Jewish literary techniques. [Ed.]

4. From the poem "Abraxas," number 62 of Goethe's special register of one hundred poems (the so-called *Wiesbader Register* or Wiesbaden Register, 1815) intended to constitute his *West-östlicher Divan*, though it is not found in the standard editions of that work. The poem is considered by some scholars to be the closest Goethe ever came to an actual religious confession (*West-östlicher Divan: Wiesbader Register*, 146). [Ed.]

5. The Tannaim (Aramaic *tanna*, 'teacher') were the legal authorities whose names and views are perpetuated in the Mishna and the baraithoth. [Ed.]

6. Better, perhaps, 'Aggada (the Aramaic form of the word), in order to distinguish this body of material from the text telling of the Exodus from Egypt, read during the Passover Seder. In the course of the Gemara, numerous digressions deal with historical events, proverbs and maxims, legends, science, and other realia. This material constitutes as much as 30 percent of the Babylonian Talmud and is known (together with the midrashic literature in general) as 'Aggada. It is opposed to Halakha, the legalistic part of the Talmud whose final interpretations were taken as binding within Jewish law. The 'Aggada and Halakha are so completely intertwined in the text of the Talmud that it is well-nigh impossible to separate the two. Nor would it be desirable to do so, inasmuch as both were directed at the same goal: instruction in how to live a good and upright life so as to serve the Creator. [Ed.]

7. Although today the term 'scribe' (Hebrew *sofer*) refers to one who has been trained in the specialized work of manually transcribing a Torah scroll, in the time of Jesus the term was used more generally to designate those who

occupied themselves with the study of Jewish law. In the Mishna the scribes are considered to be the earliest of the authorities conversant with the entirety of the Halakha. [Ed.]

8. More is said about this in chapter 4.

9. 'Akiva Ben-Yosef (ca. 50–135 C.E.) was considered to be the greatest scholar of his generation. Shim'on Bar-Kokheva (d. 135 C.E.) was a military leader who led the revolt against Hadrian in 132 C.E. He must have been a highly charismatic individual, for he succeeded in convincing Rabbi 'Akiva that he was the Messiah. The Bar-Kokheva Rebellion, despite some initial successes, is today viewed as one of the great catastrophes in Jewish History, for it led to the complete devastation of Judea and sealed the fate of the Jews as a wandering people, uprooted from their own land, over the next two millennia. Rabbi 'Akiva was subsequently executed by the Romans for refusing to comply with their ban on the study of Torah. To this day, he is considered one of the greatest of Jewish martyrs. [Ed.]

10. Malachi 3:23 in the Hebrew Bible. [Ed.]

11. The Zohar (lit. 'brightness') is the most important work of Kabbala, the tradition of Jewish mysticism. It first appeared in Leon, near Castile in Spain in the late thirteenth century, circulated by a Spanish Jew named Moses de Leon. He claimed to have "discovered" the ancient wisdom of Rabbi Shim'on Ben-Yochai (fl. 2d cent. C.E.), written during the thirteen years when the great Torah sage hid in a cave, together with his son, in order to avoid the Romans. Aside from Talmud and Midrash, there is no work in Judaism that has exerted greater influence in the past 600 years. [Ed.]

12. There is no historical relationship between these two meanings. Rather, the word *mikve* represents a derivative of separate, homophonous Hebrew roots, respectively 'wait for, hope' and 'gather.' [Ed.]

13. To this day, *tevila,* immersion in a *mikve* ('ritual bath'), is a critical part of the process of conversion to Judaism. Upon emerging from the bath, the convert is in a sense "newly born" as a Jew. [Ed.]

14. We shall have more to say about this in the following chapter, dealing with the wedding at Cana.

15. Such denomination by folk etymology or meaningful appellation is widespread in the Hebrew Bible, most notably in the naming of the twelve sons of Jacob (Gen. 29:32–30:24). [Ed.]

16. Micah 5:1 in the Hebrew Bible. [Ed.]

17. Codex Bezae (also known as Codex Cantabrigiensis) is a Greek-Latin

bilingual manuscript containing, in its present form, the Gospels and Acts, which is known for its significant deviations from the normal New Testament text. The most recent monographic treatment of this manuscript (Parker 1992) concludes that it was written in Berytus (Beirut) around 400 C.E. and reflects a still-fluid oral tradition of Christian scripture. The passage cited by Ben-Chorin represents one of its most notable additions: paralleled in no other Gospel manuscript, it is interpolated between Luke 6:4 and 6:6, whereas Luke 6:5 of our canonical text has been moved in Codex Bezae to follow 6:10. [Ed.]

18. With regard to John, there is no mention of the prohibition against cutting hair, although that also belongs within the sphere of prohibitions affecting the Nazirite.

19. The Book of Tobias or Tobit is an apocryphal work included in the Septuagint and canonized by the Catholic Church. As is the case with all works written after the period of Ezra the Scribe (5th cent. B.C.E.), the Book of Tobit has remained outside the Jewish canon, for the Rabbis viewed the period of prophetic revelation as having definitely passed with the reconstitution of a Palestinian Jewish community under the leadership and guidance of Ezra. [Ed.]

20. Ben-Chorin's use of this phrase as a quasi title makes sense within Jewish tradition. Beginning with the seventeenth day of Tammuz and ending with the ninth day of Av (a period of three weeks, which falls on the solar calendar anywhere from late June to mid-August), Judaism observes a period of mourning commemorating the destruction of the two temples, which tradition says were both destroyed on the ninth of Av. The first and last days of this period, referred to as *beyn hametzarim*, 'between the straits,' are observed as fast days. On the first Sabbath after the ninth of Av and continuing for six more weeks, the *haftaroth* read in the synagogue following the Torah readings from Deuteronomy are all taken from chapters 40–63 of Isaiah (Deutero-Isaiah), and all include messages of consolation. The first verse of the "Consolation Scripture" (Isa. 40:1) begins with the famous "Comfort ye, comfort ye, my people" (Hebrew, *Nachamu nachamu 'ami*), and the Sabbath on which this portion is read is known accordingly as *shabbath nachamu*. [Ed.]

21. From the King James Version, which reflects the error of the Septuagint reading. [Ed.]

22. The Masoretic text (Hebrew *masora*, 'tradition') of the Hebrew Bible

is the pointed text established in its final form in the tenth century by a school of redactors centered in Tiberias. The "Tiberian vocalization" provides the original, almost totally consonantal text with a series of signs (points) denoting the proper vowel sounds to be read. At the same time, this school provided a system of notational signs of a musical nature (*ta'amei-hamikra'*) to be intoned in the public oral recitation of the text. These "cantillation marks" provide a relatively detailed syntactic analysis of the (punctuationless) text, which is what Ben-Chorin is here referring to. A less detailed system of "intonation" was adopted as well for reading the Talmud within the *yeshivoth,* the seminaries where the Talmud is studied, with the result that one who listens to a talmudic discourse by a rabbi or yeshiva student is likely to come away with the distinct impression that the text is being, as it were, sung. [Ed.]

23. The placement of John's imprisonment and death in the fortress palace of Machaerus, located high above the Dead Sea and about fifteen miles southeast of the mouth of the Jordan River, comes from Josephus (*Jewish Antiquities,* 8.5.2). [Ed.]

24. These pericopes (Hebrew *sidroth* or *parashiyoth*) consist today of fifty-four sections into which the Pentateuch is divided; they are given Hebrew names corresponding to a distinctive initial or near-initial word of the Hebrew text. In principle, one is read every Sabbath; however, since Judaism follows a lunar calendar, necessitating seven leap years (consisting of an extra inserted month) every nineteen years, and since special sections outside the regular pericope cycle are read on holidays, many of which fall on the Sabbath, regular Sabbaths may number from forty-seven to fifty-four in any given year. For this reason it is common practice to double up the pericopes when necessary, a procedure that is not random; only certain adjacent pericopes may be read together. [Ed.]

25. In modern traditional Jewish practice, the Torah cycle is initiated on the first Sabbath following the Feast of Tabernacles (late September to late October). The final pericope is not read on a regular Sabbath but rather on the holiday immediately following the seven-day Feast of Tabernacles, called in Hebrew *Shemini 'Atsereth* (the Eighth Day of Assembly) and additionally designated *Simchath-Torah* (Rejoicing of the Law). The Palestinian triennial cycle has not been continued in modern Judaism, owing primarily to the ascendancy of Babylonian practice, which had become completely predominant by the thirteenth century. Although in recent times some conserva-

tive and reconstructionist congregations have adopted a triennial cycle, this should be viewed as a modification of the annual cycle rather than a return to the Palestinian triennial cycle as such. See note 29 below. [Ed.]

26. For more information, cf. Mishna, Yadayim ('Hands') 3.4–5, and BT, Shabbath 14a. Detailed commentary concerning the religious-historical background can be found in Gerhard Lisowsky, *Die Mischna, Jadajim* VI/11, pp. 50 ff.

27. According to this view, the reason for the institution of a prophetic reading or *haftara* with thematic links (often not more than a phrase here or there) to the Torah pericope was presumably to remind the people of the proscribed Torah portion, but modern scholarship places little credence in this explanation. [Ed.]

28. The Torah pericope is divided into seven parts or *parashiyoth.* A different member of the congregation is called up to the *bima,* the raised platform from which the Torah is publicly read, to recite a blessing prior to the reading of each part. Each summons (Hebrew *'aliya*) is considered an honor, with the first two being reserved for a priest and a Levite, respectively. It was originally the custom that each individual summoned to the Torah would read his own portion; at a later date, however, a particular individual (a *ba'al keri'a,* lit. 'master of the reading') was designated and sometimes paid to learn to read the entire weekly portion, so as not to embarrass someone who might be called up and then found incapable of reading on his own. Following the reading of the pericopes, an eighth individual is called up. This is the *maftir* (lit. 'concluder' from the same Hebrew root as *haftara,* 'conclusion'). This person repeats the last few sentences of the weekly portion (at least three, the minimum to be read in order to justify a blessing) and then proceeds to recite the pericope from the Prophets. To this day, it is considered a particular honor to be designated *maftir.* [Ed.]

29. This paragraph contains several factual inaccuracies. First, in those years when *Nitsavim* is coupled with another portion, it is invariably the following *Vayelekh* and not the preceding *Ki-thavo'.* Second, Isaiah 61:1–2 is not actually the *haftara* to any of the portions mentioned. Thus, to *Ki-thavo'* is adjoined Isaiah 60, to *Nitsavim* (*-Vayelekh*) Isaiah 61:10–63:9. All of this, however, applies to the Babylonian (one-year) cycle rather than the Palestinian (three-year) cycle, which would have been in use in Galilee during Jesus' lifetime. Moreover, there is a great deal of evidence, albeit no earlier than the sixth or seventh century, that the triennial cycle (its pericopes, called *sedarim,*

number 141, 154, or 167, depending upon which extant list one follows) was not completed in precisely three years but required three and a half years or so and hence was not linked at all to the calendar. It also appears that the cycle was not fixed throughout Palestine but varied from region to region. Consequently, there is no basis for correlating pentateuchal readings and calendar dates in Palestine in the time of Jesus (Heinemann, "Triennial Lectionary Cycle").

Regarding the *haftaroth* then associated with the various Torah pericopes we know even less. Ironically, however, an argument for Ben-Chorin's contention that the episode in question occurred in the (late) summer can be constructed independently on the basis of the *haftaroth* alone. Luke 4:17 states that Jesus was handed the book of Isaiah. This apparently means that on that Sabbath in the synagogue in Galilee, the *haftara* was meant to be read from that book. This is in itself significant, since evidence from post-talmudic times shows that 50 percent of the *haftaroth* of the Palestinian cycle were taken from Isaiah, but only 25 percent of those of the Babylonian cycle. Wacholder ("Prolegomenon," xxi–xxx) concludes that unlike the Babylonian *haftaroth*, whose links to the Torah portion were primarily thematic, those of Palestine centered more on the theme of the messianic kingdom. Luke goes on to say that Jesus, "unrolling" the scroll, "found" the passage Isaiah 61:1–2. Given the way one opens a scroll, this could not have been a completely random event. Moreover, it agrees with post-talmudic evidence indicating that two-thirds of the Palestinian *haftaroth* from Isaiah were taken from chapters 40–66 (Deutero-Isaiah). Even more important, however, it appears that from a period as early as the fifth century C.E. the *haftaroth* for the three Sabbaths preceding the Fast Day of the Ninth of Av (roughly corresponding to the period from late July to mid-August; see note 20 above), commemorating the destruction of both temples (in Jesus' time only the first, of course) and the seven that follow it were fixed and identical in both Palestine and Babylonia; and it is at the end of this period that Isa. 61:10–11 (but not 61:1–2) is recited. If we are entitled to project this situation backward by a half-millennium, it raises the question as to whether Jesus purposely altered the accepted reading for the day in order to announce his own prophetic mission—and thereby aroused the ire of those in attendance, who might have perceived this as an act of arrogance. A final point here is not without interest. BT, Megilla 23a, states that a *haftara* should have a minimum of twenty-one verses. JT, Megilla 4.3, on the other hand, states that the *haftara* could have as few as three verses, and some lists of Palestinian *haftaroth* include readings consisting of only two verses (Wacholder, "Prolegomenon," xxxiv). It is therefore perhaps no accident that Luke 4:17 gives precisely Isaiah 61:1 and most of 2 as the prophetic pericope read by Jesus, after which he closed the scroll and sat down. [Ed.]

30. I myself witnessed a magical competition in Jerusalem between the chasidic rabbi of Belz and the rabbi of Satmar. Both attempted to free a woman possessed of a demon. The rabbi of Satmar emerged the victor from this competition.

31. Jonah 2:1 in the Hebrew Bible. [Ed.]

32. "Rav" is the honorary title of 'Abba 'Arikha, one of the towering personalities among the first generation of 'Amoraim or interpreters whose teachings figure prominently in the Babylonian Talmud. In 219 C.E. he founded the famous Sura Academy in Babylonia, which continued in existence for eight centuries. [Ed.]

33. "Rabbi" is the honorary title of Rabbi Yehuda ha-Nasi' (ca. 135– 220 C.E.), redactor of the Mishna and head of the Palestinian Jewish community. [Ed.]

34. Vayikra' Rabba (or Leviticus Rabba) is a midrashic commentary on Leviticus. This and its companion volumes on the remaining four books of the Pentateuch (the "Five Books of Moses"), plus those on the so-called five scrolls (Ecclesiastes, Esther, Lamentations, Ruth, and Song of Songs), form the Midrash Rabba or "Great Midrash," a corpus of 'aggadic or homiletical literature composed between the sixth and twelfth centuries C.E. This body of texts stands beside an earlier corpus known as halakhic midrashim dating from the tannaitic period, first to third centuries C.E. The latter are concerned with the derivation of legal prescriptions from scripture and emanate from the same circles that produced the Mishna, the Tosefta, and the various *baraithoth*. Halakhic midrashim are found for all books of the Pentateuch except Genesis (which is overwhelmingly nonlegalistic): they include the Mekhilta (on Exodus), Sifra (on Leviticus), and Sifrei (on Numbers and Deuteronomy). [Ed.]

35. Despite its classification as a halakhic midrash (cf. previous note), the Mekhilta (Aramaic, 'measure') is nevertheless filled with 'aggadic material. [Ed.]

36. Ben-Chorin is presumably referring here to Zechariah 14:21, which

foretells an age when every pot in Jerusalem shall be holy and thus fit for boiling the flesh of the sacrifice. Yet the prophet nowhere here or elsewhere speaks specifically of "boiling blood." [Ed.]

37. I am fully aware of a certain anachronism, for the *masora* in its modern form derives from a somewhat later period. But already in Jesus' day there was, of course, a text of the Torah and of the Prophets that he considered authoritative.

38. This commandment is reminiscent of the biblical injunction to (hate and) blot out the memory of the Amalekites, stated in Deuteronomy 25:17–19; v. 19 takes the curious form "you shall blot out the remembrance of Amalek from under heaven; do not forget." The Amalekites were the first nation to attack Israel following the Exodus, and their manner of doing so was considered particularly heinous: they attacked the weak and infirm at the very rear of the fleeing host, those who could hardly keep up. In accordance with the biblical injunction, Jewish tradition treats the Amalekite as the eternal enemy of the Jews, the very paradigm of the anti-Semite. Thus Haman, the sworn enemy of the Jews in the Book of Esther, was taken to be a descendant of the Amalekites, and Deuteronomy 25:17–19 is read in the synagogue every year on the Sabbath before Purim, the festive holiday commemorating the salvation of the Persian Jews from the hands of Haman. That Sabbath is called *shabbath zachor* from the first word (meaning 'remember') of the Deuteronomic passage. Whether in fact this passage is the ultimate source of Jesus' statement in Matthew 5:43 can of course not be known. [Ed.]

39. By the Writings, also known as Hagiographa (Hebrew *Kethuvim*), are meant those parts of the Hebrew Bible not included in the Pentateuch (*Torah*) and the Prophets (*Nevi'im*). They comprise Psalms, Proverbs, Job, Daniel, Ezra, Nehemiah, and the so-called *Chamesh Megilloth* (Five Scrolls) (cf. note 34 above). From the designations Torah, Nevi'im, Kethuvim comes the acronym *Tanakh*, used to refer to the Hebrew Bible in its entirety. [Ed.]

40. I follow in this selection the excellent compilation of parallels in the little book *Judentum und Christentum: Parallelen*. There are, of course, many such parallels in the scholarly *Kommentar zum neuen Testament aus Talmud und Midrasch*, by Hermann L. Strack and Paul Billerbeck.

41. Verse 19 in the Hebrew Bible. [Ed.]

42. For an overview of the contents of this work, see Klausner, *Jesus*, 48–51. [Ed.]

43. The second of these prayers is, of course, uttered only by men. Women, who are also obliged to say the morning prayers, are at this point given their own blessing in the orthodox prayerbook: "Blessed art thou, Lord our God, King of the Universe, who has created me according to his will." [Ed.]

44. Josephus (*Jewish Antiquities,* 11.8.2) says that the Samaritans built a temple there in the fourth century B.C.E. The Samaritan woman makes reference to it as an ancient place of worship (John 4:20). [Ed.]

45. According to the version we have of this parable, that of the pagan-Christian Luke, the priest and the Levite are going *down* to Jericho (10:30). Luke is missing an important point here. I would guess that in the original version the priest and the Levite went *up* to Jerusalem (i.e., in the opposite direction). At any rate, priests and Levites would have carefully avoided any contact with a corpse, since this led to ritual defilement. Even today an orthodox Jew of priestly caste immediately leaves a house in which there is a corpse and participates in no burial other than that of a close blood relative.

46. More generally, priest and Levite represent the two distinguished castes of Judaism; all other Jews belong to an undifferentiated mass called simply *Israel.* The priests were of course officiants: they uttered the blessings over the nation in the temple ritual and do so still today in the synagogue service. The Levites were the attendants of the priests. In the temple they performed various ministering tasks, such as transporting the Ark and ritual objects, and today they minister to the priests by assisting them in washing their hands prior to the performance of the priestly blessing. The hierarchical order priest, Levite, Israel is reflected in the sequence in which members of the congregation are called up during the Torah reading in the synagogue (see note 28 above). [Ed.]

47. Samson Raphael Hirsch (1808–88), rabbi of the congregation of Frankfurt am Main, was the uncontested leader of orthodox Jewry in Germany in the nineteenth century. [Ed.]

48. The contemporary prayer for the State of Israel instituted by the Chief Rabbinate of Israel begins with the phrase *'Avinu shebashamayim.* [Ed.]

49. We adopt here the alternative reading offered in the NRSV. [Ed.]

50. Rabbi Gamaliel indeed praised the Creator with a blessing at the sight of a lovely heathen woman (JT, Berakhoth 9.1).

51. In BT, Berakhoth 10a, Rabbi Me'ir is said to have been vexed with some hooligans living in his neighborhood and to have prayed for them to die. His wife, Beruria, upbraided him for this with reference to Psalm 104:35: "Let

sinners be consumed from the earth," where the Hebrew word treated as *chatta'im* in the Masoretic text but taken in the sense of *chot'im* and universally translated "sinners" could also be read in the unredacted text as *chata'im* (sins). Beruria was thus exhorting her husband to pray not that the offending sinners should die but that they should repent and their sins therefore disappear from the earth. Few indeed were the women of that period (late second century C.E.) with the linguistic training to engage in such homiletic perspicacity. [Ed.]

52. Cf. Job 22:28. [Ed.]

53. According to (post-talmudic) legend, Beruria is said to have derided certain statements of the rabbis censuring women for their frivolity. Rabbi Me'ir then tested her mettle by persuading one of his students to attempt to seduce her. Feeling compromised by his advances, she committed suicide. [Ed.]

54. Of all the teachers of the Talmud known to us, only one was unmarried: Ben-'Azzai (second century), who was accordingly held up to ridicule (BT, Yevamoth 63b).

55. Hosea 2:1 in the Hebrew Bible. [Ed.]

56. As late as the Revised Standard Version. [Ed.]

57. In more recent times, the late Lubavitcher Rebbe, Menachem Mendel Schneerson (1902–94), was thought by many of his followers to be the Messiah. [Ed.]

58. Naturally, one could adduce here the Aramaic form *Kephas* (John 1:42), which John Allegro ("Secret Code") considers to be a designation for an Essene office.

59. Robert Henning, "Das Bildnis Jesus," in *Der christliche Sonntag*, 25 December 1966, 414.

60. The traditional vocalization of this mishnaic formula is "'Ani *Vaho* hoshi'a na." As such, it cannot mean "I and He (= 'Ani *vehu*), save us," but is usually explained as a substitute for the straightforward phrase "'Anna YHWH hoshi'a na" (Ah now, YHWH, save, we pray). The tetragram (YHWH) was of course deemed ineffable by Jews and was therefore not pronounced except by the high priest during the Yom Kippur rite. Otherwise, it was euphemistically replaced, even in ancient times, by *'Adonai*, 'My Lord.' In a classical case of secondary taboo, this euphemism was itself replaced, except in the context of prescribed prayer, by *hashem* (lit. 'the name'). One possible explanation for the substitution of *'ani vaho* for *'anna YHWH* involves the widely practiced procedure of the rabbis known as *gematria*, in which the

Hebrew letters are assigned numerical values, and words having identical values are homiletically associated. Applying this method here, we find that *'ani vaho* and *'anna YHWH* possess the same numerical value: 78. The phrase *'ani vaho hoshi'a na* is found not within the Hallel Prayer proper (see note 62) but rather in a supplementary processional occurring later in the service. It is therefore likely that this formula was devised in order to avoid repeating the divine name, which (albeit euphemized as *'Adonai*) had already been uttered in the original phraseology of the Hallel entreaty. [Ed.]

61. Hebrew: "They shall look upon *me* whom they have pierced." See note 95 below. [Ed.]

62. The Hallel Psalms are Psalms 113–18, and the recitation of these Psalms is known as the Hallel Prayer. This prayer is one of the most distinctive features of the liturgy of the festive holidays, which include, in addition to the pilgrimage feasts (Passover, Pentecost, and Tabernacles), Chanukah, and new moons. A shortened version of Hallel, omitting verses 1–11 of Psalms 115 and 116, is recited on new moons (because of their status as lesser holidays) and also on the last six days of Passover. The latter shortening stems from the conception of divine love for all mankind: according to the Talmud (BT, Megilla 10b), when the angels sang for joy after the Children of Israel had crossed safely over the parted waters of the Red Sea, God rebuked them, saying that it was not right for them to rejoice while his creatures, the Egyptians, were drowning as the sea surged back over them. The crossing is commemorated on the seventh day of Passover, and the Hallel is therefore abridged on that day. But in order not to make the intermediary days of the festival (*chol hamo'ed*, lit. 'profane [part] of the festival') seem more important than the seventh day of 'holy convocation' (*mikra' kodesh*), the Hallel is abridged on those days as well. [Ed.]

63. The hosha'na (*hoshi'a na*) formula, which is recited not only on the three pilgrimage festivals but also on each new moon and throughout all eight days of Chanukah, is only weakly characterized on all occasions except the Feast of Tabernacles, where it is especially ritualized in two ways. First, the *lulav* is waved up and down on the very words *hoshi'a na* during the actual recital of the Hallel Prayer in which it is embedded; on no other occasion are these words accompanied by any ritual act. Second, only on the Feast of Tabernacles is there a special service (called in Hebrew *hosha'noth*) in which the *bima* is encircled while prayers for salvation are uttered with *'ethrog* and *lulav*

in hand. Finally, the seventh day of Sukkoth is known as *Hosha'na Rabba* (lit. 'The Great [or, better, Manifold] Hosha'na') because during the morning service of this day all the *hosha'noth* prayers recited individually for each particular day of Sukkoth are recited together, as well as numerous other prayers—some messianic in nature, others supplicative for rain—unlike anything else recited during the rest of the year. Moreover, this day is deemed to be a time of great solemnity, sometimes referred to as Little Yom Kippur, because of a tradition that on this eleventh day after Yom Kippur the Book of Life, in which Jews hope to be registered for the coming year, is finally and irrevocably closed. Symbolizing this final opportunity for divine forgiveness, a bundle consisting of five willow branches (*'aravoth*) is beaten on the ground toward the end of the special Hosha'na Rabba service, an act of transferred self-castigation. This ritual is reported in the Mishna (Sukka 4.6) to have occurred already within the temple service. By a process of metonymy, the willow bundles themselves became known as *hosha'noth*. [Ed.]

64. Perhaps a group of people, a *minyan* (prayer quorum), who had gathered to recite the holiday prayer service apart from the overcrowded confines of the temple. It is further likely that at the point when Jesus and his disciples encountered this group, they were reciting the Hallel Prayer, with palm branches in hand, and had just come to that section in which the phrase *barukh haba' beshem YHWH* (blessed be he who comes in the name of the Lord) is proclaimed. [Ed.]

65. Friedrich Pzillas ("Messiaskönig") provides a clear summary of Eisler's theses and shows, among other things, that the overrated Joel Carmichael has followed directly in Eisler's footsteps.

66. This statement was uttered by Hillel upon seeing a skull floating on the surface of the water. The first part of the saying is, "Because thou hast drowned [others], they have drowned thee." Apparently, Hillel knew the man whose skull it was, and his character as well. [Ed.]

67. The Hagana ('defense') was the forerunner, in British Mandatory Palestine, of the modern Israeli defense forces (Tseva Hagana Leyisra'el). Both the Irgun Tsevai Leumi ('national military organization') and the Stern Gang (the British designation for the Lochamei-Cheruth Yisra'el, 'freedom fighters of Israel') were right-wing forces that remained outside the Hagana and operated independently of it. They were disbanded upon the formation of the State of Israel in 1948. [Ed.]

68. It is not a question here of a variant reading but rather of a metonym. Similar usages of "Canaanite" for "merchant" in the Hebrew Bible are found in Proverbs 31:24 and Job 41:6 (Job 40:30 in the Hebrew Bible). [Ed.]

69. Papyrus Egerton 2, a fragment of a papyrus code of unknown provenance purchased by the British Museum in 1934, contains four text fragments, three of which have parallels in the canonical Gospels. One of these is a version of the tribute coin pericope. Its date has been placed variously from around 100 to around 150 C.E. If the former, it would be one of the earliest Christian texts in existence; however, its status relative to the canonical Gospels is a matter of intense debate. For an assessment of the issues, cf. Charlesworth and Evans, "Jesus." In any event, Ben-Chorin's characterization of this papyrus as "later tradition" is one-sided. [Ed.]

70. On the problem of the Qumran calendar, see Schubert, *Dead Sea Community*, 57–58.

71. Rabbi Elijah Ben-Solomon Zalman, called "the Vilna Ga'on" (1720–97), was the leader of Lithuanian Jewry in the eighteenth century. [Ed.]

72. A *Ga'on* (pl. *Ge'onim*; lit. 'pride,' 'eminence') was an intellectual leader of Babylonian Jewry in the post-talmudic period (sixth to eleventh centuries). Rabbi 'Amram Bar-Sheshya Ga'on headed the prestigious Sura academy from 856 to 874 C.E. [Ed.]

73. There is an argument concerning whether there should be four or five cups at the Seder, based on textual attestations in the Bible. As is often the case in the Talmud, when a point cannot be resolved one way or the other, one finds the statement *teyku* (lit. 'let it stand!'). A folk etymology later understood this term to be an acronym for the sentence "*Tishbi yetarets kusheyoth uve'ayoth*" (The Tishbite [i.e., Elijah, son of Tishbi] will solve difficulties and problems): hence the cup of Elijah, who will come and solve the legal question of four versus five cups. [Ed.]

74. Kosmala here modifies Mark 14:24: "This is my blood of the covenant, which is poured out for many." [Ed.]

75. The designation "four questions" for this catechistic recitation must be understood loosely. The text runs as follows (we quote from *The Hirsch Haggadah*, 61, 63):

> Why is this night different from all other nights? On all other nights, we may eat leavened or unleavened bread; tonight we must eat only matsa. On all other nights, we may eat all kinds of vegetables; tonight we must

eat bitter herbs. On all other nights, we are not required to dip even once; tonight we are required to dip twice. On all other nights, we may eat either sitting or reclining; tonight we must all recline.

From this it appears at first that there are not four questions here but only one, followed by four answers. Even if, as is more likely, the Hebrew particle *she-*, which introduces each of the four apparent answers, should be translated 'inasmuch as,' we still have a single question, albeit a highly complex one with four subparts, each designating an aspect of the uniqueness of the night, which still needs an explanation. When understood in this way, the real answer is the narration or *maggid* (from the same Hebrew root as *haggada*) that immediately follows: "We were slaves unto Pharaoh in Egypt." Placing the conjunction "because" before this clause would do justice to the contextual meaning implicit in its juxtaposition to the "four questions." [Ed.]

76. The ultimate source of this midrash is the formulation in the Torah, Deuteronomy 6:20: "When your children ask [Hebrew: 'your son asks'] you in time to come, 'What is the meaning of the decrees and the statutes and the ordinances that the Lord our God has commanded you?' . . ." [Ed.]

77. This command is a direct quotation from the Haggada. Its ultimate scriptural source is Exodus 13:8: "You shall tell your child [Hebrew: 'son'] on that day. . . ." [Ed.]

78. The two dippings involve, first, the dipping of fruits of the earth (*karpas* = parsley, celery, or the like) into saltwater, symbolic of the tears of those forced into hard labor by Pharaoh; then, the dipping of the bitter herb (*maror* = horseradish, romaine lettuce, etc.) into a puree of apples, nuts, and wine called *charoseth*. The bitter herb is, of course, symbolic of the bitterness of slavery; the *charoseth* symbolizes the mortar that the Hebrew slaves were forced to make as they built the storerooms of Pharaoh. [Ed.]

79. The NRSV, used as the base translation, is modified here as necessary to conform to Buber. [Ed.]

80. Or better, *epikomon*, a so-called delocutive formation derived from an uttered phrase *epi komon*, 'to the revels!' (these being understood here as after-meal entertainment). The phrase *epi komon badizein*, 'to proceed to the revels,' is actually used in classical Greek literature by the playwright Aristophanes. Ironically, the revels in question were often enacted in honor of Greek deities, particularly Dionysus, god of wine and fertility, the orgiastic worship of whom was proverbial. [Ed.]

81. The *kos hatarʿela;* cf. Isaiah 51:17, 22. [Ed.]

82. These passages are the key ones, though variations and additions to the narrative appear here and there elsewhere in the Gospels, as well.

83. Cf. Klausner's chapter "The Trial" in *Jesus,* 339–48. [Ed.]

84. To be sure, a classical precedent already existed in Jeremiah's sharp words regarding the temple (7:4–15).

85. The same sort of evasive or ambiguous formula is also attested in the Talmud, as in BT, Kethuvoth 104a (in the plural form): "You all say so."

86. Greek *lampros* ('bright', 'shining'; said of garments, esp. white ones; cf. vulgate *veste alba*). The NRSV translates it as 'elegant'; the RSV, 'gorgeous'— both missing the nuance here, as Ben-Chorin explains. [Ed.]

87. This refers to his reading the portion from the Torah dealing with the Day of Atonement. [Ed.]

88. In his book *On the Trial of Jesus,* Paul Winter dedicates an entire chapter (91–99, notes 198–201) to this *privilegium paschale.*

89. The Swedish poet Pär Lagerkvist expresses the idea in this fashion in his novel *Barabbas* (1951).

90. It often happened in the calendar, reckoned according to the official dating of the temple authority, that the first day of the Passover celebration was a Sabbath. The slaughtering of the Passover lamb in such instances had to take place somewhat earlier than on other days.

91. The *ʾAmoraim* (Aramaic *ʾamora,* 'interpreter') were the group of learned men who were active in Palestine and Babylonia from about 200 to 500 of our era, following the compilation of the Mishna. The names of hundreds of these scholars are preserved in the Talmud. [Ed.]

92. I have not been able to date this midrash passage precisely; it belongs, however, to the Christian era.

93. We wish to emphasize that Ben-Chorin is using the term *midrash* here and in the following paragraphs loosely and imprecisely. In its strict usage, midrash refers to a body of literature, of widely diverse origin in both space and time, which exists in a large number of books and collections (for a reasoned assessment of these, see Strack and Stemberger, *Introduction to the Talmud and Midrash*). Ben-Chorin's contention seems to amount to a claim that some now lost midrashic material dealing with Zechariah (and Psalms) may have existed around the time of the Evangelists and have been incorporated into the Gospels. Although not out of the question, this cannot of course be proved. [Ed.]

94. Psalm 22:19 in the Hebrew Bible. [Ed.]

95. The NRSV has mistranslated here. The Hebrew text says very clearly "And they shall look upon Me [i.e., the Lord]." What follows is less clear and may be translated either "whom they have thrust through" or "because they have thrust [him] through." As noted above, the Talmud refers this passage to the Messiah, son of Joseph, who will die in battle. Modern Jewish commentators are inclined to see here a reference to a sense of national remorse over the execution of some leader whom the people have rejected. Cashdan, "Zechariah," questions whether this may have been Zerubbabel, the satrap of Davidic descent who took some of the first steps toward the restoration of the Temple in Jerusalem following the Babylonian captivity. [Ed.]

96. Mark reads, "Eloi, Eloi, lema sabachthani." Matthew employs the shorter (Hebrew) form of the *nomen Dei: 'El* + first person possessive suffix *i*, whereas Mark employs the longer (Aramaic) form *'Elah* (or *'Eloh*) + *i* (since Greek has no medial *h*, *'Elahi* [or *'Elohi*] is reproduced as *elōi*). The verb of this final cry, *sabachthani*, is to be equated with Aramaic *shevaktani*, the precise semantic equivalent of Hebrew *'azavtani*, which is the verb employed in Psalm 22:1. It is found, as well, as a variant reading of both the Matthaian and Marcan passages in the Codex Bezae, where it takes the form *zaphthani*. This important manuscript also provides the reading *lama* for 'why.' [Ed.]

97. Harris Birkeland disagrees in his book *The Language of Jesus* (1954).

98. Psalm 31:6 in the Hebrew Bible. [Ed.]

99. Cf. here the talmudic passages to which we have already made reference in BT, tractate Sukka 51b–52a.

100. According to Jewish law, Passover is a seven-day festival, but only on the first and seventh days are Jews enjoined to have a holy convocation and not to perform halakhically defined work (*mele'kheth-'avoda*). The intermediate five days, less charged with religious restrictions, are termed in Hebrew *chol hamo'ed* (lit. 'profane [part] of the festival'; see note 62 above). In the year of Jesus' crucifixion, Sunday would have been the first such intermediate day, when his women followers would have been free to visit his burial site. [Ed.]

101. The enlightened position was represented by Lessing against the orthodox Hamburg preacher Johann Melchior Goeze, and the entire affair became known as the Goeze controversy.

102. *Wichtige historische Enthüllungen über die wirkliche Todesart Jesu, nach*

einem alten, zu Alexandrien gefundenen Manuscripte, von einem Zeitgenossen Jesu aus dem heiligen Orden der Essäer (Important historical revelations on the true manner of death of Jesus, according to an old manuscript found at Alexandria by a contemporary of Jesus from the Holy Order of the Essenes).

103. Kosmala ("Conclusion of Matthew") notes that in the oldest versions the passage referred to here contains no injunction to baptize but speaks rather about gaining disciples from all nations in the name of Jesus, and it omits all reference to the Trinity. This original version is cited by Eusebius.

104. A rich body of literature exists on the subject of the sayings of Jesus. For an orientation to the most recent scholarship on this still controversial subject, consult Burton Mack's books *The Lost Gospel* (1993) and *Who Wrote the New Testament?* (1995). [Ed.]

Bibliography

Achad Ha'am (Asher Hirsch Ginzberg). "Worte des Friedens." Hebrew, 1894; in *Am Scheideweg: Gesammelte Aufsätze,* translated into German by Israel Friedländer and Harry Torczyner, 1: 215–35. Berlin: Jüdischer Verlag, 1923.

Allegro, John M. *Die Botschaft vom Toten Meer: Das Geheimnis der Schriftrollen.* Frankfurt am Main: Fischer, 1957.

——. *The Dead Sea Scrolls and the Christian Myth.* 2d rev. ed. Buffalo, N.Y.: Prometheus Books, 1992.

——. "Secret Code of the New Testament." *Jerusalem Post,* 13 January 1967, 8.

Aron, Robert. *Jesus of Nazareth: The Hidden Years.* Translated by Frances Frenaye. New York: William Morrow, 1962.

Augstein, Rudolf. *Jesus Son of Man.* Translated by Hugh Young. Preface by Gore Vidal. Afterword by David Noel Freedman. New York: Urizen Books, 1977.

The Babylonian Talmud. Translated with notes, glossary, and indexes under the editorship of Rabbi Dr. Isidore Epstein. 18 vols. London: Soncino Press, 1961.

Der babylonische Talmud. Translated and edited by Lazarus Goldschmidt. 12 vols. 1929–36. Reprint, Königstein: Taunus, 1980–81.

Baeck, Leo. "The Gospel as a Document of the History of the Jewish Faith." In *Judaism and Christianity,* translated by Walter Kaufmann, 39–136. New York: Atheneum, 1970.

——. *Paulus, die Pharisäer und das Neue Testament.* Frankfurt am Main: Ner-Tamid, 1961.

Biblia Hebraica Stuttgartensia. Edited by Hans Bardtke, Karl Elliger, et al. Stuttgart: Würtembergische Bibelanstalt, 1968–75.

Birkeland, Harris. *The Language of Jesus.* Avhandlinger utgitt av Det Norske

Videnskaps-Akademi i Oslo, II, Hist-Filos. Klasse, 1954, no. 1. Oslo: I kommisjon hos Jacob Dybwad, 1954.

Blinzler, Josef. *Der Prozeß Jesu: Das jüdische und das römische Gerichtsverfahren gegen Jesus Christus auf Grund der ältesten Zeugnisse.* 3d ed. Regensburg: Friedrich Pustet, 1960.

Blüher, Hans. *Die Aristie des Jesus von Nazareth: Philosophische Grundlegung der Lehre und der Erscheinung Christi.* Prien, Bavaria: Kampmann & Schnabel, 1921.

Bornkamm, Günther. *Jesus of Nazareth.* Translated by Irene and Fraser McLuskey, with James M. Robinson. New York: Harper, 1960.

Braun, Herbert. *Jesus of Nazareth: The Man and His Time.* Translated by Everett R. Kalin. Philadelphia: Fortress Press, 1979.

Buber, Martin. "Geltung und Grenze des politischen Prinzips." In *Gedenkschrift zur Verleihung des Hansischen Goethe-Preises 1951 der gemeinnützigen Stiftung F. V. S. zu Hamburg an Martin Buber, überreicht am 24. Juni 1953.* Hamburg, 1953.

———. *Two Types of Faith.* Translated by Norman P. Goldhawk. New York: Harper, 1961.

Buber, Martin, and Franz Rosenzweig, trans. *Schrift verdeutscht.* Cologne: J. Hegner, 1954.

Bultmann, Rudolf. *Jesus and the Word.* 1926. Translated by Louise Pettibone Smith and Erminie Huntress Lantero. New York: Scribner, 1989.

———. *Jesus Christ and Mythology.* New York: Scribner, 1958.

———. *Kerygma and Myth: A Theological Debate.* Translated by Reginald H. Fuller. Edited by Hans Werner Bartsch. London: S.P.C.K., 1960.

———. *New Testament and Mythology and Other Basic Writings.* Selected, edited, and translated by Schubert M. Ogden. Philadelphia: Fortress Press, 1984.

Carmichael, Joel. *The Death of Jesus.* New York: Macmillan, 1962.

Casanova, Giacomo Girolamo. *The Memoirs of Jacques Casanova de Seingalt.* Translated by Arthur Machen. Vol. 4. New York: Putnam, 1959.

Cashdan, Eli. *Zechariah. Introduction and Commentary.* In *The Twelve Prophets,* edited by A. Cohen, 266–322. London: Soncino Press, 1948.

Chajes, Hirsch Perez. *Markus-Studien.* Berlin: Schwetschke, 1899.

Charlesworth, James H., and Craig A. Evans. "Jesus in the Agrapha and Apocryphal Gospels." In *Studying the Historical Jesus: Evaluations of the State of Current Research,* edited by Bruce Chilton and Craig A. Evans, 479–533. Leiden: E. J. Brill, 1994.

Cohen, Hermann. *Reason and Hope: Selections from the Jewish Writings of Hermann Cohen.* Translated by Eva Jospe. New York: Norton, 1971.

Cohn, Haim. "Reflections on the Trial and Death of Jesus." *Israel Law Review* 2 (1967): 332–79.

———. *The Trial and Death of Jesus.* New York: Harper & Row, 1971.

Daube, David. *The New Testament and Rabbinic Judaism.* 1956. Reprint. Peabody, Mass.: Hendrickson, 1994.

[*Dead Sea Scrolls*]. *A Facsimile Edition of the Dead Sea Scrolls.* Edited by Robert H. Eisenman and James M. Robinson. 2 vols. Washington, D.C.: Biblical Archeology Society, 1991.

Deschner, Karlheinz, ed. *Jesusbilder in theologischer Sicht.* Munich: List, 1966.

Eisler, Robert. *The Messiah Jesus and John the Baptist.* Translated by Alexander Haggerty Krappe. New York: Dial, 1931.

Elliger, Karl. *Das Buch der zwölf kleinen Propheten, II.* 2d ed. Göttingen: Vandenhoeck & Ruprecht, 1951.

[*Evangelien*]. *Die vier Evangelien ins Hebräische übersetzt.* Translated by Franz Delitzsch. Turnhout, Belgium: Brepols, 1984.

Exodus Rabbah. Translated by Simon Maurice Lehrman. Vol. 3 of *Midrash Rabbah,* edited by Harry Freedman and Maurice Simon. 3d ed. London: Soncino Press, 1961.

Flusser, David. *Jesus in Selbstzeugnissen und Bilddokumenten.* Reinbek bei Hamburg: Rowohlt, 1968.

———. *Judaism and the Origins of Christianity.* Jerusalem: Magnes Press, Hebrew University, 1988.

———. "Qumran und die Zwölf." In *Studies in the History of Religions X: Initiation* (supplements to *Numen,* no. 10), edited by Claas Jouco Bleeker, 134–46. Leiden: E. J. Brill, 1965.

France, Anatole. "The Procurator of Judaea." In *Golden Tales of Anatole France,* 1–25. New York: Dodd, Mead, 1927.

Freud, Sigmund. *Moses and Monotheism.* Translated by Katherine Jones. New York: Knopf, 1939.

Genesis Rabbah. Translated by Harry Freedman. Vols. 1 and 2 of *Midrash Rabbah,* edited by Freedman and Maurice Simon. 3d ed. London: Soncino Press, 1961.

Goethe, Johann Wolfgang von. *West-östlicher Divan.* 1819. Edited by Hans-J. Weitz. Insel Taschenbuch 75. Frankfurt am Main: Insel Verlag, 1974.

———. *West-östlicher Divan: Wiesbader Register.* Edited with commentary by Konrad Burdach. In *Zur Entstehungsgeschichte des West-östlichen Divans,* edited by Ernst Grumach. 2d ed. Berlin: Akademie-Verlag, 1959.

Goldberg, Oskar. *Die Wirklichkeit der Hebräer: Einleitung in das System des Pentateuch.* Berlin: David, 1925.

Grant, Frederick C. *Ancient Judaism and the New Testament.* New York: Macmillan, 1959.

Graves, Robert. *King Jesus: A Novel.* New York: Farrar, Straus & Giroux, 1981.

[*Haggadah*]. *The Hirsch Haggadah.* 2d ed. New York: Feldheim, 1989.

Harnack, Adolf von. *What Is Christianity? Lectures Delivered in the University of Berlin during the Winter-Term, 1899–1900.* Translated by Thomas Bailey Saunders. 2d ed. New York: Putnam, 1902.

Hegemann, Werner. *Christ Rescued.* Translated by Gerald Griffin. London: Skeffington, 1935.

Heinemann, Joseph. "The Triennial Lectionary Cycle." *Journal of Jewish Studies* 17, no. 4 (1966): 41–48.

Higgins, Angus John Brockhurst. *Jesus and the Son of Man.* Philadelphia: Fortress Press, 1964.

———. *Menschensohn-Studien.* Franz Delitzsch-Vorlesungen. 1961. Stuttgart: Kohlhammer, 1965.

Hirsch, Samson Raphael. *Horeb [Chorev]: A Philosophy of Jewish Laws and Observances.* Translated with an introduction and annotations by Dayan I. Grunfeld. 2 vols. London: Soncino Press, 1962.

Horowitz, David. *The Bible in the Hands of Its Creators: Biblical Facts as They Are.* New York: Society of the Bible in the Hands of Its Creators, 1943.

Hurwitz, Siegmund. *Die Gestalt des sterbenden Messias: Religionspsychologische Aspekte der jüdischen Apokalyptik.* Zürich: Rascher, 1958.

Jeremias, Joachim. *The Eucharistic Words of Jesus.* Translated by Norman Perrin. London: SCM Press; Philadelphia: Trinity Press International, 1990.

Jerusalem Talmud. *The Talmud of the Land of Israel: A Preliminary Translation and Explanation.* Chicago Studies in the History of Judaism, 35 vols., ed. Jacob Neusner. Chicago: University of Chicago Press, 1982–94.

Josephus, Flavius. *Jewish Antiquities.* Translated by H. St. J. Thackeray, Ralph Marcus, and Louis H. Feldman. 7 vols. Cambridge, Mass.: Harvard University Press, 1930–65.

————. *The Jewish War.* Translated by H. St. J. Thackeray. 2 vols. Cambridge, Mass.: Harvard University Press, 1927–28.

Judentum und Christentum: Parallelen. Jüdische Volksbücherei 4. Zurich: Jüdischer Volksschriftenverlag, 1952.

Jung, C. G. *Answer to Job.* Translated by R. F. C. Hull. London: Routledge & Paul, 1954.

Justin Martyr. *The First and Second Apologies.* Translated with introduction and notes by Leslie William Barnard. Mahwah, N.J.: Paulist Press, 1997.

Käsemann, Ernst. *Essays on New Testament Themes.* Translated by W. J. Montague. Philadelphia: Fortress Press, 1982.

Kerr, Alfred. "Jeruschalajim." 1903. In Kerr, *Gesammelte Schriften,* 7:153–79. Berlin: S. Fischer, 1920.

Klausner, Joseph. *Jesus of Nazareth: His Life, Times, and Teaching.* 1922. Translated by Herbert Danby. New York: Macmillan, 1925.

Kosmala, Hans. "The Conclusion of Matthew." *Annual of the Swedish Theological Institute* 4 (1965): 132 ff.

————. *Hebräer—Essener—Christen: Studien zur Vorgeschichte der frühchristlichen Verkündigung.* Leiden: E. J. Brill, 1959.

La Farge, Henry Adams. *Lost Treasures of Europe: 427 Photographs.* New York: Pantheon Books, 1946.

Lagerkvist, Pär. *Barabbas.* Translated by Alan Blair. New York: Random House, 1951.

Landau, Herbert. "Jesus in jüdischer Sicht." In *Jesusbilder in theologischer Sicht,* edited by Karlheinz Deschner, 299–343. Munich: List, 1966.

Lauterbach, Jacob Zallel. "Jesus in the Talmud." In *Rabbinic Essays,* edited by Lauterbach, 473–570. Cincinnati: Hebrew Union College Press, 1951.

Leviticus Rabbah. Edited by Jacob Israelstam and Judah Jacob Slotki. Vol. 4 of *Midrash Rabbah,* edited by Harry Freedman and Maurice Simon. 3d ed. London: Soncino Press, 1961.

Lisowsky, Gerhard. *Die Mischna, Jadajim.* Berlin: Topelmann, 1956.

Lohse, Eduard, ed. *Die Texte aus Qumran: Hebräisch und Deutsch. Mit masoretischer Punktuation: Übersetzung, Einführung und Anmerkungen.* 2d ed. Munich: Kosel, 1971.

Ludwig, Emil. *The Son of Man.* Translated by Eden and Cedar Paul. Garden City, N.Y.: Garden City Publishing, 1928.

Luther, Martin. *Die gantze Heilige Schrifft Deudsch.* 1545. Edited by Hanz Volz,

with Heinz Blanke. Reprint, Herrsching: Manfred Pawlak, Verlagsgesell-
schaft Mbh., n.d.

Mack, Burton L. *The Lost Gospel: The Book of Q and Christian Origins.* San
Francisco: HarperSanFrancisco, 1993.

———. *Who Wrote the New Testament? The Making of the Christian Myth.*
San Francisco: HarperSanFrancisco, 1995.

*Mekilta de Rabbi Ishmael: A Critical Edition on the Basis of the MSS and Early
Editions with an English Translation, Introduction, and Notes.* 3 vols. Philadelphia: Jewish Publication Society of America, 1933–35.

The Midrash on Psalms. Edited by W. G. Braude. 2 vols. 3d ed. New Haven:
Yale University Press, 1976.

Midrash Rabbah: Translated into English. Edited by Harry Freedman and
Maurice Simon. 10 vols. 3d ed. London: Soncino Press, 1961.

The Mishnah. Translated by Herbert Danby. Oxford: Oxford University Press,
1933.

Mishnayoth. Edited by Philip Blackman, with translation and notes. 7 vols.
2d ed. New York: Judaica Press, 1963–64.

Montefiore, Claude Joseph Goldsmid, ed. *The Synoptic Gospels.* 1909. 2 vols.
2d ed. 1927. Reprint, New York: Ktav, 1968.

Otto, Gert. *Glauben heute: Ein Lesebuch zur evangelischen Theologie der Gegen-
wart.* Hamburg: Furche, 1965.

Parker, D. C. *Codex Bezae: An Early Christian Manuscript and Its Text.* Cambridge: Cambridge University Press, 1992.

Pentateuch with Targum Onkelos, Haphtaroth and Rashi's Commentary. Vol. 5.
Translated and annotated by M. Rosenbaum and A. M. Silbermann. New
York: Hebrew Publishing, 1935.

Die Pessach-Haggadah. Edited with commentary by E. D. Goldschmidt. Berlin: Schocken, 1936.

Philo of Alexandria. *De legatione ad Gaium.* Vol. 10 of *Philo.* Translated by
F. H. Coulson. Loeb Classical Library. Cambridge, Mass.: Harvard University Press, 1962.

Pines, Shlomo. *The Jewish Christians of the Early Centuries of Christianity
according to a New Source.* Israel Academy of Sciences and Humanities
Proceedings 2, no. 13. Jerusalem: Israel Academy of Sciences and Humanities, 1966.

Pzillas, Friedrich, "Der Messiaskönig Jesus." In *Jesusbilder in theologischer
Sicht,* edited by Karlheinz Deschner, 181–206. Munich: List, 1966.

Rad, Gerhard von. *Deuteronomy: A Commentary.* Translated by Dorothea Barton. Philadelphia: Westminster Press, 1966.

Ragaz, Leonhard. *Die Gleichnisse Jesu.* Bern: Herbert Lang & Cie, 1944.

Raschke, Hermann. "Der ungeschichtliche Jesus." In *Jesusbilder in theologischer Sicht,* edited by Karlheinz Deschner, 343–444. Munich: List, 1966.

Reimarus, Hermann Samuel. *The Goal of Jesus and His Disciples.* Translated with introduction by George Wesley Buchanan. Leiden: E. J. Brill, 1970.

Rienecker, Fritz. *Das Evangelium des Lukas erklärt.* Wuppertaler Studienbibel. Wuppertal: R. Brockhaus, 1959.

Riethmüller, Helmut, ed. *Das Neue Testament für Menschen unserer Zeit.* Stuttgart: Quell-Verlag, 1964.

Rosenzweig, Franz. *The Star of Redemption.* Translated from the second edition of 1930 by William W. Hallo. New York: Holt, Rinehart & Winston, 1970.

Rousseau, Jean-Jacques. *Emile; or, On Education.* Translated with introduction and notes by Allan Bloom. New York: Basic Books, 1979.

Salkinson, Isaac Edward. *Ha-Berith ha-Chadashah* [The New Testament]. London: Trinitarian Bible Society, 1885.

Sandmel, Samuel. *A Jewish Understanding of the New Testament.* 1956. Reprint, New York: Ktav, 1968.

Schechter, Solomon. *Studies in Judaism.* 2d series. Philadelphia: Jewish Publication Society of America, 1938.

Schiller, Friedrich. *Gedichte.* Vol. 1 of *Sämtliche Werke.* Berlin: Aufbau-Verlag, 1980.

Schmidt, Heinrich. *Die vier Evangelien.* Leipzig: Alfred Kröner, 1910.

Schoeps, Hans-Joachim. "Jesus." 1950. In *Die großen Religionsstifter und ihre Lehren,* rev. ed., 35–69. Munich: List, 1967.

———. *Jewish Christianity: Factional Disputes in the Early Church.* Translated by Douglas R. A. Hare. Philadelphia: Fortress Press, 1969.

Scholem, Gershom. *Sabbatai Sevi: The Mystical Messiah, 1626–1676.* Bollingen Series 93. Princeton: Princeton University Press, 1973.

Schonfield, Hugh. *The Passover Plot: New Light on the History of Jesus.* New York: Bernard Geis, 1965. Reprinted as *A New Interpretation of the Life and Death of Jesus,* Shaftesbury, Dorset, U.K.; Rockport, Mass.: Element, 1993.

Schubert, Kurt. *The Dead Sea Community: Its Origins and Teachings.* Translated by John W. Doberstein. New York: Harper, 1959.

Schweitzer, Albert. *The Kingdom of God and Primitive Christianity.* Edited by

Ulrich Neuenschwander. Translated by L. A. Garrard. New York: Seabury Press, 1968.

———. *The Quest of the Historical Jesus: A Critical Study of Its Progress from Reimarus to Wrede*. Translated by W. Montgomery. New York: Macmillan, 1950.

Sigge, Franz. *Das neue Testament*. Cologne: Jakob Hegner, 1958.

Sölle, Dorothee. *Christ the Representative: An Essay in Theology after the Death of God*. Translated by David Lewis. Philadelphia: Fortress Press, 1967.

Song of Songs Rabbah. Edited by Maurice Simon. Vol. 9 of *Midrash Rabbah*, edited by Harry Freedman and Maurice Simon. 3d ed. London: Soncino Press, 1961.

Spong, John Shelby. *Liberating the Gospels: Reading the Bible with Jewish Eyes*. San Francisco: HarperCollins, 1996.

Stauffer, Ethelbert. *Jerusalem und Rom*. Bern: Francke, 1957.

———. *Jesus and His Story*. Translated by Richard and Clara Winston. New York: Knopf, 1967.

———. *Die Theologie des Neuen Testaments*. 3d ed. Stuttgart: W. Kohlhammer, 1947.

Strack, Hermann L. *P^E SAHIM: Der Mišnatraktat Passafest*. Leipzig: J. C. Hinrichs'sche Buchhandlung, 1911.

Strack, Hermann L., and Paul Billerbeck. *Kommentar zum neuen Testament aus Talmud und Midrasch*. 6 vols. Munich: Beck, 1922–61.

Strack, Hermann L., and Günter Stemberger. *Introduction to the Talmud and Midrash*. Translated by Markus Bockmuehl. Minneapolis: Fortress Press, 1992.

Tertullian, Quintus Septimius Florens. *De Baptismo Liber: Homily on Baptism*. Translated and edited with commentary by Ernest Evans. London: S.P.C.K., 1964.

The Tosefta. Translated by Jacob Neusner et al. 6 vols. New York: Ktav, 1977–86.

Unnik, Willem Cornelis van. *Evangelien aus dem Nilsand*. Frankfurt am Main: Scheffler, 1960.

Vermes, Geza. *Jesus the Jew: A Historian's Reading of the Gospels*. New York: Macmillan, 1973.

Voigts, Manfred. *Oskar Goldberg: Der mythische Experimentalwissenschaftler: Ein verdrängtes Kapitel jüdischer Geschichte*. Literaturwissenschaftliche Schriften 10. Berlin: Agora, 1992.

Wacholder, Ben Zion. "Prolegomenon." In *The Bible as Read and Preached in the Old Synagogue*, vol. 1 of *The Palestinian Triennial Cycle: Genesis and Exodus*. New York: Ktav, 1971.

Wellhausen, Julius. *Einleitung in die drei ersten Evangelien*. Berlin: G. Reimer, 1905.

Werfel, Franz. *Paulus unter den Juden: Dramatische Legende in sechs Bildern*. In *Franz Werfel: Die Dramen*, 1: 468–534. Frankfurt am Main: Fischer, 1959.

Westermann, Claus. *The Old Testament and Jesus Christ*. Translated by Omar Kaste. Minneapolis: Augsburg, 1970.

Wildberger, Hans. *Die Handschriftenfunde beim Toten Meer und ihre Bedeutung für die Erforschung der Heiligen Schrift*. Stuttgart: Calwer, 1956.

Winter, Paul. *On the Trial of Jesus*. Studia Judaica 1. Berlin: De Gruyter, 1961.

Zahrnt, Heinz. *The Historical Jesus*. Translated by J. S. Bowden. New York: Harper & Row, 1963.

Zehren, Erich. *Der gehenkte Gott*. Berlin: Herbig, 1959.

The Zohar. Translated by Maurice Simon and Henry Sperling. 5 vols. London: Soncino Press, 1931–34.

Zweig, Stefan. *Mental Healers: Franz Anton Mesmer, Mary Baker Eddy, Sigmund Freud*. Translated by Eden and Cedar Paul. New York: F. Ungar, 1962.

Index of Biblical Citations

Index of Citations from Classical Jewish Texts
(other than the Hebrew Bible)

Index of Ancient and Classical Texts, Exegetical Sources, and Translations

Haggada. *See* 'Aggada
Haggada of Passover, 126, 132, 136, 137, 140, 141, 147, 148, 203 (n. 77)
Hagiographa. *See* Writings
Halakhic Midrash(im), 196 (n. 34), 196 (n. 35)
Hebrew Bible, x, 7, 10, 27, 97, 191 (n. 10), 191 (n. 15), 191 (n. 16), 192 (n. 22), 196 (n. 31), 197 (n. 39), 197 (n. 41), 199 (n. 55), 202 (n. 68), 205 (n. 94), 205 (n. 98)
Hebrews, 150, 153, 167
Hosea, 25, 33, 108

Isaiah, 9, 53, 195 (n. 29)

Jeremiah, 9, 33, 47
Jerusalem Talmud (Palestinian Talmud; Talmud Yerushalmi), 13, 100, 189–90 (n. 1)
Job, 141, 197 (n. 39)
Joel, 33
John (Epistles), 30
John (Gospel), 36, 43, 64, 65, 67, 69, 72, 81, 99, 115, 140, 142, 154, 159, 183
John's Apocalypse (Revelation), 30, 134
Jonah, 50
Joshua, 81, 82
Judas, 144

Kethuvim. *See* Writings
King James Version (KJV), xiii, 192 (n. 21)
Ki-thavo', 41, 194 (n. 29)

Lamentations, 196 (n. 34)
Law of Moses. *See* Torah
Leviticus, 80, 196 (n. 34)
Leviticus Rabba (Vayikra' Rabba), 54, 196 (n. 34)

Luke, 30, 43, 49, 50, 51, 61, 87, 91, 95, 98, 105, 108, 109, 123, 180, 181, 185

Magnificat, 97
Mark, 34, 105, 108, 109, 129, 205 (n. 96)
Masoretic Text, 32, 56, 57, 192 (n. 22), 199 (n. 51)
Matthew, 24, 34, 50, 51, 52, 61, 91, 92, 108, 109, 139, 141, 165, 205 (n. 96)
Mekhilta, 196 (n. 34), 196 (n. 35)
Midrash, x, xi, xiii, 3, 23, 26, 42, 63, 72, 99, 103, 128, 136, 140, 141, 142, 173, 178, 182, 191 (n. 11), 203 (n. 76)
Midrash Rabba (Great Midrash), 178, 196 (n. 34)
Mishna, x, 22, 28, 31, 33, 89, 113, 114, 129, 131, 136, 166, 175, 189–90 (n. 1), 190 (n. 5), 191 (n. 7), 196 (n. 32), 196 (n. 34), 201 (n. 63), 204 (n. 91)

Nachum Commentary, 177
Nazir, 28
Nehemiah, 197 (n. 39)
Nevi'im. *See* Prophets
New Revised Standard Version (NRSV), xiii, 186, 198 (n. 49), 203 (n. 79), 204 (n. 86), 205 (n. 95)
New Testament, xi, 2–21 passim, 25, 30, 31, 33, 36, 43, 44, 45, 47, 52, 64, 65, 75, 82, 97, 99, 102, 106, 109, 126, 141, 144, 158, 159, 165, 168, 184, 192 (n. 17)
Nitsavim, 41, 194 (n. 29)
Numbers, 196 (n. 34)

Old Testament, 8, 9, 14, 15, 20, 26, 27, 56, 78, 81, 106, 107, 121, 141, 170

Palestinian Talmud. *See* Jerusalem Talmud

Index of Hebrew, Aramaic, Greek, and Latin Words and Phrases

Index of Persons

Aaron, 55, 78
'Abba 'Arikha (Rav), 54, 92, 196
  (n. 32)
'Abba Sha'ul Ben-Botnith, 162
'Abba Yosef Ben-Chanin, 162
Abednego, 183
Abel, 170
Abijah, 27
Abraham, 13, 23, 28, 33, 36, 37, 46, 99,
  178
Achad Ha'am, 59
Adam, 37, 99
Adonis, 25
Aegaeus of Athens, 24
Agrippa I, 159
Ahasuerus, 181
'Akiva Ben-Yosef (Rabbi), 13, 17, 21,
  22, 46, 56, 69, 80, 91, 102, 148, 191
  (n. 9)
Alexander Jannaeus, 11, 177
Alfasi, Isaac Ben-Jacob, 133
Allegro, John, 199 (n. 58)
Amos, 54
'Amram Bar-Sheshya Ga'on (Rabbi),
  133, 202 (n. 72)
'Anath, 142
Andrew, 49
Annas, 30, 160, 161, 162, 163, 164
Antiochus Epiphanes, 41

Apollos (Alexandrian Jew), 31
Aristophanes, 203 (n. 80)
Aron, Robert, 4

Baal, 121
Baeck, Leo (Rabbi), 4, 76
Balaam, 8
Barabbas, Jesus, 167, 168, 169, 170,
  179, 180
Bar-Kokheva, Shim'on, 17, 148, 191
  (n. 9)
Belial, 60
Ben-'Azzai, Shim'on, 199 (n. 54)
Ben-Chorin, Schalom, x, xi, xii,
  xiii, 189–90 (n. 1), 192 (n. 17), 192
  (n. 20), 193 (n. 22), 195 (n. 29), 196
  (n. 36), 202 (n. 69), 204 (n. 86),
  204 (n. 93)
Ben-Yochai, Shim'on (Rabbi), 21, 191
  (n. 11)
Beruria, 97, 101, 198–99 (n. 51), 199
  (n. 53)
Billerbeck, Paul, 197 (n. 40)
Birkeland, Harris, 205 (n. 97)
Blau, Amram (Rabbi), 118
Blinzler, Josef, 157, 158
Blüher, Hans, 48, 137, 143
Boethos, 162
Bornkamm, Günther, 112, 125, 187

Braun, Herbert, 6
Buber, Martin, viii, 5, 22, 48, 52, 80, 105, 119, 141, 203 (n. 79)
Bultmann, Rudolf, 2, 56, 57, 59, 61, 89, 95, 96, 105, 106, 188

Caesar, 104, 116, 119, 121, 122, 123, 159, 167, 172, 173
Caiaphas, 30, 130, 155, 157, 158, 159, 160, 161, 162, 164, 165, 172
Carmichael, Joel, 4, 16, 118, 201 (n. 65)
Casanova, 101
Chajes, Hirsch Perez, 73
Choni the Circle Drawer (Choni Hame'aggel), 100
Chrysostom, John, 49
Chuza (Herod's steward), 95
Clemens of Alexandria, 111
Cohen, Hermann, 86
Cohn, Haim, 157, 158, 163, 164, 178
Cozbi, 14

Danby, Herbert, x
Daniel, 106, 110, 183
Darius the Great, 177
Daube, David, xi
David, 5, 23, 25, 78, 99, 127, 128, 170
Delitzsch, Franz, 65
Dionysus, 203 (n. 80)
Dosa Ben-Harkinas (Rabbi), 127

Eichmann, Adolf, 85
Eisler, Robert, 4, 16, 116, 117, 118, 201 (n. 65)
'El'azar (Rabbi), 88
Eli (Heli; father of Joseph), 23, 30
Elijah ('Eliya, 'Eliyahu), 9, 20, 28, 32, 36, 42, 45, 104, 107, 133, 149, 183, 202 (n. 73)

Elijah Ben-Solomon Zalman (Rabbi; 'the Vilna Ga'on'), 133, 202 (n. 71)
Elisha, 9, 11, 42, 45
'Elisha' Ben-'Avuya, 12, 13, 56
Elizabeth ('Elisheva'), 27, 28
Elliger, Karl, 141
Enoch, 20
Ephraim, 48, 49
Esau, 78
Esther, 21
Eusebius, 48, 206 (n. 103)
Ezekiel, 9, 34, 107, 135
Ezra, 11, 40, 192 (n. 19)

Faust, 90
France, Anatole, 173
Francis of Assisi, 53
Freud, Sigmund, 4

Gabriel (angel), 27
Gamaliel (Rabbi), 10, 54, 144, 198 (n. 50)
Gandhi, Mahatma, 122
Gechazi (servant of Elisha), 11
Gibori, Moses, 90
Goethe, Johann Wolfgang von, 7, 190 (n. 4)
Goeze, Johann Melchior, 205 (n. 101)
Goldberg, Oskar, 144
Goldschmidt, E. D., 133, 134
Goldschmidt, Lazarus, 127
Graves, Robert, 4
Groskamp, Robbé, 156
Grüber, Dr. Heinrich, 85

Hadrian, 191 (n. 9)
Haman, 197 (n. 38)
Hannah, 97

La Farge, Henry, 143
Lagerkvist, Pår, 204 (n. 89)
Laius of Thebes, 24
Landau, Herbert, 169
Lazarus, 9, 45, 97, 98
Leon, Moses de, 191 (n. 11)
Lessing, Gotthold Ephraim, 187, 205
(n. 101)
Levi (an 'Amora), 172
Levi (tax-collector, disciple), 50
Lichtenstein, Yechiel, 130
Lisowsky, Gerhard, 194 (n. 26)
Loyson, Father Hyacinthus, 5
Lubavitcher Rebbe (Menachem
Mendel Schneerson) 199 (n.57)
Ludwig, Emil, 18
Luke, 23, 24, 26, 29, 30, 42, 49, 104,
115, 128, 129, 151, 158, 167, 182, 184,
186, 198 (n. 45)
Luther, Martin, 48
Lysanias, 30

Mack, Burton, 206 (n. 104)
Maimonides, 133
Malachi, 20, 28, 32
Malchus, 154
Manasseh, 48, 49
Mark, 104, 115, 157, 182, 184
Martha (sister of Mary), 97
Mary (disciple), 96
Mary (Miriam, mother of Jesus), xii,
23, 28, 30, 42, 66, 67, 96, 97, 113,
182
Mary Magdalene (Miriam of
Migdal), 95, 96, 97, 98, 182
Matthew, 23, 42, 50, 61, 104, 105, 107,
114, 115, 121, 129, 141, 142, 143, 158,
182, 184, 186
Me'ir (Rabbi), 56, 97, 101, 198 (n. 51),
199 (n. 53)

Mephistopheles, 90
Meshach, 183
Micah, 25
Montefiore, Claude J. G., x, xi
Mordecai, 20, 21
Moses, 4, 14, 23, 24, 29, 36, 40, 69,
78, 99, 102, 151, 152, 154

Naaman, 42
Nakdimon. See Nicodemus
Naphtali, 36
Nathanael, 67
Nathan of Gaza, 108
Nicodemus, 20, 21, 22, 120, 186
Nitheza, 13
Noah, 68
Nordau, Max, 5

Oedipus, 24
'Onkelos, 3

Pan, 104
Pandera/Panthera, 23
Paul, xii, 10, 59, 72, 96, 144, 187, 188
Peter (Simon; Shim'on Bar-Yona),
3, 5, 16, 45, 47, 48, 49, 101, 104, 108,
109, 110, 111, 117, 136, 137, 138, 153,
154, 155, 169
Pharaoh, 24, 69, 203 (n. 75), 203
(n. 78)
Philip (brother of Herod), 30
Philip (Tetrarch, son of Herod),
104
Philo of Alexandria, 159
Phinehas, 13
Pilate, Pontius, 30, 130, 155–75
passim, 179, 180, 181
Pines, Shlomo, 115, 188
Plato, 131
Pzillas, Friedrich, 201 (n. 65)

Index of Subjects

149, 152, 173, 177, 184, 197 (n. 38);
modern state of, xii, 7, 19, 82, 85,
132, 156, 186, 198 (n. 48), 201
(n. 67); national resurrection of,
15; and prophets, 55, 73; sacred
scriptures of, ix, 41; sons of, 177;
spared by God, 148, 152; tribes of,
50; as vineyard of God, 75; wise
men in, 101
Israeli Defense Forces (Tseva
Hagana Leyisra'el), 201 (n. 67)
Istanbul, 115

Jericho, 79, 81, 84, 85, 198 (n. 45)
Jerusalem: old city, 179, 180; pilgrimage to, 99, 112–25 passim,
148, 159; site of Last Supper or
Seder celebration, 129, 136; site of
temple, 39, 68, 83, 161, 177, 205
(n. 95); temple cult in, 122
Jordan (River), 22, 36, 104, 193
(n. 23)
Judaism: and afterworld, 93; after
Babylonian exile, 12; baptism in,
20; castes of, 198 (n. 46); celibacy
not idealized in, 103; chasidic, 44;
and Christianity, x; and commandment to honor parents, 66;
contemporary, 97; conversion to,
191 (n. 13); diaspora, 72; fasting in,
35; Jesus as prophet in liberal
theology of, 8; and justification
by works, 88; Kabbala in, 191
(n. 11); and loyalty of disciples, 55;
and lunar calendar, 193 (n. 24);
masculine conception of God in,
67; and mourning, 192 (n. 20);
number four in, 135; and Palestine, 121; and Palestinian triennial
cycle, 193 (n. 25); and parables of

Jesus, 73; pharisaic, 41, 60; priest
and Levite in, 85; rabbinic, 51;
rebirth concept in, 20; and Sermon on the Mount, 51; synagogue
service in, 39; and term *hosanna*,
114; *teshuva* as motif in, 37
Judea, 37, 140, 191 (n. 9)

Kabbala, xiv, 21, 191 (n. 11)
Kefar-Nachum (Capernaum), 36
Kidron Valley, 146
Kinnereth, Lake/Sea of. *See* Yam
Kinnereth
Kuta, 83
Kutim. *See* Samaritan(s)

Lake Kinnereth. *See* Yam Kinnereth
laryngeals, xiii
Last Supper, 36, 67, 125–41 passim
Law of Augustus, 171
Leon, 191 (n. 11)
Levite(s) (Hebrew: Levi, pl. Levi-
yim), 11, 39, 40, 79, 84, 85, 133, 134,
194 (n. 28), 198 (n. 45), 198 (n. 46)
Lex Iulia, 165
lex talionis, 54, 58, 59, 168
Lishkath-Hagazith. *See* Hall of Hewn
Stones
Little Yom Kippur (Hosha'na
Rabba), 201 (n. 63)
Lochamei-Cheruth Yisra'el. *See*
Stern Gang
Lord's Prayer (Our Father), 87, 89,
92, 93, 94
Lot's wife, 33

Machaerus (Fortress of), 35, 193
(n. 23)
Magi, 24
Mariology, 66

Messiah: Bar-Kokheva thought
to be, 17, 191 (n. 9); as born in
Bethlehem, 26; disciples on Jesus
as, 111, 155, 161; Elijah as herald of,
149; of the House of David, 127;
Jesus as not, 5, 6, 8; Jesus not self-
proclaimed as, 7, 106, 128, 164;
John on Jesus as, 35; Lubavitcher
Rebbe thought to be, 199 (n. 57);
New Testament proclaims Jesus
as, 126; Peter on Jesus as, 104, 108;
priestly vs. kingly, 167; "Son of
Man" and Jesus as, 105, 107;
suffering of, 123, 127, 167, 185
Messiah (talmudic; Ben-Josef, son
of Joseph), 127, 128, 205 (n. 95)
Mitsrayim. See Egypt
Mt. Gerizim, 82, 83
Mt. Horeb, 36, 51
Mt. Moriah, 152, 178, 183
Mt. of Olives, 118, 131
Mt. Sinai, 34, 36, 51
Mt. Zion, 108, 132

Nablus. *See* Sychar
Nag Hammadi, 25, 66
Nativity, 24
Nazareth, 26, 27, 36, 37, 39, 42, 43, 44, 67
Nazirite, 28, 68, 192 (n. 18)
new moons, 200 (n. 62)
Nicea, Council of, 188
Nile, 24
Ninth of Av (fast day), 192 (n. 20),
195 (n. 29), 200 (n. 63)

Our Father. *See* Lord's Prayer

Palestine, 112, 117, 121, 122, 177, 195
(n. 29), 204 (n. 91)
Palestinian cycle (Triennial cycle),
40, 193–94 (n. 25), 194–95 (n. 29)

Pandera (Panthera) tradition, 23
parable(s), 9, 36, 67, 71–85 passim,
93, 102, 109, 113, 172, 198 (n. 45)
Paschal privilege (privilegium
paschale), 168, 204 (n. 88)
Passion, 17, 141, 142, 150, 151, 173, 178,
179, 182
Passover (Pesach, Chag Ha'aviv,
Chag Hamatsoth, Zeman
Cheruthenu): amnesty on, 167,
168; blood on posts on, 145; as
celebration of nature, 147; eve of,
170; Haggada of, 148; Jesus' intent
regarding, 139; last six days of,
200 (n. 62); and Last Supper, 125,
126; liturgy of, 116; meal (Seder),
130, 132, 147, 149, 164; Mishna
discussion of, 131; night of, 144,
150, 152, 153, 164, 183; number four
in celebration of, 135, 138, 144; and
pilgrimage to Jerusalem, 112, 113,
115, 200 (n. 62); preparation for,
129, 179, 185; sacrifice on, 82, 129,
204 (n. 90); as seven-day festival,
205 (n. 100); unleavened bread
of, 133; wine on, 68; in year of
crucifixion, 187, 204 (n. 90)
Pentecost. *See* Feast of Weeks
Pesach. *See* Passover
Pharisee(s): ix, 11, 12, 13, 14; "colored" (in Talmud), 61; distinguished from Sadducees, 15; fasts
of, 35; Jesus' links to, 16; and
leadership, 76; nonviolent, 122;
as opponents of Jesus, 120; and
prophetic writings, 41; in Sanhedrin, 163, 164; as separated from
masses, 46–47
priest(s), 11, 39, 76, 79, 84, 85, 130,
194 (n. 28), 198 (n. 45), 198 (n. 46)
prophet(s), 8, 9; God of, 122; and

immersion bath, 34; Jesus considered to be, 20, 43, 104; Messiah promised by, 26; not accepted, 37, 43; and parables, 73; persecution of, 55

Protestantism, 2

pseudepigraphy, 62, 63

Purim, 197 (n. 38)

Qumran: influence on last Seder of Jesus, 131; papyrus rolls or texts from, 60, 128, 177; on priestly and kingly Messiah, 167; relation of John the Baptist to, 28, 29, 33, 53; sect(s) or community of, 22, 131, 132, 155, 160; solar calendar used in, 131, 202 (n. 70); sons of darkness tradition of, 140, 144; war scroll of, 142

Quamranians, 16, 33, 53, 60

rebirth, 20, 21, 22, 23, 26, 27, 36, 41, 107

Rechabites, 28, 32, 68

red heifer, 34

Red Sea, 200 (n. 62)

reincarnation, 21, 140

Rejoicing of the Law (Simchath-Torah), 193 (n. 25)

repentance, 31, 37, 78

resurrection(s), 15, 19, 181, 186, 187, 188

Roman centurion, 43, 45

Rome, 16, 116, 163, 166, 169, 173, 174

Sabbath: and blessing over wine, 68; healings of Jesus on, 45, 101; Jesus in synagogue on, 39; Jewish week ends with, 65; and Passover in year of crucifixion, 172, 179, 187, 204 (n. 90); purpose of, 46;

recitation of *haftaroth* on, 192 (n. 20), 195 (n. 29); recitation of Torah portion on, 40, 197 (n. 38); timing of, 130

Sadducee(s), 11, 14, 15, 41, 122, 131, 160, 163

Samaria, 83

Samaritan(s) (Kutim; Good Samaritan), 79, 80, 81, 82, 83, 84, 85, 86, 159, 198 (n. 44)

Samaritan woman, 81, 100, 198 (n. 44)

Sanhedrin, 100, 141, 157, 158, 159, 160, 161–62, 163, 164, 165

Sarepta (Zarephath), 42

scribes (soferim), 11, 190–91 (n. 7)

Sea of Galilee. *See* Yam Kinnereth

Sea of Kinnereth. *See* Yam Kinnereth

Sermon on the Mount, 6, 16, 50–63 passim, 69, 73, 92, 94, 154

Seventeenth of Tammuz (fast day), 192 (n. 20)

Shavu'oth. *See* Feast of Weeks

Shechem. *See* Sychar

Shemini 'Atsereth (Eighth Day of Assembly), 193 (n. 25)

Sicarians. *See* Zealots

Sichem. *See* Sychar

Sidon, 42, 82

Simchath-Torah (Rejoicing of the Law), 193 (n. 25)

sinful woman of Bethany, 98

soferim. *See* scribes

Spain, 191 (n. 11)

Stern Gang (Lochamei-Cheruth Yisra'el), 117, 201 (n. 67)

Sukkoth. *See* Feast of Tabernacles

Sura Academy, 196 (n. 32), 202 (n. 72)

Sychar (Nablus, Shechem, Sichem), 81, 82, 83, 100

synagogue, 39, 160; appearance of Jesus in, 41, 60; *haftaroth* read in, 192 (n. 20); in Nazareth, 27, 39; institution of, 11; liturgy of, 94, 105; as metonym for Judaism, 12, 78, 117; prayer tunic worn in, 182; service in, 198 (n. 46); as site of laical cult of rabbis, 68

Syrophoenician woman. *See* Canaanite woman

Tabernacles, Feast of. *See* Feast of Tabernacles

Tannaitic period, 196 (n. 34)

temple(s): announcement of birth of John in, 27; at Beth-El, 83; court located in, 100; cult, ritual, or service in, 11, 15, 68, 122, 198 (n. 46), 201 (n. 63); destruction of, 39, 119, 163, 192 (n. 20), 195 (n. 29); disputation in, 25; Hall of Hewn Stones in, 100; Jeremiah's words regarding, 204 (n. 84); Jesus provokes commotion in, 118; Jesus teaches in, 113, 118, 119; male prostitutes of, 31, 62; money-changers and merchants in, 115, 119; pilgrimage to, 112, 116; profanation of, by Jesus, 160; and Qumran sect, 160–61; reconstruction of, 83, 90, 177; Samaritan (on Mt. Gerizim), 83, 198 (n. 44); and Samaritans, 83; as site of judicial hearings, 162; as site of

sacrifices, 40; synagogue in, 39, 160; treasury of, 141

Ten Commandments, 62

Tetragram, 69, 90, 135, 180, 181, 199 (n. 60)

Tiberian vocalization, 193 (n. 22)

Tiberias, 193 (n. 22)

Tomb Church, 180

Tomb of David, 132

Torah cycle, 193 (n. 25)

transliteration, 13

transmigration of souls, 20, 21, 21–22

Triennial cycle. *See* Palestinian cycle

Tseva Hagana Leyisra'el (Israeli Defense Forces), 201 (n. 67)

Tyre, 42, 82

Visitation (of Elizabeth and Mary), 28

Weeks, Feast of. *See* Feast of Weeks

Widow in Sidonean Zarephath, 42

Yam Kinnereth (Lake/Sea of Kinnereth, Gennesaret, Sea of Galilee), 36, 37, 47, 49, 50, 51, 97

Yemen, 133

Yom Kippur. *See* Day of Atonement

Zarephath (Sarepta), 42

Zealots (Sicarians), 16, 50, 53, 117, 122, 140

Zeman Cheruthenu. *See* Passover